Robert Nourse

Plain Lectures on the Pilgrim's Progress

Robert Nourse

Plain Lectures on the Pilgrim's Progress

ISBN/EAN: 9783337291976

Printed in Europe, USA, Canada, Australia, Japan

Cover: Foto ©Andreas Hilbeck / pixelio.de

More available books at **www.hansebooks.com**

ON THE

Pilgrim's Progress.

ROBERT NOURSE.

SPRINGFIELD, ILL.:
H. W. ROKKER, PUBLISHER.
1878.

Entered according to Act of Congress, in the year 1878,
BY ROBERT NOURSE,
in the office of Librarian of Congress, at Washington. All rights reserved.

DEDICATION.

TO MY SAINTED MOTHER,

Who, in my earlier years, guided me into the

WAY OF RIGHTEOUSNESS,

And to

MY GLORIFIED CHILD,

Who is one of my chief attractions to the

CELESTIAL CITY,

This Volume is lovingly and reverently dedicated,

BY THE AUTHOR.

ERRATA.

Page 38, line 8 from top, for *immortal* read *immoral*.
Page 42, line 7 from bottom, for *Arguntin* read *Augustine*.
Page 42, line 3 from bottom, for *Corpernicus* read *Copernicus*.
Page 57, line 17 from top, for *possess* read *possesses*.
Page 63, line 19 from top, for *accomplishes* read *accomplish*.
Page 115, line 13 from top insert *of* after *think*.
Page 202, line 3 from top, insert *call* after *shall*.
Page 330, line 2 from top, read *how* for *hows*.
Page 287, line 13 from bottom, for *has* read *hast*.
For *Presumptious* read *presumptuous*, wherever found.
For *harbour* read *arbour* in Lecture 9.

PREFACE.

The following lectures are substantially those which I delivered on Sabbath evenings in the city of Springfield, Illinois, during the winter months of 1877–'78.

I have added fresh literary material to the first Lecture, in the hope that it may meet the need of Clerical Brethren, who may wish to deliver a similar course, but who possessing small libraries themselves, and living too far from city libraries, are unable to consult authorities or collate opinions on the subject. It is thought that sufficient has been brought together in this way to enable any brother to form an independent estimate of John Bunyan, his book, and its influence.

The reader will doubtless discover a difference in the style of the later lectures. This is owing to the fact that they were stenographically reported by Mr. Volney Hickox. The earlier ones are re-composed from my manuscript notes and from reports which appeared in the *Illinois State Journal*.

In delivering these Lectures I used as text-book an edition of "Pilgrim's Progress," published by Cassell, Petter & Galpin. For the purpose, I knew of no better one. The Allegory is admirably arranged in chapters, the typography exceedingly clear, the notes by Rev. Robert Maguire very suggestive, while the illustrations are so true to the conceptions of Bunyan as to afford in themselves a valuable commentary on "The Immortal Dream."

It was my habit to read a chapter, as there arranged, in lieu of the Scripture lesson, and I have the satisfaction of knowing that, in the opinion of one little girl at least, the "story book" was "splendid."

The "Synopses of Chapters" preceding the following Lectures do not give the contents of the Lectures, but are abbreviations of the chapters read, and intended to give the reader the pith of the story.

I have not intentionally plagiarized the words or thoughts of other men. Where I have used their thoughts or words, I have made acknowledgment in the usual manner. No doubt if certain authors honor these Lectures with a reading, they will find much that they have written. I hope that they will feel complimented by the resurrection of their works in this way.

Such as it is, I commit this little production to the cause of GOD and man, with the humble prayer that it may be acceptable to Him whose I am, and whom I serve—a blessing to those who are living in the City of Destruction, and a comfort to those, who, like myself, hope to reach the Celestial City.

> "The Book is written. Much is left unsaid;
> Much said amiss;
> Some pages, blurred with tears, can scarce be read;
> What's left? Why, this.
> To learn the lessons which are graven there."
>
> ANON.

LIST OF SUBJECTS.

		PAGE.
1.	JOHN BUNYAN AND HIS IMMORTAL DREAM,	9
2.	THE PILGRIM STARTS FROM THE CITY OF DESTRUCTION,	25
3.	THE SLOUGH OF DESPOND,	40
4.	MR. WORLDLY-WISEMAN,	53
5.	THE WICKET-GATE,	69
6.	THE INTERPRETER'S HOUSE,	80
7.	THE CROSS,	94
8.	THE HILL DIFFICULTY,	104
9.	THE PALACE BEAUTIFUL,	118
10.	APPOLYON,	130
11.	CONFLICTS,	148
12.	FAITHFUL,	163
13.	TALKATIVE,	179
14.	VANITY FAIR,	192
15.	THE HILL LUCRE,	206
16.	DOUBTING CASTLE AND GIANT DESPAIR,	217
17.	THE DELECTABLE MOUNTAINS,	231
18.	THE ENCHANTED GROUND,	249
19.	IGNORANCE, FEAR, AND TEMPORARY,	264
20.	THE CELESTIAL CITY,	280

"Doubt and discuss, examine and believe:
But, if thy judgment falter, turn with trust
Unto the staff our ancient guides relied on,
And paths that in the wilderness bear
The pilgrim's track.   If thine own wisdom fail thee,
Put confidence in wisdom tried by Time."

SIR AUBREY DE VERE.

LECTURE I.

JOHN BUNYAN

AND HIS

IMMORTAL DREAM.

"Would'st see
A man i' the clouds, and hear him speak to thee?"

"He being dead yet speaketh." Heb. 11 : 4.

"Jesus spake unto the multitudes in parables, and without a parable spake he not unto them." Matt. 13 : 34.

"Ah Lord God! they say of me, Doth he not speak parables?" Ezekiel 20 : 49.

THE BOOK, upon which I shall discourse for several successive Sabbath evenings, is thought by some of the best literary judges to be one of the most remarkable productions in existence.

The Pilgrim's Progress is read by English speaking people more than any other book, except the Bible. It has a circulation next to it in numbers, and is regarded by the devout with a sanctity only second to that which they feel towards the Word of God. It has been translated into every European language, and portions of it into Pagan tongues. It is a favorite with men and children.* You may find cheap copies of it in the saddle-bags of the prairie wanderer, the knapsack of the sol-

---

* The object of this production, it is hardly necessary to say, is to give an allegorical view of the life of a Christian, his difficulties, temptations, encouragements and ultimate triumph; and this is done with such skill and graphic effect that the book, *though on the most serious subjects, is read by children with nearly as much pleasure as fictions professedly written for their amusement.*—CHAMBERS.

—2

dier, the locker of the sailor, and the trunk of the servant girl. Did I say *cheap?* Well, they are so, if mothers' tears and prayers are cheap; but if they are sacred and precious, so are the books, for mothers place them there with prayers and tears. You may also find well-worn copies of it in the study of scholars and men of letters. Again, it may be found bound in vellum, embossed with gold, enriched with ornament, decorated by art, hard by the throne of kings. Its early editions are among the treasures of nations. For a copy of the first edition an assembly of rulers would halt in its ordinary business and bid a price for its possession.

And yet what is it? Simply the relation of a man's experience arising out of his endeavors to live a true Christian life. These experiences are covered with allegory. They are narrated under the form of a pilgrimage, and in such a way that whenever the book is read, and by whomsoever, the meaning is seen and felt, notwithstanding the parable. He writes as though he dreamed it, and this, says Lord Macaulay, "is the highest miracle of genius that the dreams of one man should become the experience of others."

We are naturally curious about this man. What manner of man is he? If scholars sit at his feet, we think he must be learned. If genius and philosophy crown him as a literary king, he must be great. If men and women feel this book to be the dream of their lives; if the old find it to be a record of their sweet and bitter memories; if the young find in it safe directions to the "Strait Gate" and the "Celestial City;" if it be one of the first books a young convert will read and the last he will lay aside—we think that a study of the life and character of its author is likely to profit us.

John Bunyan was born at Elstow, Bedfordshire, England, in the year 1628; a child of the poor and the low. His father was a traveling tinker,* and John became one. Generally this class are quite ignorant and unprincipled. They live profess-

---

* "For my descent then it was, as is well known by many, of a low and inconsiderable generation; my father's house being of that rank that is meanest and most despised of all the families of the land."—BUNYAN.

edly by their trade, but really much more by poaching and pilfering.* It may be said of them that they have no abiding city, although I fear it cannot be uttered with equal truth that they "desire a better country—that is a heavenly."

But Bunyan, senior, appears to have possessed a little more sense than usual with his fraternity, for we find Bunyan, junior, at school in early life, where he learned to spell, and probably to write. These accomplishments appear to have been neglected.‡ I should say that the lad, from his earliest memory, had conviction of sin. At the age of ten he was subject to religious terrors. This is due partly to the theology of his day, which required a sinner to be well beaten by the pedagogue law, as a prerequisite to his finding peace in Christ, and partly to his vivid imagination. He was always ruled by his impressions. His dreams and imaginations were facts to him. So sensitive was he, that on one occasion, thinking the devil struck at him with sharp claws, he adds, in apparent sincerity, that he felt them strike into his flesh. It appears to me that at this time, and for years subsequent thereto, he was a religious monomaniac.

He grew up a very profane‖ young man, so much so that a woman of loose character reproved him, saying that his lan-

---

* Sir Thomas Overbury thus quaintly describes them: "The tinker is a movable, for he hath no abiding in one place; he seems to be devout, for his life is a continual pilgrimage, and sometimes, in humility goes barefoot, therein making necessity a virtue; he is a gallant, for he carries all his wealth upon his back; or a philosopher, for he bears all his substance with him. He is always furnished with a song, to which his hammer keeping time, proves that he was the first founder of the kettle-drum; where the best ale is, there stands his music most upon crotchets. The companion of his travels is some foul, sun-burnt quean, that, since the terrible statute, has recanted gypsyism, and is turned pedlaress; so marches he all over England with his bag and baggage. His conversation is irreprovable, for he is always mending. He observes truly the statutes, and therefore would rather steal than beg. He is so strong an enemy of idleness, that in mending one hole, he would rather make three than want work; and when he has done he throws the wallet of his faults behind him. His tongue is very voluble, which, with canting, proves him a linguist. He is entertained in every place, yet enters no farther than the door, to avoid suspicion. To conclude, if he escape Tyburn or Banbury,† he dies a beggar."—*Whittier's Prose Works, vol.* 1, *p.* 209.

† Two noted places where criminals were hanged.

‡"Though to my shame I confess I did soon lose that I had learned, even almost utterly; and that long before the Lord did work a gracious work of conversion upon my soul." BUNYAN.

‖ "It was my delight to be taken captive by the devil. I had few equals, both for cursing and swearing, lying and blasphemy."—BUNYAN.

guage made her tremble. He tells us that he was guilty of breaking every command of the decalogue, but whether this is to be taken in a theological or literal sense, I hardly know—for Macaulay affirms that when he was charged with particular sins, he denied them.

He enumerates other delinquencies, such as dancing, tip-cat, bell-ringing, and reading Sir Bevis of Southampton. His views were imaginary, as well as real. You see he takes his idea of sin from society, as well as from the Word of God.

He regarded himself as the subject of special Providences. About this time we find him in the parliamentary army at the siege of Leicester, as Carlyle says, "living out the Pilgrim's Progress with a matchlock on his shoulder." Here a comrade volunteered to take his place in the line, and was shortly after shot dead. This remarkable preservation made a deep impression on his mind as well as on others.

On his return home he gave up bell-ringing, tip cat playing, dancing, swearing, and novel reading. Did I say gave them up? He tried honestly to do so, but learned swiftly and sorely that the hardest thing any poor sinner can do is to give up his sins and break from his habits. Until the sin of the heart is taken away by the Lamb of God, and the soul is filled with the Holy Ghost, there can be no giving up. The heart can not remain empty. God, nature and man abhor a vacuum. A man is not saved by merely giving up his sins, but by giving himself up to Christ to receive Christ.

But behold the man who has given up bell-ringing, going up the belfry steps to watch his old companions pull the ropes. See the change on his face as he thinks a bell may fall and dash life from his body. He moves away to the church-yard only to imagine the steeple may fall on him. From thence to the village green to bury his fears, convictions and resolves in the excitement of tip-cat.* He is about to strike, when he is suddenly arrested by a voice from heaven saying, "John Bunyan, wilt thou cleave to thy sins and go to hell, or wilt thou leave

---

* A game similar to "hockey."

thy sins and go to heaven?" John left the village green no more to profane and desecrate the day of holy rest. He chose the latter alternative.*

In his youth he married a girl as poor as himself; so destitute were they that to begin life they had not so much as "a dish or a spoon between them." She carried him something better than gold or accomplishments: piety, good sense and two good books. Half the bridegrooms to-day are not so fortunate as he. Her parents were righteous.

Immediately before he became a christian he passed through a strange series of religious vagaries. He wanted proof that he was a saved soul. He believed the Jews would be saved, and then sought to prove himself a Jew. This failing, he argues: "Christians possess faith; if I have faith I am a christian." He therefore bade the road puddles to be dry, and the dry places of the road to become puddles. As they did not obey him, he concluded he had no faith. Then he believed he had committed the unpardonable sin—and was encouraged in his belief by a professor of religion, who was old enough to have known better. This was his Slough of Despond. While in this condition, it happened that he overheard some godly women talking of the peace which possessed their hearts through faith in Christ. He inquired into this secret of Divine peace. They directed him to "that good minister of Jesus Christ" Mr. Gifford, Baptist minister of Bedford, who finally succeeded in

---

* Now you must know that before this I had taken much delight in ringing, but my conscience beginning to be tender, I thought such practice was but vain, and therefore forced myself to leave it; yet my mind hankered; wherefore I would go to the steeple-house and look on, though I durst not ring; but I thought this did not become religion neither; yet I forced myself, I would look on still. But quickly after I began to think, "How if one of the bells should fall?" Then I chose to stand under a main beam that lay over-thwart the steeple, from side to side, thinking here I might stand sure; but then I thought again, should the bell fall with a swing it might first hit the wall and then rebounding upon me, might kill me for all this beam. This made me stand in the steeple door; and now, thought I, I am safe enough; for if a bell should then fall, I can slip out behind these thick walls, and so be preserved, notwithstanding.

So after this I would get to see them ring, but would not go any farther than the steeple door. But then it came into my head, "How if the steeple itself should fall?" And this thought (it may, for aught I know, when I stood and looked on) did continually so shake my mind that I durst not stand in the steeple door any longer, but was forced to flee, for fear the steeple should fall on my head.—BUNYAN.

leading him into the way of righteousness, peace and joy, through faith in Jesus.

Soon after his baptism and reception into the church, he did what all church members are bound to do—began to work, and from the day he began, he labored till death. He preached with wonderful acceptance in the adjacent villages. Houses, barns and conventicles were too strait for his congregations. With them he repaired to the village green, the grove, and market place. He had "a circuit" before Wesley was born. So many congregations grew up under him that he was called "Bishop Bunyan."

His prosperity was not to flow unchecked, however. God intended him to preach to a larger congregation—to the whole world. And for this he must pass through great tribulation. It was then a crime to preach outside of "The Church." The clergy of "The Church," therefore, arrested Bunyan for the unpardonable sin of preaching where man first worshiped his Maker—in the open air. As John would not promise to desist, they sentenced him to prison, with the promise of ultimate hanging.

Think of it! *"The Church" persecuting piety!* Is it not contrary to the Spirit of God? And yet the history of all churches* manifests this spirit. We may think with much feeling of the inquisition of the reign of Bloody Mary; our indignation may rise as we remember the banishment of the Pilgrim Fathers and their subsequent sufferings, but do not let *us* forget the history of New England. If we, as Congregationalists, had been in the same position as the Presbyterians, we would as soon have put him in prison. Let any Church have the sanction of law to make deviation from its standard of opinion a penal offense,

---

* Except Baptist churches. I believe there is no historical record of persecution on their part. This was for a long time inexplicable to me, and would still remain a mystery had I not heard the following anecdote: A Baptist clergyman, in addressing a denominational meeting, took occasion to say that all the churches had persecuted except their own; whereupon there was great applause. He proceeded thus: "My brethren, I will tell you *why* the Baptist churches have never persecuted—(profound sensation)—*it is because they never had a chance!*" The germ of this story may be found in Southey's Common-place Book.

and the human depravity of that Church will forget the *love and mercy of the Gospel, to attend to the weightier matters of the law.*

John Bunyan was sent to prison for conscience sake, and had to leave to the care of a careless world, and to the tender mercies of a less merciful church, a frail wife and four children, one of whom (evidently his favorite) was blind. He had better speak for himself in this connection. Hear him:

"I found myself a man compassed with infirmities; the parting with my wife and poor children hath often been to me in this place as the pulling the flesh from the bones; and also it brought to my mind the many hardships, miseries, and wants that my poor family was like to meet with, should I be taken from them, especially my poor blind child, who lay nearer my heart than all beside. O, the thoughts of the hardships I thought my poor blind one might undergo, would break my heart to pieces. Poor child! thought I, what sorrow art thou like to have for thy portion in this world! thou must be beaten, must beg, suffer hunger, cold, nakedness, and a thousand calamities, though I cannot endure the wind should blow upon thee. But yet, thought I, I venture you all with God, though it goeth to the quick to leave you. Oh! I saw I was as a man who was pulling down his house upon the heads of his wife and children; yet I thought on two milch kine that were to carry the ark of God into another country, and to leave their calves behind them. But that which helped me in this temptation was divers considerations: the first was the consideration of these two Scriptures, "Leave thy fatherless children, I will preserve them alive; and let thy widows trust in me;" and again, "The Lord said, verily it shall go well with thy remnant; verily I will cause the enemy to entreat them well in the time of evil."

The charge brought against him, and on which he was tried before Judge Wingate, was, that "John Bunyan hath devilishly and perniciously abstained from coming to church to hear divine service, and is a common upholder of several unlawful meetings and conventicles, to the disturbance and distraction of the good subjects of this kingdom, contrary to the laws of our sovereign lord and king."

He was found guilty, after a trial, which probably gave him the idea of the one he has wrought into his allegory at Vanity Fair. His sentence was perpetual imprisonment, with the probability of hanging, but was reduced to twelve years on the intervention of good Bishop Barlow.

Here, in Bedford jail, with sixty DISSENTERS,* who had sinned, and were suffering, alike, for conscience sake, he lived and wrote his Immortal Dream. While here he preached to the prisoners, and inside the walls of his "den" established a church. During the day he made tagged laces and wire snares, and by this means supported his family.

What a noble fellow! Look at him suffering for his principles; preaching his Master's name and grace; working daily to support his bereaved and afflicted family, and writing one of the few books the world possesses.

Ah, noble John Bunyan; hero! martyr! devoted father! faithful disciple! prince of allegorists! heavenly dreamer! thou subtle analyst of spiritual conflict, thou who didst nobly meet and conquer thine every foe, whether in human or diabolical shape; though thy birth was so low that the great and high despised it; thy dreaming place a "den" so much bereft of heavenly associations that men thought it had no connection therewith; we revere thy memory, admire thy work, and thank God that though the den was dark, and thy life a sorrow, yet thy mind was a medium through which the light of heaven has come to us, and the joy unspeakable has filled our souls! With the angels who crowned thee we sing, "Well done, thou good and faithful servant, enter thou into the joy of thy Lord!"†

Good Bishop Barlow interceded for him with the authorities and succeeded in getting his sentence remitted, and then from

---

* Print that heroic name in capitals. They were the fathers of America.

† Few who read Bunyan now-a-days think of him as one of the brave old English confessors, whose steady and firm endurance of persecution, baffled, and in the end overcame, the tyranny of the established church in the reign of Charles II. What Mil-

prison he went forth to preach, furnished with a wonderful vocabulary of pure Saxon, a vivid imagination chastened by suffering, an extraordinary knowledge of the Word of God, deep religious experience, and the love of God in his soul. Well might Dr. Owen tell King James that he would gladly sacrifice his learning for Bunyan's power.

As a preacher he penetrated vast tracts of country. His visits to London were events. He wrote as many books as he lived years. He wrote against Episcopalianism, the Quakers, and the Close Communion of his own church, besides his wonderful allegories and theological treatises.

The last act of his life is simply sublime. He rode to Reading, amidst heavy rains, to plead with a father who had disinherited and disowned his son. His efforts were successful, and he had the pleasure of seeing the disgraced child in the loving embrace of the angered parent. Had he not the spirit of his Master? Look now from John Bunyan to his Lord. Let us for one moment contemplate *Him* in his last work of love. The cases are alike, with differences. The servant sought to reconcile the father to the abandoned child. The Master sought to reconcile the children who had abandoned and disowned their loving Father. The servant died in doing his work—the Lord Jesus sacrificed himself for us. "God was in Christ, reconciling the world to Himself." Do you admire the act in John Bunyan? Oh! then fall at the feet of his Master, and from your hearts say in loving faith—*My Lord and My God*.

The general effect of his book on English Literature is such

---

ton and Penn and Locke wrote in defense of liberty, Bunyan lived out and acted. He made no concessions to wordly rank. Dissolute lords and proud bishops he counted less than the humblest and poorest of his disciples at Bedford. When first arrested and thrown into prison he supposed he should be called to suffer death for his faithful testimony to the truth ; and his great fear was, that he should not meet his fate with the requisite firmness, and so dishonor the cause of his Master. And when dark clouds came over him, and he sought in vain for a sufficient evidence that in the event of his death it would be well with him, he girded up his soul with the reflection that as he suffered for the word and way of God, he was engaged not to shrink one hair's breadth from it. "I will leap," he says, "off the ladder blindfold into eternity, sink or swim, come heaven, come hell, Lord Jesus, if thou wilt, catch me, do ; if not, I will venture in Thy name !" —*Whittier's Prose Works, pp.* 231-2, *vol.* 1.

that any one who has not read it cannot be said to have received a liberal education. If we were to eliminate its parables, phrases, names of its various characters, particular words and events from our literature, much of it would become unintelligible.

Says Hallam: "John Bunyan may pass for the father of our novelists. His success in a line of composition like the spiritual romance or allegory, which seems to have been frigid and unreadable in the few instances where it had been attempted, is doubtless enhanced by his want of learning, and his low station in life. He was therefore rarely, if ever, an imitator. Bunyan possessed in a remarkable degree the power of representation: his inventive faculty was considerable; but the other is his distinguishing excellence. He saw and makes us see what he describes; he is circumstantial, without prolixity; and in the variety and frequent change of his incidents, never loses sight of the unity of his allegorical fable. His invention was enriched, or rather his choice determined, by one rule he had laid down for himself—the adaptation of all the incidental language of scripture to his own use. There is scarce a circumstance or metaphor in the Old Testament which does not find a place bodily and literally in the story of the Pilgrim's Progress; and this peculiar artifice has made his own imagination appear more creative than it really is. In the conduct of the romance, no rigorous attention to the propriety of the allegory seems to have been uniformly preserved. Vanity Fair, or the Cave of the two Giants, might, for anything we see, have been placed elsewhere; but it is by this neglect of exact parallelism that he better keeps up the reality of the pilgrimage and takes off the coldness of mere allegory. It is also to be remembered that we read this book at an age when the spiritual meaning is either little perceived or little regarded. In his language, nevertheless, Bunyan sometimes mingles signification too much with the fable; we might be perplexed between the imaginary and the real Christian; but the liveliness of the narration soon brings us back, or did, at least, when we were young, to the fields of fancy."

This is an abstract of the events: "From highest heaven a voice has proclaimed vengeance against the City of Destruction, where lives a sinner of the name of *Christian*.* Terrified, he rises up amid the jeers of his neighbors and departs, for fear of being devoured by the fire which is to consume the criminals. A helpful man, *Evangelist*, shews him the right road. A treacherous man, Worldlywise, tries to turn him aside. His companion, Pliable, who had followed him at first, gets stuck in the Slough of Despond, and leaves him. He advances bravely across the dirty water and the slippery mud, and reaches the Strait Gate, where a wise *Interpreter* instructs him by visible shows, and points out the way to the Heavenly City. He passes before a Cross, and the heavy burden of sins which he carried on his back is loosened and falls off. He painfully climbs the steep hill of Difficulty and reaches a great Castle, where Watchful, the guardian, gives him in charge of his good daughters, Piety and Prudence, who warn him and arm him against the monsters of hell. He finds his road barred by one of these demons, Appolyon, who bids him abjure obedience to the Heavenly King. After a long fight he conquers him. Yet the way grows narrow, the shades fall thicker, sulphurous flames rise along the road; it is the valley of the *Shadow of Death*. He passes it and arrives at the town of Vanity, a vast fair of business, deceits, and shows, which he walks by with lowered eyes, not wishing to take part in its festivities or falsehoods. The people of the place beat him, throw him into prison, condemn him as a traitor and rebel, burn his companion, *Faithful*. Escaped from their hands he falls into those of Giant Despair, who beats him, leaves him in a poisonous dungeon without food, and giving him daggers and cords, advises him to rid himself from so many misfortunes. At last he reaches the Delectable Mountains, where he sees the holy city. To enter it he has only to cross a deep river, where there is no foothold, where the water dims the sight, and which is called the river of Death."†

* This is a mistake. His original name was Graceless.
† Taine.

Coleridge says: "I know of no book, the Bible excepted, as above all comparison, which I, according to my judgment and experience, could so safely recommend as teaching and enforcing the whole saving truth according to the mind that was in Christ Jesus, as the Pilgrim's Progress. It is, in my conviction, incomparably the best *Summa Theologicæ Evangelicæ* ever produced by a writer not miraculously inspired. It is composed in the lowest style of English, without slang or false grammar. If you were to polish it you would at once destroy the reality of the vision, for works of imagination should be written in very plain language; the more purely imaginative they are, the more necessary it is to be plain. This wonderful book is one of the few works which may be read repeatedly, at different times, and each time with new and different pleasure. I read it once, as a theologian, and let me assure you there is a great logical acumen in the work; once with devotional feelings, and once as a poet. I could not have believed, beforehand, that Calvinism could be painted in such delightful colors."

The manner in which he wrote it is best told by himself:

"When at the first I took my pen in hand,
Thus for to write, I did not understand
That I at all should make a little book
In such a mode: nay, I had undertook
To make another; which, when almost done,
Before I was aware, I this begun.

And thus it was: I, writing of the way
And race of saints in this our gospel-day,
Fell suddenly into an allegory
About their journey and the way to glory,
In more than twenty things which I set down:
This done, I twenty more had in my crown;
And these again began to multiply
Like sparks that from the coals of fire do fly.
Nay, then, thought I, if that you breed so fast
I'll put you by yourselves, lest you at last

Should prove *ad infinitum* and eat out
The book that I already am about.

Well, so I did: but yet I did not think
To show to all the world my pen and ink
In such a mode; I only thought to make
I knew not what; nor did I undertake
Thereby to please my neighbour; no, not I;
I did it mine own self to gratify.

Neither did I but vacant seasons spend
In this my scribble; nor did I intend
But to divert myself, in doing this,
From worser thoughts, which make me do amiss."

It appears that he was advised by some of his friends not to print it; others, however, advised him to do so. In order to decide the wisdom of their opinions, he printed it.

Some objected to this form of presenting truth. These he successfully combats. Then, in the following earnest words, states his purpose:

"And now before I do put up my pen
I'll show the profit of my book, and then
Commit both me and it into that Hand
That pulls the strong down, and makes the weak ones
    stand.

This book it chalketh out before thine eyes
The man that seeks the everlasting prize:
It shews you whence he comes, whither he goes;
What he leaves undone; also what he does;
It also shews you how he runs and runs
'Till he unto the Gate of Glory comes.
It shews, too, who set out for life amain,
As if the lasting crown they would obtain.
Here also you may see the reason why
They lose their labour, and like fools do die."

I have lessons to teach from this life for young men, young women, parents and the church.

Young men, be true. John Bunyan had convictions, and was true to them; he had genius and was true to it. You can never be like him, except in this one particular. This was the foundation of his Christ-like character, his fortitude, his usefulness, his influence. He did not bemoan that he was not a great man; nor did he think himself one. He did his duty. Like all great men, he was a great servant. Like his Master, he was not ministered unto, but he ministered. Be yourselves sanctified; yourselves sanctified to the duty that is next you. This only is acceptable service. Many young men are ruined because they do not use the talents they have. Thou shalt not covet, applies to brain and opportunity and circumstance, as well as to goods.

Employ your leisure. The Pilgrim's Progress was written in leisure hours, at odd moments, which too many young men waste. His advantages were exceedingly few. His study was a dungeon. His books, the Bible and Fox's Book of Martyrs. You are all better off than he, but probably none of you are quite so wise as he. Lose not a moment. Life is precious. Begin now to seek wisdom; exalt her and she shall promote thee. If you still halt for want of instruction as to what you shall do in spare moments, do as he did: Read the Bible; pray for God's Holy Spirit; and then, like him, you shall see visions and dream dreams.

Maidens, be good. John Bunyan's wife's dowry was not large; estimated in the market, it was nothing. And yet we know not how much it contributed to his immortal fame. She took him her loving heart, enriched with piety, two small books and a godly father's blessing. Believe me, there is nothing that will make home so home-like and heaven-like as these. You may take into your future home, gold, silver, jewels, music, flowers, culture, grace; but unless you take a meek and quiet spirit, you do not take the pearl of great price; you leave outside the better part.

Parents: *Counteract the effects of bad literature by giving your children this book.* It costs no more than rubbish. The children will be charmed with it; it will not corrupt them; you will not then have cause to fear that your sons will run away to be pirates or robbers, or remain at home to be idle spendthrifts, gamblers and drunkards; rather may you expect that they will start from the City of Destruction, fight Appolyon, and live and die heroes of Vanity Fair; while your daughters, instead of being poisoned by false ideas of life, will cultivate the solid virtues and emulate the sisters of the Palace Beautiful.

It would be an interesting study for some one to look up the great men who read Pilgrim's Progress in youth. It was the first book Franklin possessed, and we agree with Everett, that it could not have been a better. Hallam and Dean Stanley, historians and divines, acknowledge its influence over them in youth. Sir Titus Salt, who rose to eminence from obscurity, from a poor boy to the front rank of inventors, manufacturers and philanthropists, ever regarded it as one of his favorites. I have read of many others, but now cannot call them to mind.

A word to the Church: *Fetter no genius.* The Established Church imprisoned him; they put fetters on his body; but when his genius gave birth to this child, his Baptist friends, like the Egyptian midwives, thought they had an ordinance to put it to death. What to them was an impious form of stating the truth, has been the divine message to many souls. Christ once needed the foal of an ass; He once needed the dreams of a tinker; He may need now some form of truth which is obnoxious to the church. Let us not stereotype mind; let it follow its bent; provided it be sanctified, God will use it.

Despair of no one: Bunyan was converted. The town sinner; the blaspheming tinker. This man, very low in the social scale, was saved, and has saved many others. Let us not despair. Christ shall yet bring many such sons to glory; for the joy set before Him of saving them, He endured the cross, despised the shame, and is now at the right hand of God.

Read it, and then—

> "The book will make a traveler of thee,
> If by its counsel thou wilt ruled be;
> It will direct thee to the Holy Land,
> If thou wilt its direction understand.
> Yea, it will make the slothful active be;
> The blind also delightful things to see."

[The attempts which have been made to improve this book are not to be numbered. It has been done into verse; it has been done into modern English. The "Pilgrimage of Tender Conscience," the "Pilgrimage of Good Intent," the "Pilgrimage of Seek Truth," the "Pilgrimage of Theophilus," the "Infant Pilgrim," the "Hindoo Pilgrim," are among the many feeble copies of the great original. But the peculiar glory of Bunyan is that those who most hated his doctrines have tried to borrow the help of his genius. A Catholic version of his parable may be seen with the head of the Virgin in the title page. On the other hand, those Antinomians for whom his Calvinism is not strong enough, may study the pilgrimage of Mephzibah, in which nothing will be found which can be construed into an admission of free agency and universal redemption. But the most extraordinary of all the acts of vandalism by which a fine work of art was ever defaced, was committed so late as the year 1853. It was determined to transform The Pilgrim's Progress into a Tractarian book. The task was not easy, for it was necessary to make the two sacraments the most prominent objects in the allegory, and of all Christian Theologians, avowed Quakers excepted, Bunyan is the one in whose system the sacraments held the least prominent place. However, the Wicket Gate became a type of baptism, and the House Beautiful of the Eucharist. The effect of this change is such as assuredly the ingenious person who made it never contemplated. For, as not a single pilgrim passes through the wicket in infancy, and as Faithful hurries past the House Beautiful without stopping, the lesson which the fable, in its altered shape, teaches, is that none but adults ought to be baptized, and that the Eucharist may safely be neglected. Nobody would have discovered from the original Pilgrim's Progress that the author was not a Pædo-Baptist. To turn his book into a book against Pædo-Baptism was an achievement reserved for an Anglo-Catholic divine. Such blunders must necessarily be committed by every man who mutilates part of a great work, without taking a comprehensive view of the whole.]

MACAULAY.

[Rev. W. SHRUBSALL, the first pastor of Bethel Chapel, Sherness, England, wrote a work in imitation of this. The only departure from the original is that Mr. S. makes his Pilgrim go to the Celestial City by water. It has considerable merit.]   R. N.

LECTURE II.

THE PILGRIM STARTS FROM THE CITY OF DESTRUCTION.

[SYNOPSIS OF CHAPTER.—Bunyan, in his den, dreams that he sees a man named Graceless, of the City of Destruction, clothed with rags, standing with his face from his own house, a book in his hand, and a great burden on his back. He reads, weeps, and cries out frequently and lamentably, saying, "What shall I do?" for he has learned from The Book that the city in which he lives will be destroyed by fire from heaven. Thereupon he tells his fears to his wife, children and neighbors, who, instead of being alarmed, were surly to him, and derided him by turns. A man named Evangelist here meets him, who, learning his condition, exhorts him to flee from the wrath to come, and to the Wicket Gate, which he could not see. He was then directed to follow a light, which he could see, with the promise that it would lead to the gate. He started as directed. Wife, children, and neighbors called him back, but he put his fingers in his ears and ran on, crying, Life! Life! Eternal Life! Two of his neighbors, named Obstinate and Pliable, followed him, determined to bring him back. They overtook him, and after much unavailable discussion, Obstinate returned, but Pliable went on, being moved thereto by fear, and charmed with the prospect of the Celestial City held out by Christian, late Graceless—the hero of the Dream.]

BUNYAN started his Pilgrim. He made him go. He did not permit him to sit still and wait for an angel to come from the upper world and carry him along; nor wait until he was better; nor spend years in thinking about it. No! he just started.

I suppose you need not be told that if you would get to heaven you must begin to go thither. You must take the first step, and then the next, and then the next, and plod every inch of the way. The first step should be taken; and now; and the next should follow in the same manner. Every step is a beginning and an end. Each one reaches to the threshold of the other.

Begin this journey with the strength you have now. Do not think you will be lifted to the skies by some celestial agency. You will not. Begin in some way to be a Christian; no matter how you may blunder. Better blunder in the beginning, than at last discover that your life has been a blunder all the way through.

Do you say, "It needs to be thought about?" I agree with you. But please remember that all of you have had years, and some of you a long life-time, in which to think of it. Besides, this saying that you want to think about it, is frequently an excuse to banish it from your minds. I am sure if you did think seriously you would desire to "flee from the wrath to come," and manifest it by asking the old question, "What must I do to be saved?"

I. *Consider the Condition of the Pilgrim when he started.* He is described in this graphic passage: "I dreamed, and behold I saw a man clothed with rags, standing in a certain place, with his face from his own house, a book in his hand, and a great burden on his back." Here is a picture of an unsaved man's condition. Let us talk about the several items.

"*A man!*" a being made in God's image; His child. A mind incarnate; capable of holding intercourse with Deity; of exploring the universe and learning its secrets; of knowing good and evil; of choosing blessing or curse; free to obey the law, and free to break it. Such are you, such is your dignity, such are your privileges, and such your perils. He is a picture of ourselves.

"*Clothed with rags!*" You possibly object to this description. You may say in reply, "my morality is not in rags!" But can any of you say that your lives are no where torn by sins? I do not ask whether you are as good as your neighbors. Perhaps you are really better than most men. But this is the question: Have you been as good as you ought to have been? Have you not merely broken no commandment, but have you filled full the whole law?

Go home and look at one of your old coats. It was once new, clean, and good; good in material, good in fit; you were once pleased with it and proud of it. Why do you not wear it? You reply, "Why sir, it is out at the elbows, raveled at the cuffs, greasy on the collar, torn on the lapels." These are good reasons for not wearing it. None of us would wear such on the street, at church, or parties. They are only worn when we do dirty work, or when we care not for brother man to see us. But if you will look it over you will find some good in it yet. It is not all bad as cloth, but it is very bad as a coat. It was once all good, both as coat and cloth. But you don't wear it, you are properly ashamed to do so.

Your character, or your virtue, or your righteousness is like that. It is in rags. But we don't mean to say that there is no good in you, or that there never has been, but that the good you now possess is disfigured by rags; and if you would review your lives and could see your hearts as they are, you would be ashamed and afraid to go into the presence of God as you are now doing.

Have you ever told a lie? That is one torn spot in your experience! Have you told two? three? or more? Have you told one per week? per day? Have you cheated in business? Have you withheld the truth? Have you oppressed the poor? Have you broken the Sabbath; broken the seventh commandment in any of its forms? Taken God's name in vain? Been angry with a brother without cause? Have you done any unrighteousness? Have you known to do good and neglected to do it? Have you knowingly and voluntarily been on the side of might against right? Have you smothered conscience, grieved the Holy Ghost, or substituted religion for righteousness? If you have done any of these things, am I not right in saying that your righteousness is in rags? of some might I not say *filthy* rags? Will you go to God's righteous judgment thus?

"*Stood with his face from his own house.*" Why? Because

he knew that the Celestial City was not in that direction! Perhaps so. But as yet he was ignorant of its whereabouts. He only knew where it was not. This means, when applied to a sinner, that he turns his thoughts, desires and attention from sin and its pleasures.

Friends, to get a good start, you must first turn your backs on sin and sinful engagements. It is impossible to get to heaven with a sinful life. No sin, nor anything that maketh a lie (the easiest form of sin), can enter there.

Nor can you, if you keep the love of the world supreme in your heart. You must leave father, mother, brother, sister, houses and lands, to take up the cross of leaving them further and further behind daily, or you cannot attain. They must ever be less than supreme. The claims of righteousness are before blood.

And what is the use of supremely loving this world? Its pleasures pass away. Its treasures perish. Its riches are fleeting. It will be burned up. Scripture affirms it; science declares it. It must perish. Its elements shall melt with fervent heat. The heavens and earth that now are, are but reserved for the great conflagration. But before this occurs we may leave it, and to go saved or unsaved spirits into Eternity.

Had you not better turn your attention to another life! A better world! Many of you would start, if you could but turn your backs on this world. The way to do that, is, to turn your face in search of a better.

"A book in his hand." One of the beauties of John Bunyan is that he makes his Pilgrim a Bible reader from first to last. His "Christian" is never without "The Book." With all his genius he is unable to think of a Christian who neglects to read his Bible. There is much wisdom in this. If you were visiting Europe, you would procure before-hand, and carry with you, railway guides, ocean guides, hotel guides, and guides to the various countries and places of interest. When you visit a museum you ask for a guide book. This is the habit of all intelligent persons. It is just as intelligent to take "the guide" from earth

to heaven. You need this light to thy path, this lamp for thy feet. It is folly to attempt the journey without it.

"*He had the book in his hand.*" Yours, possibly, is a beautifully bound volume, lying on a shelf at home. That will do you no good there. Take it down, rub the dust off and use it, for the Book is not to be worshiped, but read. The *entrance* of the Word giveth light. Guide books are poorly bound, but always consulted. Use the lamp to be guided by the light therein, for

> "This lamp, from off the everlasting throne,
> Mercy took down, and in the night of time
> Stood, casting on the dark her gracious bow,
> And evermore beseeching men with tears
> And earnest sighs, to hear, believe and live."*

"*A great burden on his back.*" He is a burdened pilgrim. You know how awkward, depressing and wearying is a heavy burden. Those who bear them use every means they know of to relieve themselves. Those who carry heavy burdens in their daily employment, use all their ingenuity and skill to devise machinery to do their work. An honest man may have a heavy burden of debt, and this robs him of domestic comfort and hampers his business. He will do his utmost, denying himself many luxuries, that he may enjoy the greater luxury of being out of debt. Others have burdens of personal or family afflictions to bear, and they spend their fortunes in the employment of medical skill to be rid of them.

Now we have large burdens of sin. What shall we do with them? We cannot carry them with us to heaven. We must get rid of them. But, perhaps, you are unconscious of this burden. A dead man is not conscious of the marble and the soil under which he lies. Nor are men who are dead in trespasses and sin, conscious of sin.

We will suppose that a man has stolen something. The theft is not immediately discovered, so he steals again and again. So successful is he that he grows careless. His conscience becomes

* Pollock.

hardened, and he sins easier than he did. His deeds do not trouble him; judgment is not executed against his wicked work speedily, and so his heart is fully set in him to do evil. Now let us suppose he is caught in the act, or that his crimes are traced home to him, and his employers and the officers of the law say to him, as Nathan did to David, "Thou art the man." From that moment he is burdened. He is oppressed by a knowledge of his sins, a sense of guilt. He is burdened with fear, with a smiting conscience, with shame in being brought to public trial, and with fearful apprehensions as to his future doom, and then with a life-long sense of shame and disgrace.

Have you sinned? Little or much is not the question. Have you sinned? If so, are you not apprehensive of God's judgments? If you have sown to the flesh, you must from that source reap corruption.

I believe I have presented you with a fair picture of your moral condition in its judicial relations. Don't forget that by irrevocable law all sin is punishable! It brings punishment with it. Judgment may tarry, but it will surely come. Bunyan's Pilgrim perceived that he was condemned to die, and after that to judgment, and found that he was unwilling to do the first, and not able to do the second, and when Evangelist asked, "Why not willing to die, since life is attended with so many evils?" he answered, "Because I fear this burden on my back (his sins) will sink me lower than the grave. And, sir, if I be not fit to go to prison, I am not fit to go to judgment, and from thence to execution." This is a fair picture of an unregenerated man's condition. Dare you face the God of law? Dare you any longer live indifferently to Divine law? Dare you take the consequences of broken law?

II. *Let us now talk of his motives.* He was moved by FEAR. To his credit be it said, he was afraid longer to live a life that could only end in misery, in a city that was doomed to perish. It has of late been quite fashionable to deride this motive in religion. I freely grant that it may have been appealed to, to an unhealthy extent. In such cases correction is needed.

Perhaps it is too true that there are some Christians whose only idea of heaven is security from hell. A Christian of several years' standing said to me once, "Why, Mr. N., if there is no hell, I have no desire to go to heaven!" I have met with several instances of this kind, and I deplore their existence. Yet it is philosophical to appeal to this motive. You may say that men ought to be urged by higher ones. Perhaps so; but suppose this is the only one left?

The principle of fear is in us all. You fear a fire, and therefore insure your property; you fear thieves, and therefore sleep with a revolver by your side and a mastiff in the yard; you fear poverty, and therefore "lay up for a rainy day;" you fear malaria, and therefore take antidotes. Is it therefore ignoble that a man should fear hell? I trow not. Answer ye.*

But you say a man should love right for its own sake. A Christian may grow up to that, but as a rule he does not begin there. A boy goes to school because he fears his parents' displeasure if he does not, but afterwards he pursues knowledge for the joy it affords him, and the good he can do with it. So with a Christian. He may grow, from fear of punishment, into positive and noble love of God and man.

Knowing what humanity is, St. Theresa was foolish to go about with fire in one hand to burn up heaven, and water in the other to quench hell, so that room might be made for better motives. We are creatures of low motive.

Another motive is SELF-LOVE. This is not selfishness. In the latter there is always a disregard to the rights or the feelings or the good of others. But self-love is that principle which God has implanted in us all to seek our own good. This is compatible with true benevolence, yea, with the highest form of religion. It is one of God's commands, "Thou shalt love thyself." Its roots are deeper than selfishness. Selfishness is hellish, self-love is divine; self-love is a noble duty. No man hateth his own flesh. If your house were on fire, you would

---

* Voltaire is credited with the following story : "Charles XII. once read on a tombstone this epitaph, 'Here lies a man who never knew fear.' Then, said His Majesty, 'the fool never snuffed a candle with his fingers.'"

leave furniture and books, and show your love of self by your attempts to escape.

Hope is another. He left that city, hoping to find another and a better. There is a better world, an eternal city, where death never enters, and disease never comes. There the light is never dim, the riches do not escape, the beauty does not fade, the joy is never disturbed with grief. It is prepared for you: will you leave sin and a worldly life for it? This is the result of leaving sin for righteousness. These are the motives attributed to this pilgrim. Have you such? I ask, have you such? because it is frequently supposed, and the supposition finds support from the terminology of our church life, that the ordinary motives of men are not brought into operation in the matter of salvation. And fear, self-love and hope, are the most ordinary motives of life.

Take the case of an emigrant: While living and toiling for bare subsistence in old countries, he fears—especially as responsibilities grow upon him—that he will not be able to remain there comfortably and honestly. Political, social and educational rights are denied him. His self-love prompts him to seek a newer country. He asks himself, why should I, a man, with strength of sinew and brain, toil all my life for naught, to find at the end of it a poor-house and a pauper's grave? why should I, a man, bring up my children in poverty and ignorance, and then they, in their turn, be denied a righteous reward? Why should I and mine be the slaves of custom and the stereotyped opinions of men who think that because they wear the titles of rank, which they give each other, and which are often the heirlooms of crime, they are the aristocrats of the universe? Self-love rises against it.

Then he reads of a new country, where men are free and intelligent; where labor is honored and honorable; where brain and muscle bring their price; where a man can be a man, not because he is the farthest removed from him who "founded the family," but because God made him. Hope springs up within his heart. Such a man you will frequently see on the wharves in Liverpool, literally seeking his salvation. He leaves father, mother, brother and sister—the living and the dead—for this. He is moved by fear, self-love and hope.

The same may be seen in an invalid: She fears the disease of which she is a victim; she sends for a physician, and takes all manner of nauseous drugs, submits to low fare and to be treated as a child, not because she loves these things, but because she loves herself, and because she hopes they will be the means of her restoration.

These ordinary motives are the ones on which you must act, and yet, I venture to say, that many of you are waiting for some extraordinary supernatural impulse to move you before you ask what you must do to inherit eternal life! Do not wait for that. If you believe that sin is punishable, if you know that you have sinned, then let fear of the consequences, love to self, and the hope which is held out in the gospel, move you to the salvation of your soul.

III. *His hindrances.* You will observe that they arose partly from his own ignorance. He knew his condition and danger, but he knew not what to do to escape either. No sinner seems to. You may have heard the word preached for many years, and yet not know the way of salvation by faith in Christ. If you are this night aroused to a sense of your danger, you will cry out, as he did, and as Paul did, "What must I do to be saved?"

He was hindered by his family. They thought "some distemper had got into his head." They treated him harshly; tried to divert his thoughts from his convictions, and derided his fears. An unconcerned sinner does not understand an awakened one. The one is to the other an insoluble enigma. A friend of my own, in this condition, visited the clergyman of his parish. The reverend brother thought it was a case of melancholia, and forthwith supplied him with a half-dozen new novels. But a young lady broke the spell grandly. Her friends tried to stop her conversion; did their utmost to scatter her serious thoughts. To do this they took her to the theater and opera and balls;

kept her away from religious associations. One evening she was taken to a *musicale sociable*, and being possessed of a fine, cultivated voice, was led to the piano for the performance of a favorite song. She struck a few chords, and then she sang in the ears of her relatives, who threatened to expel her from her home—

> "There is my house, my portion fair,
> My treasure and my heart are there,
> And my abiding home;
> For me my elder brethren stay,
> And angels beckon me away,
> And Jesus bids me come."

And thus broke the opposition forever.

This is but an every day picture of divided families. How frequently it is that one starts alone, and starts opposed by the others. Sometimes the husband hinders the wife. Oh husbands, your wives might be Christians but for you. It is heart-breaking for them to think of a Christian profession without you. And sometimes the wife hinders the husband. Her desire for gaiety and pleasure is an obstacle. Can I not persuade you, brothers and sisters, husbands and wives, parents and children, to start together? God's old-fashioned way of saving men, was in families. Early and continuous promises are made to families. But if you will not start together, let each one start alone.

Public opinion was against him. His neighbors opposed him. They joined his family in the general derision and attempts to keep him back. Two of them, Obstinate and Pliable, started after him, determined to make him return. But of this I will say no more. "*Vox populi*" is not always "*Vox Dei.*"

LASTLY. *let us talk about his Helps.* A man, named Evangelist, saw him and heard him and came to him. This man, in Bunyan's history, was "the good Mr. Gifford," pastor of the Baptist Church at Bedford, under whose personal directions Bunyan was led to Christ. In the allegory he is the portrait of "the good minister of Jesus Christ," whose mission it is to direct souls to the Master.

Preachers should help sinners as Evangelist did, by—

1. *Looking out for burdened souls.* There are many who have not courage to come to us, and because we do not go to them, think no man cares for their souls.

2. *Entering into direct personal conversation.* So close does the physician get to his patient, and so close does the lawyer get his client, and the merchant to the buyer. There is little success in these things till this is done. While I would say nothing that appears to limit the operation of the Spirit of God, yet I do believe that success is only attained by immediate contact of soul with soul.

3. *By giving proper directions.* He gave him a parchment roll—some instruction applicable to his case. Every case is "peculiar," and demands special attention. I preached in prison a few Sabbaths ago. At the conclusion of my sermon, one of the prisoners came to me and said, "Sir, if I were to ask you, 'what must I do to be saved,' what would you reply?" I told him that I would give no reply until I knew him. He expressed his suspicion of my orthodoxy in a moment, and instructed me that the proper answer would be, "Believe on the Lord Jesus Christ, and thou shalt be saved." It was now my turn, and so I put to him this question: "Do you believe on the Lord Jesus Christ?" "Yes, sir, I do." (With emphasis.) "Well, then, how comes it that you are here?" He was emphatically silent.

Evangelist gave Christian no instruction until he discovered his condition. Here Bunyan is true to Scripture, and those who adopt the other plan of saying, "Believe on the Lord Jesus Christ and thou shalt be saved," to any and everybody, are not. Of the many examples of men seeking their salvation, given in the Scriptures, to one only was this answer given. Different answers were given to different individuals. To the people who came to John the Baptist, with the question. "What shall we do, then?" he said, "He that hath two coats, let him impart to him that hath none ; and he that hath meat, let him do likewise." To the publicans who said to him, "Master, what shall we do?" he replied, "Exact no more than that which is appointed you." To the soldiers who demanded an answer for themselves to the same question, he said, "Do violence to no man, neither accuse any falsely ; and be content with your wages." The young man whom Jesus loved, was told to sell all that he had and give it to the poor, and follow Christ. Christ said to Nicodemus, "Ye must be born again." To the penitent thief, "To-day shalt thou be with me in Paradise." To the multitudes who repented under the preaching of Peter on the day of Pentecost, and who cried out, "Men and brethren, what shall we do?" the apostles said, "Repent and be baptized, every one of you, in the name of Jesus Christ, for the remission of sins." To his own disciples the Master said, "Except ye be converted and become as little children, ye shall in no wise enter the kingdom of heaven." Does not this sustain the statement that the way of salvation for one man is different from that which will save another? There are different ways to Christ, just as there are ways to get to New York. There is a way from the prairies, a way from over the ocean, a way from north, south, east and west, by rail, by ship, by carriage. It depends upon where a man is, as to the way he must take to reach it.

If a man be drowning, you throw out a rope to save him ; if he be starving, a rope is useless, you give him bread; if fever burns in his veins, neither are helpful, we give him drugs. It is impossible to save these three men in one way. So if a man be a liar, he must speak the truth to be saved ; if he be a thief, he must become honest; if a drunkard, he must become sober; if lecherous, he must be chaste ; if selfish, he must become benevolent. All this is included in believing in Christ, but my objection is to giving a general rule when specific directions are necessary. To tell the Phillipian jailer to sell his goods and give them to the poor, would have been mockery ; not to have demanded it of the young lawyer, would have been to ruin him.

I cannot help but refer to my own history. When about thirteen years of age I decided to be a Christian. It happened in this wise: I attended a meeting with the rest of my parents' household. During the recital of religious history, my brother Samuel, who is now a preacher of the Gospel, began to weep, and finally to pray. Before the meeting was over he professed conversion.

I was moved, though stubborn. With my brother we walked home—mother between us. Samuel was happy, mother was praying, and I was miserable. I felt my mother praying for me. Now, I never could stand her prayers, and so when I reached home I was completely broken down, and instead of *saying* my prayers that night, I prayed with strong crying and tears for the Lord to save me. My prayers brought father to me. I had heard him preach many a good sermon, and received from him many a sound thrashing; but nothing that he had done ever affected me as his kneeling by my side and mingling his prayers and tears with mine. When in my intense grief and earnestness I said, "Father, what shall I do to be saved?" he replied, "My son, believe that Jesus died for you."

I shall never forget my feelings. I should have felt mocked, but father loved me too much to mock me. He assured me again and again that I must do that. On his assurance I became happy, and on this experience joined the church.

Shortly afterwards I was accused of naughtiness; and then my father corrected me. I do not now remember his words, but they were to the effect that it was of no use for me to pray and believe and join the church and go to meeting, unless I tried to be good. Here was an inconsistency which I felt, though I did not understand it.

There was no need for me to believe that Christ died for me; I had never doubted it. I had learned the whole story at my mother's knee, had heard it from her lips, warm from her heart. Believing that did not save me from sin, nor has it ever. I make the sad confession, that I have often wickedly and wilfully broke God's law, because I believed that the "blood of Christ—God's Son—cleanseth from all sin." I have sinned, and believed the consequences would amount to nothing, because I had been taught, and I believed that by some means which I could not understand, the matter was righted by Christ in His death on the cross. There are many hundreds in this condition. They cover immortal lives all over with Scripture quotations.

Think of it again for a moment. Here was my devoted father seeing his prayers answered in mine. I was just emerging from youth to manhood. Would he trifle with me? No! Let me speak that word in *thunder tones*, NO! He loved me too well for that. It was the manner in which he began the Christian life, but it was not applicable to my condition. I wanted to be saved from sin, from myself, from the thralldom of my habits, and he did not understand me. Nor do men trifle in such circumstances. They do err, not knowing the Scriptures.

I have shown from the Word of God, analogy, and my own experience, that each sinner's case is peculiar, and needs special direction, and that it is folly (if not worse) to attempt to answer the question, "What shall I do?" until the enquirer is understood. Sinners must be known, and to be known they must be studied.

He points him to "The Wicket Gate," but when the Pilgrim confessed he could not see it, he then advised him to follow the light he could see. Ah! poor soul, if thou can'st not as yet see Christ, follow the light you can see; and just as we can trace every beam of light to the suns, every rill to the ocean, every road to the metropolis, so surely will all moral and spiritual light lead thee to Him who is The Light of the world—the Sun of Righteousness.

Another help is found in his common sense. He began to cry "What must I do?" Evidently he had read the book he held in his hand. Hence he did not cry "What shall I feel," or

"What shall I believe," as men are taught to do now. Such questions are not asked in the Scriptures. Men who are led by the Holy Ghost ask what they shall do, and then rejoice in ONE in whom they believe. Doing is not a deadly thing; it does not end in death; it is a response to the breath of heaven; it results in life. They that do the commandments are blessed; shall have a right to the tree of life, and enter through the gates into the city.

But he found his greatest help in his own intense earnestness. Without this, Evangelist, the roll, the light are nothing.

He began to run. "Now he had not run far from his own door, but his wife and children perceiving it, began to cry after him to return; but the man put his fingers in his ears and ran on, crying, "Life! Life! Eternal Life!"

His life was at stake, and that made him earnest. Would to God you would so start for heaven this night; that you realized the importance of saving your lives; that these thoughts would make you as earnest as he who cried "LIFE! LIFE! ETERNAL LIFE!

LECTURE III.

THE SLOUGH OF DESPOND; THE WAY IN AND WAY OUT.

[SYNOPSIS OF CHAPTER.—Obstinate, being unable to persuade Christian to return with him, goes back to his own house. Pliable and Christian pursue the journey by themselves. They spend the time in profitable conversation, wherein Christian instructs and delights the new pilgrim. It is chiefly concerning the glories of the city to which they tend, that they talk. Pliable is so delighted, that, after every statement of Christian's, he asks, "And what else?" He becomes so eager, that he urges his companion to mend his pace. From this Christian was hindered by the burden on his back. They now reach a plain wherein is a morass called the "Slough of Despond," into which, as they were both heedless, they fell. Pliable grew angry, and after an effort or two got out the side nearest his own house, to which he immediately returned. Christian would have perished, but that One, whose name is Help, saw him and delivered him, set him on sound ground, and let him go on his way. This slough cannot be mended. For 1800 years the King's laborers have been trying to do so, but failed. It is Despond still. It is the place where the scum and filth that attend conviction of sin do continually run. Pliable, at home, is derided, mocked, and regarded as fool and coward. Presently he gained courage, and like many another, began to deride poor Christian behind his back.]

BUNYAN calls his Pilgrim a Christian as soon as he had fairly started from the "City of Destruction;" long before he had seen or heard of the "Palace Beautiful," by which is meant the Church; long before he reaches the Interpreter's house, which means that stage of Christian life in which a man receives a special enlightenment of God's Spirit; even before he trod the narrow path or passed through the Strait Gate; before he had lost his rags or burden, he received the name of "Christian."

We have greatly advanced since the days of John Bunyan. Theology, the queen of sciences, like all other sciences, has advanced. We live in an age of advanced thought. Now, no man is called a Christian until he has joined the Church; until he can give evidence of many subtle experiences, and becomes indoctrinated in the scholastic theology. We withhold the name until the Pilgrim shall be a guest instructed and armed in the Beautiful Palace.

Are we right, or is Bunyan? We conceive that his idea of a Christian was this: One who desired to leave a life of sin and live a life of righteousness; who endeavored to leave the one and attain the other through Jesus Christ. Not merely one who had accomplished this, but also one who was struggling to do so. Just as we should classify a babe under the *genus homo*, so we classify all such under the generic term, "Christian." Here Bunyan and Wesley agree. The latter admitted to his societies any who expressed a desire to "flee from the wrath to come."

Christian life begins at the lowest possible point. Its birth is always very feeble; "Thou canst not tell whence it cometh," for "it cometh not with observation." The lower we descend in the order of nature, the more perfect is the creature born; the higher we go, the more imperfect does it commence its existence. A fly is born a fly at once, wings, limbs, head, body, and all parts. It is ready for business the hour it is hatched. But it is not so with the dog, one of the most sagacious and intelligent of animals. It is born blind, helpless, stupid; we have to keep him six months before he begins to learn, and another six before he is useful. According to the same law, the mind is less at birth than the body. It takes longer for the mind to mature than the flesh. If, then, by this law the life of the spirit be higher than that of the mind or body, we ought not to be surprised to find it very feeble in its beginnings, and discovering it so feeble, acknowledge it to be Christian. We are, therefore, willing to call any man a Christian, whatever his past life may have been, or his present difficulties are, always provided that he is seeking the way of righteousness through faith in Christ.

Such, certainly, is the doctrine of Christ. His kingdom is composed of little children and child-like men. The one essential of entrance thereto is child-likeness. "Verily I say unto you, whosoever shall not receive the kingdom of God as a little child, shall in nowise enter therein." These words are very plain and unmistakable. Unless you are willing to commence the Christian life just where you commenced your ordinary life, at the weakest, most dependent, most ignorant point, you can in nowise enter therein.

Let us suppose that a man wishes to enter the kingdom of Music. He is ignorant of notations, scales, sharps, flats, and everything else pertaining to the science. Now, if he wants to be a musician, he must begin to learn and perform just where a little child does. He must be treated as a child, for he is as ignorant and as skilless. If he objects to learn music because at his first attempt he cannot sing the Twelfth Mass or play the organ accompaniment, he cannot enter therein. The most ignorant tyro in music can teach him, and he must take the lowest place, or none at all. The music-teacher from the first calls such a disciple. A Christian must first be a Christian child. He must be born anew. So soon as his desires take a practical shape, he is regarded by Christ as one of His own.

What is said of music may be said with equal truth of any other branch of art, of science and of literature. The laws by which a man proceeds to be a Christian, are the same as those by which he must become anything else; but to be a Christian he is moved by a Higher and Holier Spirit.

All the great Christians, such as Paul and John, Arguntin, Luther, Wyckliff, Wesley, Whitfield, Howard, Knox, Spurgeon, Muller;—yea, each one began as a little child. And this is the secret of their greatness.

Think for a moment of Galileo, Corpernicus, Newton, Faraday, Young, Agassiz, Tyndall, Dana and Dawson; names mighty in science, at one time knowing no more about it than we do. They had to begin as little children. This is the secret of their greatness, their great discoveries, and the great benefits given by them to the world. In the light of this eternal law, may I not beg of you to enter the kingdom of God as little children.

Let us now proceed to follow the fortunes of our Pilgrim. Obstinate has turned his back on his neighbors and gone home. Christian and Pliable attempt the journey together. They spend their time in profitable conversation, and both are helped. All went well until they came to a very miry slough, which they had not observed, and into which they both tumbled. Pliable struggled out, in high dudgeon, on the side nearest his own city, and returned; Christian was helped out the side next the Wicket Gate, and went on.

"The Slough" is a piece of rural scenery which Bunyan has wrought with consummate genius into his "dream." Scores of times in his wandering life he had to ford such boggy places. "The lily-bordered Ouse" upon which he looked through the grating of his cell, may have suggested the Slough, and the fortunes of the travelers in crossing it at low water, may have been the material out of which he has produced the misfortunes of his Pilgrim. You have possibly seen such. The prairies abound in sloughs. This offensive place in nature is made the picture of as great an offense in Christian experience. Most pilgrims fall in; some get out, but none without mire.

If we want to see the thing in a Christian's history, we may refer to the life of Bunyan. It is that period when he believed he was not "elected," and made the foolish attempt to prove himself a Jew, because he believed all the Jews were chosen people; when he believed he had no faith, and tried to work miracles to prove that he had; when he gave up trying to be good, because he believed he had committed "the unpardonable sin." David must have suffered in like manner, for he tells us that he was delivered from the "horrible pit and miry clay." Saul of Tarsus was in the "slough" when he was three days without sight, neither did eat or drink. "It is the descent whither the scum and filth that attend conviction of sin do continually run." It is the time when a man falls into himself, and finds only evil, and that continually.

> "Where hardly a human foot could pass,
> Or a human heart would dare
> On the quaking turf of the green morass;
> His all he had trusted there."

There is a cause, or there are causes, of the sloughs that abound on the prairie. It is the business of the scientist to discover, and when desirable, mend them. We propose to search for the cause of the Slough of Despond, and preach you out of it.

In our last lecture we pointed out that the Pilgrim started under the influence of fear, and we defended the wisdom of his action. When it is the best motive the preacher can appeal to, and the only one left in the man (as is frequently the case), neither is fool to do the best he can under the circumstances. But it is not the only motive that exists in Christian life. If alone, it will produce excess. It is a good stimulant, but like all stimulants, it leaves a corresponding depression. It is like a whip, a very good thing to start a stubborn horse with, but very poor corn to feed him on.

An artist desires to produce a statue; for this purpose he goes to the quarry with gunpowder, drill and match. With these he blasts the rock, and gets a block suitable for his purpose. Does he now use more gunpowder? No; he applies the chisel, and produces a model of art, resembling a thing of life. But you see he does very little of it with gunpowder. It is useful at the beginning, but would be destructive at the end. Now, unless stimulants give place to food, there can be no agreeable, healthy life; unless the whip gives way to care and corn, there can be no useful horse; unless gunpowder is quiet while the chisel performs its mission, there can be no statue; and unless fear of punishment gives way to faith in Christ, there can be no success in the Christian pilgrimage.

These are but illustrations. Come to actual experience. Let us suppose that a revival will occur in this city this winter. What do we expect? We deliberately calculate on a great falling away. So many will be moved by the ministry of fear, that, unless that is followed by the ministry of faith, the declension is inevitable.

There is a great and vital difference between galvanism and life; and yet a subject galvanized, though dead, may look like life. Place the poles of a battery on any particular organ of the brain of a corpse, and it will open its eyes and mouth; move its limbs at your pleasure; but take away the current, and the corpse will fall back to the grave.

But when a man lives, he has something behind and beneath the mere appearance of life. His life may be as feeble as a babe's, but it is life, and the life of a babe is better than the electrified movements of a corpse. Many converts are magnetized by singing, oratory and sympathy. But unless this gives place to faith in Christ, like Pliable, they will go back to the City of Destruction; and those that go on will go through the Slough of Despond. He that believeth on the Son hath life. But the ministry that never creates fear is barren of converts.

We also saw that our Pilgrim was moved by Hope. Fear sent him from the City of Destruction; Hope allured him to the Celestial City. He and Pliable spent their time in talking of the things hoped for; they became so much interested in the glories of the future, that they neglected the duties of the present, and so, by "being heedless, did both suddenly fall into the bog." They fell into this Slough, you see, under the undue influence of hope. Men frequently fail in consequence of this. If men of business send their thoughts too far into the future, give too many notes, speculate too much, instead of watching the markets and their finances closely, they quickly fall into "The Slough of Despond." Notice those men who are always going to do some grand thing in the future, and you will see that they frequently do some very foolish things in the present. They are too sanguine. It is bad policy to count your chickens before they are hatched; and it is equally unwise to think we are in heaven before we are well on the way. Let not him who putteth on the armor, boast as he that putteth it off. Paul knew a man who was caught up into the third heaven, so entranced with the glory, that whether in the body or out, he could not tell; he heard words which it is not lawful for man to utter on earth; but that man came down to receive a thorn in his flesh and meet the buffeting messenger of Satan. Peter wanted to stay on Tabor, where it was good for men to behold the glory of the Master; but with his Master and companions, he had to descend for the humbler work of casting out devils and preaching the gospel.

Suppose a farmer were to stand talking to his neighbors about the glorious harvest he expected; his hopes would soon fall into despondency. The glorious harvest will not come by expecting it. The Celestial City is not attained by exciting one's hopes concerning it, but by carefully walking in the way of righteousness now. "Ponder well the paths of thy feet."

In every little village with railroad, newspaper, saloon, fast horse, crushing tax, and other evidences of civilization; with naught but a forge, grist-mill, school house, two hundred inhabitants, four churches, and the deep mellow loam which the good Lord has been hoarding for ages, there are men to be found who believe that such a place must speedily become a second Chicago. Dear, hopeful souls, they hope against reason, and are speedily depressed; whereas if they would but just accept the situation and toil on, they might grow wealthy. Hope must have good, deep and broad foundations, for we are saved by Hope. But a babe may have too much cordial, a small ship may have too much sail, and a young Christian may be too sanguine.

Just as the excess of good, solid, nourishing food may produce disease, just as stimulants will produce depression, so surely, and in like manner, will hope and fear (though in themselves good), if unduly administered and indulged, produce that state of experience which Bunyan calls the Slough of Despond. Pliable was specially moved by hope.

But there is a way out of this condition—indeed, there are two, one backwards, the other forwards; one on the side that lies nearest the Celestial City; the other on the side nearest the City of Destruction. There is a right and a wrong way out. Which one will you take?

There came to him (Christian) a man whose name was Help. He was helped out and put on to sound ground by this man. He is the Savior revealed under this name. He was on the look-out for Christian. He permitted him to fall into the Slough, but he did not permit him to perish there. The parable of the lost sheep and lost pieces of money, illustrates the fact that Christ *seeks* to save men. A little girl was asked during the Edinburgh revival, if she had found Jesus. "I don't know," she replied, "but I know he has found me."

"Give me thy hand," said Help. Christian did so, and was delivered. This means that you are just to trust yourself and your case, with all its peculiarities, to Christ. It is His work to save; it is yours to trust him. Think of Christ. Just as thinking of your condition in the light of conscience, universal law, and the Word of God, makes you wretched, so thinking of Christ and trusting in Christ, will make you joyful. You may get out of the Slough by transferring your thoughts from yourselves to Him, if in your thoughts you completely trust Him.

Despondency takes many forms. A remarkable case is that of Robert Hall's mother. During the latter years of her life she was subject to most distressing spiritual despondency; she was convinced that she would be lost, and no arguments or pleas seemed to alter her belief. On one occasion she took her husband's watch, which hung in her chamber, and said, "I need not regard time; I am entered on an eternal state of suffering;" and throwing the watch with vehemence on the floor, she exclaimed, "I am as surely damned as that watch is broken!" But the watch was not broken; and seeing this, she said with amazement and with tears, "Well, if God save me, all Heaven will be astonished; and none will wonder at his unparalleled mercy as myself."

In a few weeks, however, her despondency returned. Again she snatched up the watch, and thinking she had not before thrown it with sufficient force, she dashed it with the utmost violence across the room. But though the enamel had been cracked by an accidental fall some years before, it now received no further injury, even the glass was unbroken, and not the least apparent damage had been done.

On another occasion, two persons were left in charge of Mrs. Hall, as it was feared she might commit suicide. But she eluded both of them, escaped unperceived from the house, and at length returned, to their great surprise, wet through. It was subsequently ascertained that she had flung herself into a deep pit, full of water. How she got out she could not tell; but she said that while in the water the words sounded in her ears, "Deliver my soul from going down to the pit."

And it was delivered. At evening time there was light; the darkness was exchanged for joy unspeakable and full of glory. Her husband records with the utmost gratitude and affection the triumph of these last hours. "Seating myself," says he, "on the other side of the chamber, she waved her hand towards me. I returned to her and eagerly taking hold of her hand, she smiled, saying, "Mercy! Mercy! Sweet Jesus! Mighty to save! Found in Him—living—dying—judgment?" So she entered the saint's everlasting rest.

Despondency takes many forms, I repeat. "*I am not elected,*" says one. And he goes about moaning and mourning. Well, how do you know you are not—supposing your conception of the doctrine to be the correct one? I would not mourn about it until I knew. Go make your calling and election sure. If you are a candidate for eternal glory, you may. If you have any faith in the promise of God; if you have desire to flee from the wrath to come, by walking in the way of righteousness; if you really want to love God, and be taught of Christ, my impression is that you may call yourselves one of "the elect."

Would to God that all who think that they are the elect of God, or the *elite* of Christendom, were like you. But look from that doctrine to Christ. Do not get away from John III. to Romans IX. so quickly. Men are not saved by believing one or all of the five points of Calvinism, nor by being Arminians; but by choosing Christ as Redeemer, Master, Example, Lord. And be sure you do not forget that you cannot receive Him as Redeemer, unless you receive Him also as Master, Example, and Lord. He is a complete Savior, and He saves from hell, only as He saves from sin. If you would be saved from sin, you have the witness within that God has called you to newness of life. Certainly you are not given over to a reprobate mind.

"*But, I have sinned against the Holy Ghost*," says another; "therefore I am unpardonable." I do bless God that the sin against the Holy Ghost is not clearly revealed. No school of divines agree as to what it is precisely. But it seems a very improbable thing for any man to do. From the penalty attached, it would seem to be the least likely sin that a man would commit. If you have a desire to repent; if you would if you could live holily, you are yourselves living proof that the Holy Ghost has not left you; if, in looking to Christ, you can see in Him any love and beauty; if He is still desired by thee, you may put the despondency from your soul. You have *not* sinned against the Holy Ghost.

But, says another, "*If I begin I cannot keep on!*" How do you know? Did you ever try? Thousands as bad as you, as weak as you, have tried to keep on, and succeeded. Babes keep on by growing. Last summer I spoke to a poor paralyzed drunkard about commencing the life. "I would," said he, "but I can't continue." I assured him he could, if he would be patient enough to take a step at a time, and every one in advance. The poor harlot would often turn from her life of shame, but knowing the power of carnal desire and the obstructions of modern society, fears that she cannot keep on. My brother and sister, you can if you will. Trust your case to Help; to the One who is mighty, and you will succeed, for He is mighty to save. "He is able to keep you from falling, and to make all grace to abound toward you; that you, always having all sufficiency in all things, may abound in every good work." "Believe ye that He is able to do this?" I knew an invalid who, in his own opinion and that of his friends, could not walk a hundred steps. But, when leaning on the arm of a friend, out in the sunshine, strength and energy came with every succeeding step, and he would walk a mile, each step growing stronger and lighter. He seemed to walk the disease out of him. So do ye. Lean on the Mighty One. "Trust in Him with all thine heart, and lean not to thine own understanding," and you will find, in the sunlight of His love, strength and energy return. But always lean on Him. His name is HELP.

But another says: "*I am too bad to be saved.*" Now, that is not true. You who say that with any regret, are not. That tone of regret is music in heaven. Are you sorry that you are so bad? Bless God; that is godly sorrow, and it will yet work repentance to life. Too bad? Will you say that, with the example of the unclean and bloody David, lecherous Magdalene, craven Peter, blaspheming Saul, before you? Will you say that you are too bad, with the parable of the Prodigal in your memory? You may be a very great sinner, but Christ is a very great Savior. You are not too bad. When Mr. Whitfield was once preaching, he said, in the excitement of the moment, that "God received the devil's castaways." The next morning at breakfast, Lady Huntington expressed her doubts both as to the propriety of this expression, and its theology. Whitfield adhered to his statement. Just at that moment he was summoned to the door, where stood a daughter of shame. "Oh, sir," she said, "I heard you preach, yesterday, that God received the devil's castaways. I have come to know if it is true. I am one such; I have lived a life of sin. Man has thrown me off; yesterday I was sent into the fields to die. Will God take me?" Whitfield led her into peace through faith; the Countess was convinced, and the poor woman lived and died a restored soul.

None of you have sinned like that; if you had, I should still preach these delightful words: "Wherefore He is able to save to the uttermost all that come to God by Him," and ask you to sing with me—

"None but Jesus can do helpless sinners good."

It may be almost necessary to say that the Slough is not essential to salvation. I say this, because I find some men and women who apparently feel at home in it. We find men in very morbid conditions; there is neither sense nor grace in them. If we heard of a city visited by cholera or some fatal epidemic, or a locality where miasmatic poison was prevalent, we would keep away, and remain at home, where it was healthful. A man would be scarcely sane to delight in such places. They are not necessary; indeed, they are fatal to health.

There are some Christians who emit nothing but miasmatic disease among those who are seeking Christ. They demand *experience*. I was once told that I could not be saved until I could say that I was the chief of sinners. Well, I never could tell that lie. A system of theology popular not many years ago, made it an item of salvation that the sinner should be willing to be damned, if God decreed it. Religious, and especially devotional books, are full of this deadly poison. It is not the will of God that any man should be in this condition. We shall meet with Pilgrims who escaped it. You may also. Men are not saved by looking within themselves, but unto Jesus, the author and finisher of faith. You will not be saved by thinking how bad you are, but how gracious He is.

Neighbor Pliable was very angry with Christian when he fell into the bog. After a struggle or two he got out on the side next his own house, and Christian saw him no more. When he reached home his neighbors visited him; some applauded him, some mocked, some called him fool and coward, and thus he sat "sneaking" among them. Then, with the others, he began to deride Christian behind his back.

He got out the wrong side, nearest his own home. That is the wrong way out, for it is the way back. How many of you, my friends, are but like him? Oh! how have you gone back! Had you but been faithful to your convictions; had you but been led by the Spirit of God, you might have been far on the road by this time. But you are in the world, of the world, living for the world, disquieted within, reckless, unhappy, dissatisfied; with cravings for higher things, which you know not how to satisfy; hardly respecting yourselves for your want of faith or courage in not living according to the light that God has given you. Possibly derided by some who knew your history, secretly despised by them, too, just as you despise others in your own condition; and then, it may be, in your turn deriding good Christians behind their backs. "And thus much concerning Pliable," and you.

But there is something worse than "The Slough of Despond," into which men fall. I mean conceit. Let the drowning man say he needs no rope; the invalid that he needs no physician; the lonely, to whom life is like a dark cave that gives not back an echo even, say that they need no friend. When they do that, you may say you have no need of Christ. A man may be saved if he falls into Despond, but if he falls into Conceit, there is more hope of a fool than of him.

LECTURE IV.

MR. WORLDLY-WISEMAN.

[SYNOPSIS OF CHAPTER.—Christian, alone, walks laboriously along in consequence of the burden on his back, towards the Wicket Gate, as he was directed by Evangelist. He now meets with Mr. Worldly-Wiseman, who has heard of his pilgrimage. This gentleman interests himself in him, inquires concerning his family, sympathizes with him, gains his ear, and then proceeds to administer "wholesome advice." He describes the way in which Christian is traveling, as being exceptionally troublesome; casts aspersions on Evangelist, and the Book which he has in his hand, and succeeds finally, by many brilliant promises, in turning The Pilgrim from the way to the town of Morality, where he may be eased from his burden, by Mr. Legality or his son Civility. Christian essays to take this advice, but to reach the town of Morality he has to pass a very high hill. When he came to do so he was much affrighted, for part of the hill that stood nearest the way-side did hang so much over, that Christian thought it would fall on his head. Then there came flashes of fire out of it, and Christian was afraid he would be burned. His burden here seemed heavier than before. He now feels sorry that he took the advice of Mr. Worldly-Wiseman. Evangelist coming to the rescue, Christian is heartily ashamed of himself. He receives the reprimands of the good man with becoming meekness. Evangelist then proceeded to give him good counsel, and to show Christian his mistake, which might have been fatal. The Pilgrim being penitent, "Evangelist kissed him, gave him one smile, and bid him God speed."]

BISHOP WILBERFORCE was once asked whether he knew the way to heaven. "Oh yes," replied the witty prelate, "I have known it from a child; take the first turn to the right, and then keep straight on." A better answer has never been given.

Our Pilgrim has taken that "turn to the right," and has been going "straight on," notwithstanding various efforts on the part of neighbors and friends to shake his purpose. He has heroically forded the Slough of Despond; his courage has won our sympathies. But what his friends, by tears and entreaties, failed to do, will be attempted by one who appears to be wise, and looks like a gentleman. He will not attempt to turn him back, but will turn him aside. He knows that Christian cannot now go back to the City of Destruction, but he is as hostile to Christ as were the ignorant neighbors; therefore he employs his craft to deceive. Being a Worldly-Wiseman, he knows that the current of a river and a beam of light cannot be sent back, but they can both be turned from their direct course. So he employs his energies to turn Christian out of the way.

Behold our Pilgrim, with burden, rags, book, and the mud of the Slough of Despond on him, going laboriously onward, with sighs, groans and tears. He is alone. Pliable has returned. Help has performed his mission, and is possibly helping another poor soul out of the Slough. He is just in the condition for sympathy and temptation. Just at this moment Mr. Worldly-Wiseman accidentally, apparently, but really by design, meets him. He knows him by his guise, for Christian's setting out has been much talked of. He sympathizes with him, gains his attention, and then, by advice and brilliant promises, succeeds in turning him from the way that leads to the Wicket Gate, whither he has been directed by Evangelist; to the town of Morality, that he may be rid of his burden at the hands of Mr. Legality, or his son Civility.

The whole of his arguments amount to these two propositions:

First—That the way to the Celestial City is essentially one of sorrow.

Second—That Mr. Legality can ease pilgrims of their burdens.

As all sinners who seek Christ will meet with much of this worldly-wisdom, and as it will have the effect, if listened to, of turning them from Christ, I shall reduce the propositions to plain statements, available for our purpose.

First—The world thinks and says that the Christian life is an unhappy one.

Second—That men can be saved by doing the works of the law.

I meet these statements by a most emphatic denial. The Christian life is not unhappy. Sinners cannot be justified or saved by doing the works of the law; by Civility, Legality, or Morality.

I. Christian life is not an unhappy one.

"Get rid of thy burden, for thou wilt never be settled in thy mind till then: nor can'st thou enjoy the benefits of the blessings which God has bestowed upon thee till then;" quoth Worldly-Wiseman.

Quite true, sir! so far we agree.

"There is not a more dangerous and troublesome way in the world, than is that unto which he hath directed thee, and that thou shalt find if thou wilt be ruled by his (Evangelist's) counsel. Hear me, I am older than thou. Thou art like to meet with, in the way which thou goest, wearisomeness, painfulness, hunger, perils, nakedness, sword, lions, dragons, darkness, and, in a word, death, and what not."

Partially true in the letter; absolutely false in the spirit, Mr. Worldly-Wiseman. Here we disagree, and must part company. I affirm the opposite. The Christian's life is essentially happy.

We appeal to the Scriptures.

When Christ began to unfold the conditions and laws of the kingdom of God, He sat down and taught men, saying, "Blessed." The word has never been changed. It is the chief word in the vocabulary of Christian experience. Its force is intense. It is all-comprehensive. Until he used it, men had described the condition of their gods, demigods and heroes in elysium thereby. They had never applied it to any men. They thought, as many do now, that a man's happiness here consists in his possessions, either mental or material; the experience of the world, notwithstanding. But Christ took a word sacred to their highest conceptions of bliss, and used it as being the only appropriate one, to convey an idea of the Blessedness of being humble-minded, pure-hearted, meek, merciful, righteous, peaceful. Happiness arises from certain spiritual conditions. It is a fountain of living water, which flows from the midst of a man. It is absolutely inseparable from them as is heat from fire, light from the sun, beauty and perfume from the rose.

But in my appeal to the Scripture, I must not forget that other words are used in connection with the Christian life; "trial," "tribulation," "anguish," "sorrow," "persecution," "peril," "death," and many others. No true history of Christian living could be recorded without the use of one, or perhaps all of them.

"In the world ye shall have tribulation," says Christ. Righteous men, says Paul, "had trial of cruel mockings and scourgings, of bonds and imprisonment. They were stoned, sawn asunder, were tempted, slain with the sword, were destitute, afflicted, tormented; they wandered in deserts, and in mountains, and caves of the earth." "These are they who came out of great tribulation," said the elder to John, of the white-robed, innumerable multitude who stood around the throne of God. The history of the Church confirms all this. And yet Christ says now, as he has from the beginning, "Come unto me all ye that labor, and are heavy laden, and I will give you *rest*. Take my yoke upon you and learn of me, for I am meek and lowly of heart; and ye shall find *rest* unto your souls. *For my yoke is easy and my burden is light.*" These two classes of statement appear contradictory. They are, however, not even inconsistent with each other.

It will be conceded that happiness is not dependent on circumstances, but on interior conditions. The rich are not all happy. The votary of pleasure is frequently most miserable. The poor are sometimes happy. The godly poor always are so. Kings wear crowns of gold before the public; crowns of thorn before God. The rich appear to have all that heart can wish, but really have not satisfied their heart's desire. They may gratify their lusts, but not satisfy their souls. They intend to build bigger barns and acquire larger stores, before they say: Soul! take thine ease; eat, drink, and be merry.

> "All the world's a stage, and
> All the men and women merely players."

To us, who look on, the curtain seems plain; to those who see it raised, there is either tragedy or comedy. No, no, my friends, happiness is so precious that God does not trust it to unstable materials; He gives it to the soul alone.

Christ, in his promise, says, "And ye shall find rest to your *souls.*" He giveth peace, but not as the world giveth. He giveth rest and peace to the soul, from whence alone happiness can flow. Christ's yoke fits the nature of man exactly. Man was made for it, and it was made for man. The burden of Christian duties is light. "His commandments are not grievous."

Let me suppose that one of you possess a very fine horse. You send him to the harness-maker's for a new set of harness, to be made expressly for him. It is made and on him. You are very particular to see that the collar fits; that it does not chafe or irritate his neck or shoulders. Being satisfied with that, you attach him to a beautifully painted, well-constructed, light carriage. As you proudly survey the "turn out," you anticipate much pleasure, for the "yoke is easy and the burden is light." Now, let me further suppose that you attempt a journey through the streets of a certain city, which, for obvious reasons, shall be nameless. I think you will at once see, that although the "yoke is easy and the burden light," you will have to go through a great trial of mud. Your fine carriage is filthy, horse spent, and yourself disappointed. But it was not caused by either horse, yoke, or burden. Given proper conditions, the ride would have been enjoyable. Such exercise we all know to be exceedingly pleasurable.

Now, a Christian life is like that. In itself it is all and more than Christ has promised it to be. The half has not been told, even by Him. Words are too few and too poor to describe it. It has to be linked to the holiest, best and richest things before a conception of it can be had. It has a peace which passeth all understanding. It gives a joy that is unspeakable and full of glory. But a Christian lives in a world opposed in its maxims, principles, and practice, to the life that Jesus lived and which He invites us to receive. Therefore, the life of a Christian in this world is attended by trial, for two cannot walk together unless they are agreed.

This happiness is not arbitrarily bestowed. It is embedded in the nature of things. A Christian is a righteous man. No unrighteous man is a Christian. I don't mean that the righteousness of another is by some pious fiction attributed to him. I do not use the word in any theological sense, but ask you to receive it as common sense suggests. He does right, and is therefore and thereby righteous. The word righteous is used to describe God's heroes, the Bible throughout. Only one kind of righteousness is acknowledged by God. But we have several kinds, or else one kind with different names, in our Church phraseology. That aside; the righteousness of which I speak is of Christ and of God. It is wrought into the soul and life by the Holy Ghost. It comes unto and upon all that believe. The Christian is clothed with righteousness, not artificially, but really and naturally. We are acquainted with two different kinds of clothing—artificial and natural. That which we wear is artificial. We can put it on and off at pleasure. We can discard it; we can assume the dress of another. Cowards may dress like heroes; traitors like kings; rogues like honest men; sinners like Christians. But we know another kind that is not so easily removed. Out in the fields you see the sheep, the ox, the horse, the birds. They are all clothed with hair, wool, or feathers. Our artificial clothing is their legacy to us. Now look at the process by which they are clothed. They eat grass and corn and herbs; it comes unto them in this way. They transform it into hair and wool and feathers; thus it comes upon them. So we receive Christ by faith. He is taken into the soul. He is the bread of our life; on Him and by Him we live.

We reproduce Him in righteousness of life, and in this way and not in any artificial manner, comes righteousness "unto and upon all who believe."

Not in fiction, but in fact, a Christian is a righteous man. Abel was *righteous* Abel; Lot is called righteous Lot; Abraham was righteous Abraham; Noah preached righteousness. God would have spared the cities of the plain if ten *righteous* men had been found there. I dare say there were plenty of religious people in those cities, as there are and ever have been in all cities given up to iniquity. Job was a righteous, or rather a right-up man.

Christ came to establish everlasting righteousness. He is the Sun of righteousness. His sceptre is a sceptre of righteousness. One of His first blessings was pronounced upon those who hungered and thirsted for righteousness. One of His first complaints was the little righteousness (not the religion) of the Scribes and Pharisees. He will bring in a new heaven and a new earth, wherein dwelleth righteousness.

Look into the matter yourselves, my hearers, and you will see it is righteousness, and not religion, that is acceptable to God. The fervent, effectual prayer of a righteous man availeth much with God. Christianity, then, is no substitute for righteousness; its foundation is righteousness; it does not overturn the throne of the Eternal, nor give society over to lawlessness. When a sinner goes to God for pardon, He sends him back to his fellow-man. "Therefore, if thou bring thy gift to the altar and rememberest that thy brother hath ought against thee, leave there thy gift before the altar, and go thy way; *first* be reconciled to thy brother, and then come and offer thy gift." God cannot establish iniquity by law or by gospel.

All the joys of righteousness—of being right and doing right—are his. The fruit of righteousness is peace and assurance forever. His peace flows as a river, because his righteousness abounds as the waves of the sea.

A Christian is more than righteous; he is a *good man*.

There is a distinction to be made between them. "Scarcely

for a righteous man will one die; yet, peradventure, for a good man some would dare to die." A man may be righteous, just in all his dealings, correct in behavior, and yet not be generous or kind. On the other hand, a man may be very generous, benevolent, and beneficent, and yet not be righteous. A follower of Christ unites the two. His deeds are good works. He therefore possesses the joys that flow from goodness, and learns practically that it is more blessed to give than to receive.

Take the element of mercifulness—

> "The quality of mercy is not strained;
> It droppeth as the gentle rain from heaven
> Upon the place beneath: it is twice blessed;
> It blesseth him that gives and him that takes."

This is one of the elements of a Christian's life. We often express our joy at being forgiven; we have received mercy; but this joy is not worthy of being compared with the blessedness of forgiving. I am never forgiven without a sense of shame, in consequence of my sin. I am ashamed to have to be forgiven. There is a privilege greater than that; I mean the Divine approval. Now, when I am merciful, when I forgive an enemy, I am enriched and ennobled in my spirit; I rise above the vengeance of my animal nature to actions and feelings akin to the Eternal God, whose son I am; Who is ever blessed, because all-merciful, and ever ready to forgive. Being thus reconciled to God in my life, I can rejoice with joy unspeakable and full of glory.

I have reasoned from Scripture and natural law that it is a mistake on the part of Worldly-Wiseman to suppose that a Christian's life is essentially sorrowful. But, perhaps, we have conveyed such an impression. If so, we are to blame.

Puritanism is not Christianity. Do we not rather seek to puritanize the Church, than to make it righteous through Christ. The Puritans were Christians, and so were many others who were diametrically opposed to them in faith and manner of life. Christian life is not made up of stern visage, rigorous self-denial, silent Sabbaths, and arbitrary habits. A puritan is like a photograph; it is a picture of life in one mood. But we are not always wearing one facial expression; not always smirking, smiling, sour, or stiff and awkward. We are not always in a ridiculous posture, flattering ourselves that we are the central figure of a work of art No. Life would be intolerable if it were so. There are many expressions of the human face divine, and many facets of the Holy Life.

Ritualism is not Christianity. By ritualists I mean all those who pay excessive attention to worship. It is our duty to worship God with becoming reverence and appropriate forms. But there is no piety in multiplying them. There is often a wicked waste of money and idle superstition in doing so. I fail to see any righteousness or mercy in making long pilgrimages, multiplying fasts, becoming learned in genuflections, making prayers, whether we desire the things for which we pray, or not. Worship is but one form and feature of the life of Christ's followers. It should always be spiritual; never formal and mechanical.

Perhaps those who think that the life we desire you to lead is joyless, have attended a prayer-meeting when a good brother addressed the Divine Being in elongated vowels and nasal consonants; when another spoke in sepulchral tones of the blessed promises, and anticipated death, as if he were afraid of it; when another defended his faith against hosts of deadly heresies, of which nobody knew and nobody cared; and when the gracious Father was praised in long-metre dirges. Perhaps he was taken to such a meeting when a boy, and is too much of a true Christian to return.

Or he may have been to some public service where the choir did all the singing; where men loved God so much that they praised Him by proxy; where, instead of the congregation shouting in thunder tones to the God of glory, and coming into His presence with gladness and a voice of triumph, a solo was substituted, which was sung correctly, as becometh a professional. And the pastor, if he were an old fogy, read a long, dry essay on predestination; and if he were a young fogy, one of the same kind, on "evolution," or the "survival of the fittest." And the congregation fell asleep, and were refreshed thereby; awoke to receive a benediction, for which they had paid; dispersed, much too respectable and too cultured to speak as Christ would have done to the strangers or the young. There are congregations like Coleridge's Ancient Mariner; the ship in a dead smooth, calm sea, and every man on board a corpse. From such burlesques on Christianity he infers that Christians are unhappy mortals; and well he may. They may have a peace which the world can neither give nor take away; but he finds it hard to believe it, and therefore is not attracted thereto.

But there is another cause for his inference. Christianity is theoretically opposed to sin, and he finds pleasure in sin. He naturally prefers a life which he knows to be pleasurable, to one of which he has just suspicion. Brethren, we ought not to allow such impressions. If we would but spend half as much time in being Christians as we do to be orthodox on the one hand, or liberal on the other, we should rejoice in the Lord always; we should serve Him with gladness. If Christian life be wholehearted, unrestrained, generous love to God and man; if this love be as steady as the sunshine, and yet as impulsive as the song of birds, there can be no essential sorrow in it. Oh! for a religion of love, instead of metaphysics; of the heart, head, and hand, instead of the head without either; a religion in which body, soul, and spirit will be freely given to God in sacrifice and service! Oh! for a Church built on Christ—with Christ, and not a creed for its chief corner-stone! Oh! for a Church of men, and not of doctrinaires, wherein the preacher, learned in the Word of God and taught by the Holy Ghost, shall take of the things of God and shew them unto the disciples, who, in their turn, shall

> "Sing their cheerful songs
> With angels round the throne."

My friends, in the name of the religion of Christ, I deny the first assumption of Worldly Wiseman.

Let us now address ourselves to the consideration of the second proposition:

II. *No sinner can be saved by the deeds of the law.*

Worldly-Wiseman taught that he could. He therefore sent our Pilgrim to Mr. Legality, or to his son Civility, to get rid of his burden, and advised him to dwell henceforth in the town of Morality. His teaching amounts to this, and is equal to that which we can hear on the streets any day. "Be moral; do nothing excessively wicked, and all will be well." Man's need of salvation is not recognized, and a Savior is ignored. This is wordly wisdom. It may be that it is foolishness with God. Understand me, God cannot make it foolish if it is not so. But if it ignores any fact, or is contrary to any universal principle, it is presumptious folly.

We are all under law. We cannot escape from it. No one can or does, on earth, in heaven or hell; neither Christian, pagan, Jew, gentile, child, devil, angel. God governs, and works by law.

Law is the rule by which God's forces accomplishes their purposes. Beneficence is in all His works. Love is the soul of the universe. The laws are the lines on which His love advances; the features through which His soul shines. Blessing and curse are the natural and not arbitrary result of keeping or transgressing law.

Christian and pagan unite in saying "We are His offspring." We are the children of Him whose law is holy, just and good. It is ordained to life. In keeping His commands there is great reward. They are not grievous. In infinite wisdom and love hath He ordained the rules of life. They are adapted to our nature, and secure our welfare. Disobedience to them perverts the order of nature. Let the sun rise in the west and set in the east; let day be changed to night; let heat freeze and cold burn, and you thereby will not procure anything more unnatural than sin.

It is unnatural to sin. We are under moral law; that law is beneficent in its designs; it is written in our souls; it is ingrained in our nature. Even the heathen, who possess not our Scriptures, are a law unto themselves. Sin, which is the transgression of the law, is therefore unnatural. All God's laws presuppose perfection. Not one is adapted to bless a sinful being. Sin destroys the sinner; its tendency is to shorten and embitter life; it degrades a man; the greater the sinner the less the man. From these premises we conclude and state that sin is unnatural.

Before we can realize what sin is, we must have clear ideas of the law. The law is expressed in many ways. It is detailed into negative and positive commands, as given by Moses. Its principle is revealed by Christ: "Thou shalt love the Lord thy God with all thy heart, and with all thy soul, and with all thy mind, and with all thy strength. This the first commandment. And the second is like, namely, this, thou shalt love thy neighbor as thyself, there is none other commandment greater than these." Here the principle of the law is love; the degree of it is with all thy heart, strength, soul, and mind to God; and as thyself to thy neighbor. Love is the fulfilling of the law. The end of the command is charity out of a pure heart He that loveth hath fulfilled the law Practically it is not in word or thought, but in deed and in truth. It is to "do unto others all things whatsoever ye would that they should do unto you." This is the law, the prophets and the rule of gospel life. For it we have the example of Christ, who came not to destroy, but fulfilled the law by loving and giving Himself for us. For it we have "Our Father;" "for God is love; and he that dwelleth in love, dwelleth in God and God in him."

To love God and man, then, is the law. Any deviation from this is sin; "Sin is the transgression of the law." "All unrighteousness is sin." "He that knoweth to do good and doeth it not, to him it is sin." Sin is therefore both positive and negative. It is not only evil done, it is good undone.

We are all under this law; it is our privilege, interest and duty to be obedient thereto; it is at our peril if we are disobedient. Now let us, who are under the law, hear what it says:

It says, "Cursed is *every* one that continueth not in *all* things which are written in the book of the law, to do them." Pay particular attention to the phraseology of the quotation, please. The curse is pronounced upon *every* one that continueth not in *all* things. Let us suppose a case. A man has lived in our city for fifty years. Hitherto he has preserved his integrity, his reputation is untarnished. But he falls; he commits some crime. At first his conscience makes him look back on the fifty years of unspotted life, and then holding up to him his sin, says, "Cursed is every one that continueth not in all things that are written in the law." His apprehension by the sheriff, the indictment laid against his fair fame; the manacles on his wrists; the boys, who wonderingly follow him to prison; his enemies, who leer on him in his dishonor; his friends, who always thought "he was not quite what he professed to be, who never had any faith in him," but who sat at his table, and were once dependent on his favor, say to him most emphatically, "Cursed is every one that continueth not in *all* things that are written in the law." The grating of the cell, prison fare, criminal notoriety, the tears of wife, the disgrace of children, trial as a felon, evidence, verdict, sentence, public opinion, life-long disgrace, banishment, a convict's home, a convict's death, and a convict's grave, pronounce him "Cursed who continueth not in *all* things that are written in the law."

Let us take the case of another. He is not a criminal. He has done naught for which the law of our courts can punish him. But he has lived for himself; he will see that right is done to him; he grows rich, has amassed gold, made it his god, and grown as cold and hard as it. The widow and orphan appeal to him in vain. Benevolent enterprises find in him no support. He grows old, and no one loves him. Hired sycophants surround him. The absence of love is a curse on him who has not continued in all things that are written in the law *to do them*. He has known to do good; has had the means and opportunity to do so, but has neglected to do it: and widows' wails and orphans' cries; hungry, ragged, ignorant men; the fawners who wait for his death, and rear a monument, which they grudge, over his grave, say, "Cursed is every one that continueth not in all things that are written in the book of the law *to do them*.

You see, my friends, the law under which we live condemns us; the law that is written on our hearts and built in our being, and which is transcribed from us to the Bible, condemns us. Visit the best law library this land or this world affords; read descriptions of various felonies and misdemeanors, and after you have read, you will find the sentence due to the guilt assumed; that is, the condemnation. But nowhere, not on a single page, will you find a line or a word that speaks of approval or forgiveness. And these; condemnation, forgiveness, or approval, are the issues to which our lives bring us.

Take another case. Here is a man who has sinned, and he is conscious of his fault; also, that the evidence is clear against him, and if presented, will convict him. What does he? He hires the most unscrupulous attorney in the profession; buys up the other side, if possible; objects to every righteous man on the jury; provides false witnesses; perjures himself, and attempts to bribe the judge! Why? History and conscience tell him that law condemns the guilty, and he needs a deliverer. Therefore the law says to such, "Ye cannot be justified by the works of the law." The term sinner implies condemnation.

> "Consider this—
> That in the course of justice, none of us
> Should see salvation."*

One sin is an eternal fact. It can never be disannulled. The king who stood on the sea-shore, and commanded the waves to roll back, was not more foolish and ignorant than he who thinks that because he forgets his sins they are destroyed. The consequences will surely come. Justice is stern and unrelenting. The law is holy. He who sins to-day may not be punished to-day. But so soon as his guilt is ripe, justice passes sentence, the holy law strikes the blow.

---

* Shakespeare.

Our law courts are but the transcript of the human heart. All our law-books came out of man. They are his inner sense translated into symbols. Judge, jury, dock, officers, are but shadows from the real spiritual court within. Man

> "Bears about
> A silent court of justice in his breast,
> Himself the judge and jury, and himself
> The prisoner at the bar, ever condemned."*

Have I not proven that the law condemns the sinner. Can you suggest any hope of escape that it holds out? Is it possible for any one to be saved by doing the works thereof? Are ye not condemned already? Have ye done—not have intended or wished or known that ye ought—but have you "done to others all things whatsoever ye would they should do to you?" Have you done it to wife, children, husband, merchant, buyer, friend? aye, even enemy? Have you given hospitality to strangers? fed the hungry? visited the sick? restored the erring? had compassion on the sinful? instructed the ignorant? been a friend to prisoners? Have you loved God with *all* your heart? Have you loved your neighbor as yourself? Have you really loved yourselves? Perhaps not that even. You may love your body (which, mayhap, after all, is not yours, but the butcher's, grocer's, and baker's,) enough to gratify its desires, feed it on luxuries, pander to its lusts, be vain of it, and even become its slave. But that is not to love yourself. It is but to love the shop you work in. You may be proud of your mental calibre and acquirements, boast of your intellectual instruments, but that is not loving yourself, it is only loving the tools you work with. Thou art yet greater than they. Thou wilt exist when they perish. Dost thou love thyself? thyself that wills and does; the Ego, the I Am that thou art? If not, how mercilessly art thou condemned, even by thyself? Dost thou feel this condemnation? Listen to the thunders of Sinai within; God is in the thunder. Let its lightnings arrest thee, God has called thee by them to see thee face to face. Oh! may

* Tennyson.

He grant that thou mayest go from His presence with the law in thy hand and heart.

Do you now wonder that Bunyan fixed the burning mountain close by the house of Mr. Legality, of the town of Morality, and that it thundered, lightened, and condemned the Pilgrim who attempted to pass it? "They are both of them a very cheat."

These are the arguments on which I rest my denial of the assumption of Mr. Worldly-Wiseman. I must leave you to judge whether or no they are conclusive.

For once and forever hearken not to the voice of the worldly-wise charmer; charm he never so wisely.

LECTURE V.

THE WICKET GATE.

[SYNOPSIS OF CHAPTER.—Christian now made the best of his way from the threatening mountain to the Wicket Gate. He speedily reached it. Over it was written "Knock, and it shall be opened unto you." He knocked, and a grave person, named Good-will, came to him and asked who was there? whence he came? and what he would have? Christian's answer being satisfactory, he was admitted, but just as he was entering, the other gave him a pull. The reason was explained to be that a little way from the gate was a strong castle, of which Beelzebub was the Captain, from which he and his minions shot arrows at those who came to the gate, if haply they might kill them before they entered in. Christian rejoiced at being delivered, and, at the request of Good-will, related the incidents of his journey and the reasons of his pilgrimage. Good-will, in his turn, pointed out to him the way in which there are no "turnings or windings," that was cast up by the patriarchs, prophets, Christ and his apostles, and is as "straight as a rule can make it;" and described it to him so well that he might distinguish it from others that abutted upon it. Then Christian desired to be relieved of his burden, but Good-will bade him be content, to bear it until he came to the place of deliverance, for then, said he, it will fall from thy back itself.]

WE left our Pilgrim under Sinai, suffering from the condemnation of the law. While there he "wot not what to do," and his burden seemed heavier than when he was on the way. He felt as we have sometimes, in sickness. We knew we were sick, but how much we could not tell until we summoned the physician, who made a diagnosis of our case, and pronounced upon our disease. The law analyzes the life; it also reveals the incapacity of the sinner. It sits like an accountant on a bankrupt's estate, who mercilessly putting down every cent that is owed, with every iota of assets; without pity or sympathy states the result to the helpless merchant, and leaves him to the mercy of his creditors. His work is done in discovering and announcing the condition of affairs. After the bankrupt has paid all he has, he yet is a debtor, and has naught wherewith to pay. So the law reveals our helpless condition.

An invalid is incapable of doing the work of a man. A man whose faculties are trained in one direction, is incapable of employing them in another. A man whose life has been disobedient, knows not how to obey God. The habit has petrified into character. It is the experience of all who attempt to lead a virtuous life on the principle of obedience, that they fail. On this point let me read you a passage from Shedd's Sermons to the Natural Man:

"There is no more touching poem in all literature than that one in which the pensive and moral Schiller portrays the struggle of the ingenious youth who would find the source of moral purification in the moral law; who would seek the power that can transform him, in the mere imperative of his own conscience, and the mere strugglings and spasms of his own will. He represents him as endeavoring earnestly and long to feel the force of obligation, and as toiling sedulously to school himself into virtue, by the bare power, by the dead lift of duty. But the longer he tries, the more he loathes the restraints of law. Virtue, instead of growing lovely to him, becomes more and more severe, austere and repellant. His life, as the Scripture phrases it, is under law and not under love. There is nothing spontaneous, nothing willing, nothing genial in his religion. He does not enjoy religion, but he endures religion. Conscience does not in the least renovate his will, but merely checks or goads it. He becomes wearied and worn, and conscious that after all his self-schooling he is the same creature at heart, in his disposition and affections, that he was at the commencement of the effort, he cries out, "O Virtue, take back thy crown, and let me sin."

Thousands continue in sin because they know they have no power to obey. This is the condition in which pastors find men and women. The good they would do, they cannot. They hate and despise themselves. Drunkards would be sober, if they could. Men would be honest, liars would be truthful; but they are too weak.

If what I have said is true; if the law condemns the sinner, finds him incapable of meeting its requirements, and leaves him as it found him, two things are clearly manifest; first, that the sinner needs a deliverance; second, he must look from the law to find it.

This is what we preach. Blessed are the people who hear the joyful sound! The law reveals the condition of the sinner; the gospel the condition of the law-giver. I said in the previous Lecture that the law was love. God is love, and His law is the expression of it. But it does not follow because law expresses the mind of God, that therefore there is no other moral expression of Him. May He not be revealed in sacrifice?

Side by side these two features of God exist. The gospel is nothing new; it is as old as the law. Most men think that the Gospel commences at the birth of Christ, and the law with Moses at Sinai. A few have traced it back through the Prophetic, Mosaic, Patriarchal, and Antediluvian age to Eden. Still fewer to the counsels of the Eternal. Let us go infinitely further back, to the existence of God Himself; for God is the Gospel. It is, then, no after-thought; with Him there can be none. He is never behindhand with His remedies. By the side of the poisonous herb grows its antidote; with sickness are the means of recovery; in ignorance is the desire for learning. Before the child is born God has provided the mother. Before man was created, the world was made ready to receive him. But man is always behindhand. Thousands of ships strike the rocks of the ocean, and property and lives are lost before man erects the lighthouse; thousands are wrecked before man constructs the life-boat. Epidemics rage, and death sweeps the carnage to the grave before man discovers a cure. For centuries nations settle their difficulties by war, and so lose the strength, glory and honor of a people, before men think that it would be wise to settle the difficulty before the war begins. Cities are destroyed by fire before fire-engines are invented or fire-companies organized. It is not so with God. Before the ship was wrecked the life-boat was on the strand ; before the disease struck the man, the remedy was prepared ; before the fire consumed He had provided a way of escape. Cotemporaneously with the possibility of His child perverting the law of His love, a Savior was provided ; not merely as a part of the plan of salvation, but as part of the constitution of nature. From everlasting to everlasting He is God. When, therefore, Evangelist found Christian at the burning mountain, it was not to strike the fatal blow, but to lead him from the condemnation which he inherited to the life of faith and love which God provided. To the sinner the law is destructive, the Gospel constructive.

From the burning mountain he was directed by Evangelist to the Wicket Gate. This is one of the most disputable points of the allegory. Artists know not what to do with it. No two give the same idea of it in their works. It is variously represented by them, while theologians have regarded it with feelings according to their doctrinal bias.

Here is another piece of English scenery. If you walk along the country roads of "Merrie England," you will frequently discover gates in the hedge-rows ; a porter's lodge is erected close by ; over the gate you will find the armorial bearings of the proprietor, and frequently a motto, in English or Latin, the supposed principle on which the proprietor lives. The public are not permitted to pass through them ; that privilege is limited to the family, friends, servants, and those who do business with the proprietor. They are generally kept locked, and are opened only to such as I have mentioned. To enter the grounds through them without permission, is a trespass, and is punishable as such in the courts of law. These gates open into a straight, narrow, clean, direct path to the mansion. There is no legal way of getting to the mansion but by them. No doubt Bunyan had often asked and been denied the favor of entering them. Men of his class were specially prohibited. In the feudal age they were protected by soldiers.

I see the same idea in every street of this city, particularly in connection with the large houses. Before the door, in the fence, stands a little gate; within the gate is a straight and narrow (when compared with the avenue) path to your door. If one of them is attached to your property, you know that you have perfect control of it; you can open or shut it, lock or bolt it, at your will. By it you can and do keep your enemies off your property, and admit your friends. To such a simple contrivance Bunyan, like his Master, attached most important truths and experiences.

"The Gate" is an era in the Progress; it is an end of one stage and the beginning of another. It separates the efforts of the Pilgrim to find the right way from his efforts to keep in the right way.

The "Wicket Gate" is Jesus Christ. Just as your gate seems to say to the public, "No man goeth to the house but me," so he says: "No man cometh to the Father but by me." "I am the door." He exhorts us to lay aside all idle and curious questions and strive to enter into the Strait Gate.

Perhaps nothing appears so much unlike Christ as a door or a gate. And yet He uses these most familiar uninspiring things to represent Him.

I have said that near the English gate a porter lives. He is there to represent the feeling of the proprietor to friends and strangers. Therefore Bunyan, in describing the feeling of God to man, names the porter of this gate "Good-will."

God's good-will is especially seen in the Gospel. When Christ first came to the earth to show by His life a new and living way to the Father; when He removed all legal difficulties out of the way of salvation; when He came to declare Himself not merely "the way," but the beginning of it, by saying, "I am the door; I am Alpha, the first, the beginning," the everlasting doors of heaven gave way and angels sang "Good will to man."

Good will is manifest in the inscription over the portal—"Knock, and it shall be opened unto you." Christian knocked again and again; and at last Good-will opened to him. The Divine Being who wrote and spake these words, fulfills them. What is knocking? It is a certain form of praying. Sometimes, as we are sitting at our meals, we hear a slight tap at the door, and going to it, find a waif begging for bread. He has been praying with his fist on our door for entrance to our houses. When a friend comes to see us, he prays in the same way. The geologist goes with his hammer to the quarry, and knocks for days and months on the doors of the rocks. He is simply praying the earth to open her treasure-house to him. What the beggar, the friend, and the geologist do literally, you must do spiritually. The only difference is this: they pray by knocking, you must knock by praying. Ask Jesus Christ to save you. "Ask, and ye shall receive." When you ask Christ, He and you are of the same mind, you cannot ask of Him without discovering that He is more willing to give than you to receive.

God's good will is manifest in the kind words spoken to the Pilgrim. The Christian confessed his sin and weakness. But he was assured by Good-will of His complete welcome. "We make no objection against any, notwithstanding all they have done before they come hither. They are in no wise cast out; therefore, good Christian, come a little way with me, and I will teach thee about the way thou mayest go." I do wish we could get out of our minds the idea that God is a hard, austere, malevolent being. God is a loving Father. Christ is a loving Savior. He receiveth sinners.

> "A wretched Magdalene or Saul
> May find in Christ a home;
> Salvation is held out to all,
> Come, guilty sinner, come."

The abundant welcome to sinners is the peculiar glory of the

Gospel. If a servant applies for a situation in your household, or a clerk wants to work in your store, you require a certificate of character before you will employ either. If you want to join any secret order, you must possess some moral character before you can do so. Men do not believe in men; Christ does; He receives men of no character; He wants them as they are. It is said that an artist desiring to produce a picture of squalid poverty, searched the dens and slums of a great city for a model. After searching a long time, he found a man in the condition that suited him. He therefore bargained with him to be at his studio at a certain hour the next day, and relieving him for the nonce, went home. The hour appointed arrived; pencils, easel, artist, were ready. True to the minute, the bell rang; the artist went to the door to admit his sitter, when, lo! and behold! he had got himself up for the occasion—he had washed himself, and by some means procured better clothing. "Oh! you have spoiled it," cried the artist, "I sought you for weeks, and wanted you as you were." Is not that what you are trying to do. The feeling is praiseworthy and honorable, but it is a mistake. Christ wants you to come to him as you are; you cannot be anything but a sinner, do as you will. He knows you exactly, and while He would have you all and more than you possibly can desire to be, yet He knows that you must begin just where and what you are now. He will cast no one out that cometh to God by Him.

And yet this may be no commendation to some. Men argue in this way: The Gospel is for the low, vulgar and depraved. We are not low, neither are we vulgar or depraved; therefore, we do not need the Savior. And because we preach to harlots, drunkards, adulterers, thieves and liars, that if they will they may lead a better life through Christ, there is almost a demand for a respectable Gospel, if not for a respectable Savior. Certainly there is a demand for respectable churches, from which such are excluded. For some sins are respectable and others are not. It is disreputable for an Irishman or German to get drunk on beer or whisky in a saloon, but it is respectable for a gentleman to be elevated with wine at his club. It is disreputable to speak to Magdalene on the streets, but it is respectable to buy carriages and furnish parlors for Delilah. It is disreputable to steal horses and wreck trains, but it is respectable to write another man's name to a bond. It is disreputable to thieve at a faro bank, but at a savings bank it is quite another thing. It is disreputable to pick a man's pocket, but to mislead a man in a business transaction, by silence or a lie, so that he loses his all, and we are benefited by that loss—what is that? We could call it by an ugly name, but we need not.

Both these classes of sinners have many things, and these, the essentials of life, in common; this is a presumption that salvation is common to all. They see by the same light, breathe the same air, eat and drink in the same manner, are moved by the same motives, have the same ends. It is therefore not strange that there is but one Savior provided for all. It were as unwise to reject common mercies as the common salvation.

What a gate is to your property, so Christ is to the way of righteousness.

A gate is an end; an end of wanderings. It opens on a direct road to your house. At the gate a man leaves behind that which he will not carry into his house. It is the door of separation. A merchant leaves his store and his office with careworn expression. The difficulties of his business perplex him, until he sees a curly head hanging over the gate, and a pair of blue eyes watching for "pa." Then he lets his business go, and taking his child's hand in his, forgets his cares in the love and duty of a parent. But it is a beginning of a man's private property. Once within it, he becomes his own true self. So Christ Jesus is the end of the old, care-worn, curse-struck life. If any man come to Him, he is a new creature. He is born again! Behold, all things are become new. He is no longer in the flesh, but of the spirit.

Two difficulties arise here. The one is practical, the other theological. The one concerns us as sinners, the other as truth-seekers. The practical difficulty is related by Bunyan in this way:

"When Christian was stepping in, the other gave him a pull. Then said Christian, 'What means that?' The other told him: 'A little distance from this gate there is erected a strong castle, of which Beelzebub is the captain; from thence both he and they shoot arrows at them that come up to this gate, if haply they may die before they enter in.'"

I suppose most Christians have had experience corresponding to this. And if some of you become Christians, you may suffer in the same manner. If you were to follow your convictions and to profess your faith in Christ, then there would come suddenly to your heart, you know not whence nor how, a number of reasons against it. And if you followed those dissuasions, your good desires, hopes and thoughts would die.

The theological difficulty is this: The Pilgrim is made to go through the "Wicket Gate" into the way of righteousness, with the burden on his back. He teaches us that a sinner may come to Christ, and be found in the way of righteousness with the burden of conscious sin; with no sense of forgiveness in his soul.

Our modern idea of a Christian is one who can say that he has lost all sense of sin, and has experienced forgiveness. Men become religious to be forgiven, whereas God forgives when men are righteous. Many are kept out of the way of righteousness because they do not possess such a sense. The difference between our theology and Bunyan's is this: We put forgiveness before righteousness; he places righteousness before forgiveness. Who is right?

If we collect evidence from the experience of notable men, we shall find that, much as it may differ in its history, yet, in fact, it is nearly the same. Bunyan, Wesley and Baxter are illustrious examples of the truth here pictured by the Great Dreamer. But to the law and to the testimony.

Saul, of Tarsus, is the pattern conversion. He is an example to all who shall hereafter believe. He was obedient to the heavenly vision before he received sight or the remission of sins.

The Savior has taught that no one will be forgiven of God

until he has first forgiven all who have trespassed against him. No one, I take it, can be forgiven until he ceases to do evil and learns to do well. But it may be asked, "Can a man who is conscious that he is a sinner, walk in the way of righteousness? Can he be obedient to Christ?" Let me answer this question by asking another: "Can a man who is sick, do as his physician directs him before he gets well?" Of course he can. That is just how he arrives at the experience of health. So you must get into the way of righteousness in order to get these experiences. A tree must be planted before it can bear fruit.

A gate shuts. You close your gates for protection at night; you lock and bolt your windows; by them you are protected and your interests secured. When the man-slayer fled to the City of Refuge, he was safe only when he was inside the gates. They forever barred his pursuers from taking vengeance on him. This gate closed on the way over which Christian had traveled, and forever shut out the experiences he had undergone. What a beautiful illustration of Christ! We run to Him, and are safe.

1. Christian feared to die. Most men do. Christ saves men from that. He delivers those who, through fear of death, are all their lifetime subject to bondage. Ah! poor, sinful brother, the sentence of death is in you. The wages of sin is death. The soul that sinneth shall die; but a Christian never dies; Christ gives to him eternal life; he shall never perish. Whosoever believeth in Christ shall never die, though he were dead.

2. Christian despaired of ever being saved. He fell into the Slough of Despond; the gate closed on that; a soul that believes on Christ cannot despair; Christ to such is an Almighty Savior; He saves to the uttermost.

3. The Christian was condemned by the law. But the gate closed on that experience also. There is no condemnation to them who are in Christ Jesus; He is the end of the law for righteousness; no one can condemn a believer in Him, for He hath died.

A gate opens; it is a means of ingress. Christ opens the way of righteousness. We are not made righteous by knowing the law, but by faith in Him. Faith brings us into fellowship with God, and the Great Being who demands a perfect obedience to His law, makes our service possible by a simple faith in His Son. We can none of us get to heaven by a perfect obedience, but we may by a simple faith and honest love.

He openeth, and no man shutteth; and shutteth, and no man openeth. Your salvation and mine is abolutely in the hands of Christ. His Spirit will not always strive with man. May God grant that none of you may knock at the gate which is so absolutely under His control, and read, not "Knock, and it shall be opened unto you," but "Too late, too late, you cannot enter now."

LECTURE VI.

THE INTERPRETER'S HOUSE.

[SYNOPSIS OF CHAPTER.—The hero of the allegory reaches the Interpreter's House, where he knocks over and over for admission. The Interpreter comes to him, grants him entrance, lights a candle, and proceeds to show him the wonders of the house, as follows: 1. A picture of a very grave person, hanging against the wall. 2. A room full of dust, which one attempted to sweep before it had been sprinkled with water. 3. Two children, named Passion and Patience, the former of whom was wretched in abundance, the latter of whom was content to wait with nothing, for the riches promised him. 4. A mysterious fire against a wall, on one side the devil attempting to extinguish it by pouring on water; on the other side Jesus Christ keeping it up by pouring on oil. 5. A beautiful palace, guarded by soldiers; a man at the door with ink-horn and book, to take the names of all who would enter; a stout-hearted man who had his name put down, and who, to reach the palace, fought his way through the soldiers. 6. A miserable man in an iron cage. He was formerly a professor of religion, had backslidden, was wretched in consequence, and was afraid of Eternity. 7. A man who trembled in consequence of having had a dream of the final judgment. After he had seen these things he went on his way.]

GOOD-WILL directed Christian to the house of the Interpreter. To it he came, and at the door knocked over and over again, as instructed. Ultimately he was admitted.

In our last, we saw that knocking meant praying. The Interpreter's House is that stage of discipleship in which the Christian receives the enlightenment of God's Spirit. Therefore to say that the Pilgrim knocked at the door of the Interpreter's House, is that a Christian must pray for like experiences.

We ought not to forget that the Holy Ghost is our teacher; there is no disciple that does not need to learn of Him.

After admitting the Pilgrim, the first thing the Interpreter did was to light a candle. This may seem to be too insignificant to notice; it is such a common-place action, but upon it depends the value of the things he was to see. A room may be beautifully furnished, but if we go into it when in darkness, and carrying no light, its beauty is naught. The things of the spirit exist, but they have to be spiritually discerned. The spirit of the man is the candle of the Lord. That candle must be lighted before these things can be discerned. The natural man knoweth not the things of the Spirit of God.

In the phenomena of sight there is the thing seen and there is the eye that sees. Each is necessary to the other. We can imagine an eye mechanically perfect, and yet without the power to see; it lacks the gift or sense of sight. So we can conceive an ear perfectly made, and yet deaf to music; in that case the musical sense is defunct. In the midst of beauty we know that men may live untouched by it, unblessed by its mission. In such a case the aesthetic sense needs cultivation. So, I am not uttering a theological dogma, but a philosophical necessity when I say that we must receive the light within to see the things of God without. No man knoweth the things of God but the Spirit of God. "Eye hath not seen, nor ear heard, neither have entered into the heart of man, the things which God hath prepared for them that love Him. But God hath revealed them unto us by His Spirit, for the Spirit searcheth all things, yea, the deep things of God. For what man knoweth the things of a man, save the Spirit of man which is in him, even so, the things of God knoweth no man, but the Spirit of God. Now we have received the Spirit which is of God that we might know the things that are freely given to us by God."

Observe, the Spirit of God is not given to any who are out of the way of righteousness. Mark, learn, and inwardly digest the fact that the Interpreter's House is in this way; so if any one, no matter how sacred his office, how well his condition, has not enough righteousness between man and man to practice it, the law of righteousness between man and God enough to honor it: if such an one, I say, professes to have the Spirit of God, believe him not; he is a liar. The fruit of the Spirit is righteousness. By their fruit know all men.

Christ is the way into righteousness; therefore none who refuse Christ can receive the Holy Ghost. No one had the liberty to go to such mansions as I described last week, pluck the flowers, and enjoy the hospitality, but those who went in at the gate; those who get in any other way, are breakers of law. Christ makes the same assertion in the words, "I am the Door, he that entereth in any other way, the same is a thief and a robber." God's Spirit reveals nothing to that man who refuses Christ. God is one. He who refuseth Christ rejecteth the Father.

The conditions, then, upon which we may see and enjoy the sights of the Interpreter's House, are, that we pray for the Spirit of God, and that we receive the Spirit of God.

The first thing shown to the Pilgrim was a picture of a very grave person, hanging up against the wall, and this was the fashion of it: "It had eyes lifted up to heaven, the best of books in its hand, the law of truth was written upon its lips, the world was behind its back, it stood as if it pleaded with men, and a crown of gold did hang over its head.

This is Bunyan's description of a Christian minister. It was the ideal to which he strove, and which, in the judgment of posterity, attained; for on St. Peter's green, Bedford, England, "the glorious dreamer is standing in a most natural attitude, holding an open Bible in his left hand, the finger of his right hand resting upon the page, his face turned upwards, yet not averted from the persons with whom he is supposed to be pleading, radiant with the truth he is setting forth. There is, perhaps, less of robust vigor in the expression than we look for in a man of Bunyan's mould, and a more strongly pronounced smile than would often be seen lighting up the features, which are described by cotemporaries as habitually grave and even stern; yet the moment seized by the artist is one in which implicit faith and exultant joy are animating the soul of the preacher as he tenderly pleads with men; and there cannot be two opinions as to the strong moral impression which the countenance of this earnest preacher is calculated to make on the beholder. The effect is exceedingly vivid and pleasing."

"The idea which the sculptor has striven to work out is embodied in the inscription at the back of the pedestal, which is taken from Bunyan's description of the picture he saw hanging up against the wall in Interpreter's house."*

"Now," said the Interpreter, "I have shown you this picture first, because the man, whose picture this is, is the only man whom the Lord of the place whither thou art going, hath authorized to be thy guide in all difficult places thou mayest meet with in the way; wherefore take good heed to what I have shewed thee, and bear well in mind what thou hast seen; lest in thy journey thou meet with some that pretend to lead thee right, but their way goes down to death."

Evidently his design was to show by contrast *the clergy* of his day; the false and blind guides to whom the ministry of the gospel was but a profession.

Being a Baptist, he believed as we do, that the choice of a pastor is entirely with the Church. It became necessary, therefore, that the Pilgrim should be taught the true features of an ambassador of Christ. It is not necessary that a preacher should be rich, or well dressed, or even learned; of elegant manners or eloquent; but it is absolutely essential for him to be thoughtful, truthful, taught in the Word, careless of gold and silver, compassionate with men, and heavenly-minded. There are such men to be found; Churches should seek them. If the Churches asked of God and demanded of men a spiritually robust ministry, a ministry of men who hated sin, loved righteousness, who could stand behind the words they uttered with these credentials of heaven; in short, if John Bunyan's ideal

---

* Book of the Bunyan Festival.

were attempted, it would be realized, and the works of John Bunyan again would follow. As it would not become me to say more on this point, we will pass to

THE ROOM FULL OF DUST.

This teaches him—

1. The state of man's heart; "*full of dust*, because never swept." And let me remind you that we are talking about the heart, its thoughts, desires, affections, and imaginations, rather than the outer conduct.

2. The operation of the law of God upon the heart. Just as in sweeping a dusty room, you discover the amount of dust therein, so the law of God reveals the condition of a sinful soul. But the law cannot of itself cleanse the heart.

3. The sweet influences of the Gospel. One came and sprinkled water upon the dust and the room was cleansed. Here our Dreamer teaches that the heart can only be made clean under the purifying influences of grace.

Punishment of itself has a hardening effect. The worst criminals are those who have been punished most. If criminals are saved, it is by the power of love. The world will be saved by revealing the love of God, not by preaching the law, nor by uttering the Gospel; for much preaching of the Gospel gives no thought of love; but by ourselves loving men; loving men because God has first loved us. Love is of God; God is love. This is the commandment which we have from Him: "That he who loveth God love his brother also."

To illustrate this better than I can explain it, let me give an incident from my early ministry. When I was about to leave a district where I had labored as an Evangelist for eighteen months, a gentleman sought an interview with me. He reminded me of a series of meetings I had conducted a few months previous, and then related the following: "I had been drinking hard for several weeks, was out of employment, and myself and family were fast coming to want. One Sunday I was without money, and consequently without drink. The only funds available were in the shape of 'rent,' which my wife had saved out of her earnings. I determined to steal that, and nerved, by drink, end my life. I went to the spot where my wife kept this money; to my surprise it was not there. She had anticipated me. I was angry, and left the house, intending to take my life. Just at that moment I heard some singing. I traced it to a certain room, and discovered that a religious service was being held. I went in. Well, sir, you preached. Do you remember the text?" "No, I do not," I replied. He then repeated it: "Hell is moved from beneath for thee, to meet thee at thy coming." Well, sir, I thought the text and sermon were both for me. I went home, but could not rest. The next day I wandered about, to drown my senses in drink or to kill myself. I went on the railroad several times to lay myself on the rails for a train to pass over me, but somehow I could not. I thought of the consequences you preached. On the next night you preached again. Do you remember the text?' "No." Well, sir, it was this: 'Come now, and let us reason together, saith the Lord; for, though your sins were as scarlet, they shall be as wool; though red like crimson, they shall be as white as snow.' I saw that though my sins were great, God's love could save me from them. That night I began a new life, and a few months ago I joined a Baptist Church."

You see, one night I preached the law; it revealed the man to himself, but it drove him nearly to despair. The next I preached the Gospel; it revealed God to the man, and resulted in a new life. The law is weak through the flesh, but the Gospel is the power of God. Wherefore I am not ashamed of the Gospel of Christ. It may be folly to the cultured, a stumbling-block to the legal, but to the sinner who believes, it is the power of God unto salvation. When a man can receive into his soul the thought that though a sinner, God loves him, so as to touch his affections and turn them to believing and righteousness and truth and wisdom and beauty, he has received a power by which he will become a son of God. He is converted and made a new creature by that love of God which passeth knowledge.

The Interpreter then took him by the hand and led him into a little room where sat two children named

PASSION AND PATIENCE.

"Passion seemed to be much discontent, but Patience was very quiet." Christian asked, "What is the reason of this discontent of Passion?" The Interpreter answered, "The governor of them would have him stay for his best things to the beginning of the next year; but he will have them all now; but Patience is willing to wait. Then one came to Passion and brought him a bag of treasure, and poured it down at his feet; the which he took up and rejoiced therein, and withal laughed Patience to scorn. But I beheld but a while, and he had lavished all away, and had nothing left him but rags."

This represents the folly of worldliness and the wisdom of goodness. The things of this life do perish in their using; the fashion of them passes away; they can never satisfy the spirit made for God. If I were asked to select the most miserable person on earth, it would be one who had all the world could give; one whose mental pabulum was the latest novel, the sensational drama, and the artificial pretensions of what is called society. If you want to see misery, go and look, not at the gutter children of large cities, but at the men and women who have "seen the world;" those who risk eternity for it.

We often depict and describe the miseries of the poor; we spend money to relieve their wants; we form societies to strike at the root of their evils; all this is well enough, but we have left one field untilled, the world needs a mission to the rich, to the prosperous, the worldly, for if I am asked to select the happiest, I should find them in prison, among the sick, in heathen lands. Sacrifices, yea, living sacrifices, who, like their Master, go about doing good. The boy who truants sacrifices all the intellectual pleasures of manhood for the pleasure of amusement. The Prodigal took his portion and went into a far country and spent it in riotous living; did it at the expense of future happiness. It is better to be happy in eternity than in time, and better to be miserable in time than in eternity. Let us beware of a passionate, worldly life; let us rather live for the things that are unseen and eternal.

I found a perfectly happy human creature once. She was a poor old woman, dependent upon the public for support. As she was a member of my congregation, I visited her one afternoon. She lived in a very small cottage. The moment I entered I saw that it was scrupulously clean; the dear old creature had just been gathering sticks from the lanes with which to prepare her evening meal. Her face was the heavenliest I ever saw. It was surrounded by the white fringe of her cap. On the table lay a well-worn copy of God's Word; she was so old that I involuntarily looked for the entrance of a daughter or a friend, who, I thought, had charge of her. As no one appeared, I said, "Mother Ansel, you don't live alone, do you?" "Live alone! Live alone!" she said, first in gentle correction, and then, with a smile, a ray of light from the inner heaven, "Live alone! *Me* live alone! No, my son. *Me* and the Lord live together." Now, she had nothing, and was contentedly happy, for she had all that can make happiness, in her Lord, and naught to substitute for the chief good.

You may think that this is all very well to preach. Friends, I utter facts. The experience of every man who neglects the future for the present, confirms them. The life of a worldling is my proof. This world is soon spent, and the spender quickly comes to want. Not so he who lives to God. He who lives for righteousness; he who receives God in His law and love. His soul lives richly and forever. He can sing from his heart—

>O wealth of life beyond all bound!
>Eternity each moment given!
>What plummet may the Present sound?
>Who promises a *future* heaven?
>Or glad, or grieved,
>Oppressed, relieved,

In blackest night, or brightest day,
   Still pours the flood
   Of golden good,
And more than heart-full fills me aye.

My wealth is common; I possess
   No petty province, but the whole;
What's mine alone, is mine far less
   Than treasure shared by every soul.
     Talk not of store,
     Millions or more,
Of values which the purse may hold—
     But this divine!
     I own the mine
Whose grains outweigh a planet's gold.

I have a stake in every star,
   In every beam that fills the day;
All hearts of men my coffers are,
   My ores arterial tides convey.
     The fields, the skies,
     And sweet replies
Of thought to thought are my gold dust,—
     The oaks, the brooks,
     And speaking looks
Of lovers' faith and friendship's trust.

Life's youngest tides joy brimming flow
   For him who lives above all years,
Who all immortal makes the Now,
   And is not ta'en in Time's arrears:
     His life's a hymn
     The seraphim
Might hark to hear or help to sing,
     And to his soul
     The boundless whole
Its bounty all doth daily bring.

"All mine is thine:" the sky-soul saith,
 "The wealth I am, must thou become
Richer and richer, breath by breath,
 Immortal gain, immortal room!"
  And since all his
   Mine also is,
Life's gift outruns my fancies far,
  And drowns the dream
   In larger stream
As morning drinks the morning star.

Then he was taken to see

THE UNQUENCHABLE FIRE.

A fire against the wall, over which one stood, and on which he continually poured water; but instead of putting it out, it burned the more. The Pilgrim was much amazed, until he was taken to the other side, where the secret was revealed. There stood One, and he the Lord Jesus, pouring on oil. This is to show that an effort is constantly made to put out the spiritual life of a man. He will find the law of his flesh contrary to the law of his mind. The maxims, the temptations of the world are against him. At the end of life the wonder to him will be that he is a Christian. But God sustains us by His grace. Bunyan's life is an illustration of this. The World, the Church, and Satan did all they could to extinguish the work of grace in his soul. Persecution, poverty, threats, promises, were tried from without; temptations, fierce and strong, from within; but without avail. Trust Christ, though invisible. The greatest forces we know of are unseen. The less material and the more etherial the source of power the greater is it. His is an invisible, though constant supply. "He is able to make all grace to abound towards us, that we, having all sufficiency in all things, may abound in every good work."

In an early edition of Wycliffe's Bible is a frontispiece, consisting of a fire; and an atheist, the pope, and the devil, blowing on it with all their might to put it out; but instead of blowing it out they blow it on; the flame grows fiercer and hotter. Christ is watching his chosen ones, and every soul he secretly sustains. His grace is all-sufficient; we can endure and do all things through Him who strengthens us. Let each soul say, "My sufficiency is of God."

THE INK-HORN AND THE BOOK.

Next he saw a man sitting in a room, the door of which was guarded by soldiers. At his side was an ink-horn and a book; beyond him was a mansion, and shining ones walking on the battlements of it. Many desired to reach the mansion, but were intimidated by the guard. At last came a man of very stout countenance, who said to the man with the ink-horn and book: "Put my name down, sir." Then, drawing his sword, he fought fiercely till he made his way through the soldiers to the mansion; so he went in and was clothed with such garments as the inmates. Christian smiled, and said, "Verily, I think I see the meaning of this." I do not know whether you do, my friends. The meaning is, that there are difficulties to be met constantly, and if we would get to Heaven we must as constantly fight and conquer them.

I have seen boys enlist in the army, and they were pleased and proud as though they were veterans of a hundred battles. A man gets possession of a farm, and thinks his fortune is made. Two dear souls get married and think their troubles are over. A man gets converted and thinks he is all right forever and ever. Poor things, they will soon be undeceived. Their troubles have only just commenced, and will probably last a life-time. The only way to conquer them is to fight, and fight constantly. There is no "rest and be thankful business," in a Christian's life, this side the grave; he must fight if he would reign. Those who do not will fail, as may be seen in the next parable, of

"THE MAN IN THE IRON CAGE."

"So the Interpreter took him by the hand and led him into a very dark room, where there sat a man in an iron cage. Now, the man to look on, seemed very sad; he sat with his eyes looking down to the ground, his hands folded together, and he sighed as if his heart would break. Conversation elicited that he was once a flourishing professor of religion, but having left off to watch and be sober, he gave way to his lusts, tempted the devil, provoked God to anger, hardened his heart, so that he could not repent." He had no hope of salvation. He had grieved away the Spirit of God, and he sat with his head upon his knees, crying, "Oh, Eternity! Eternity!"

I do not care to discuss the doctrine of the Perseverance of the Saints. I take it the Saints will persevere. I shall state a fact with which we are well acquainted, that men who have professed religion have turned round and are living in sin; there are others who, while keeping up the appearances of a religious life, know very well that they have lost all interest in the matter. They lost their treasure by not attending to the keeping of it. If a man neglect to eat he will starve. If a man neglect to study, he will become incapable and ignorant. If a prosperous man neglect to work, he will become poor; so, if a Christian neglect the means of grace, the communion of Saints, private prayer, and reading of the Bible, he will fall, and the last state of that man is worse than the first, for men who go back are miserable; to hide this they seek pleasure and repose in all manner of means. Frequently they land in infidelity. Most of the infidels I have known—and I have known many—have once been professed followers of Christ. Professedly led there by intellectual questionings, but more frequently to quench their conscience in the darkness of naught.

But the thought of eternity troubled him. Eternity! How long is eternity? We can easily speak the word, and as easily repeat it, and then as easily forget it. But we can form no conception of it. Figures of speech and numerals will not express it. It defies analysis. But let us analyze a portion of it, if it is worth being called a portion. Let us dissect an English billion.* Write it on paper—a modest 1 with a dozen ciphers attached. Let us first try to show what it is as applied

---

* Here I use the illustration of Mr. Bessemer.

to Time, Distance, and Weight. When, for example, we speak of a billion of seconds, we, perhaps, suppose that since our era, such a number has long since been measured out. Arithmetic shows us, however, that we have not even passed one-sixteenth of that number in all these long eventful years; for it takes just 31,687 years, 17 days, 22 hours, 45 minutes and 5 seconds to constitute a billion of seconds. A billion of sovereigns (20-cent pieces will do,) would extend, when ranged side by side, in piles of twenty feet high, so as to form two parallel walls, a distance of 2,386½ miles; or, if placed on the ground so as to form one continuous chain by each sovereign touching the one next to it, such a chain would encircle the earth 763 times. The weight of the same sovereigns would be 6,975,447 tons. As to altitude, a billion sheets of the *Times*, or any first-class newspaper, superimposed upon each other, and pressed into a compact mass, would reach to the height of 47,348 miles. A billion is a fearful thing, and as for quadrillions and trillions, they are simply words wholly incapable of impressing themselves on the human intellect. But one thing is thinkable concerning them; somewhere they end. But Eternity means endlessness; it has no end. Mere astounding figures give no idea of it. They are but the starting points of eternity. When the Egyptians expressed this idea in their hieroglyphical language, they did it by a circle, denoting, without beginning and without end forever. Measure it! Suppose we gather every beam of light that ever came from the sun, every ear of corn, every blade of grass, every feather of flying fowl, every drop of the ocean, every grain of sand, that ever existed; call each a year, and spend this time in eternity—and then eternity is to come! The thought is overwhelming—it is awful! How will you spend it? With whom, and where? Let controversialists treat the subject with becoming reverence. It is a matter to feel, rather than to dispute about.

The Interpreter then took him to a man who had been dreaming of the final judgment. The dream is told in Bunyan's own dramatic manner. But I have trespassed too much on your time. As this subject will occur again in our progress, we will discuss it then.

These are the truths wrought into the soul by the Holy Ghost; they become the intuitive sense of the child of God. They are spiritual, and are felt, rather than understood. We need the direct personal teaching of the Holy Ghost. We need spiritual discernment, for this we must have spiritual enlightenment.

In conclusion, let me say, that I am reminded I have two congregations—one that has *heard* what I have said, the other has *felt* my utterances; the one is spiritual, the other is carnal. To feel the truth is evidence of spiritual-mindedness.

Some excuse themselves, saying they have not the Holy Ghost. Is not a man responsible for his poverty, if he might be rich; for his ignorance, if he might be learned? Is he less responsible, who has not the Spirit of God? Certainly not. God has promised to all who ask, "If ye being evil know how to give good gifts to your children, how much more will your Heavenly Father give THE SPIRIT to those who ask Him.

LECTURE VII.

THE CROSS.

[SYNOPSIS OF CHAPTER.—The Pilgrim entered the Interpreter's House by knocking, and left it singing. With a song, he marches an highway, fenced in on either side by a wall called Salvation. His burden is still a difficulty. But he soon comes to a little ascent, where stood a Cross, and a little below, in the bottom, a Sepulchre. Here the burden falls off by itself into the Sepulchre, and he saw it no more. Christian stands in amazement and weeps and sings for joy. Three shining ones come to him and salute him with "Peace be unto thee." The first said unto him, "Thy sins be forgiven thee." The second gave him a change of raiment. The third set a mark on his forehead, and gave him a roll with a seal on it. From hence he proceeds with much joy, and sees, to his sorrow, a little out of the way three men, named Simple, Sloth, and Presumption, asleep, with fetters on their heels. He awoke them, shewed them their danger, but was unsuccessful in getting them concerned. Then two others, Formalist and Hypocrisy, came tumbling over the wall. These he sought to instruct and correct, and got derided for his pains.]

WE bring our Pilgrim to the Cross to-night. He came to it soon after he left the "Interpreter's House." The instruction and enlightenment he received there were esential to the experiences which we now study. It is indispensable that a man be divinely illuminated in order to see that his salvation from sin is in Christ. The mission of the Spirit of God is to take of the things of God and show them to us. We cannot of ourselves unravel the meaning of the life of Christ and the tragedy of Calvary. He, however, is possessed of the secret, and He conveys it to all those who fear God. I shall not be able to communicate it. Without controversy, great is its mystery. To reveal it is the work of the Holy Spirit.

It may be necessary to review. Christian fled from the wrath to come—from the condemnation of the law. He entered at the Wicket Gate, and passed through the Interpreter's House. Now, a man must leave sin, acknowledge Christ, and become His disciple, before he can enjoy the experiences of spiritual life. Christ taught men righteousness before He died for them. They followed Him before they received the Holy Ghost. So with our Pilgrim; he left sin and followed after righteousness before he found peace and joy in Christ Jesus.

But there are crosses which are not "The Cross." They need to be pointed out, so that you may not make a fatal mistake. One of the most common and fatal of all mistakes is to come to the Cross as theologians, and not as sinners. Our Pilgrim came as a burdened sinner. Do thou likewise.

I. There is the literal fact: Christ was put to death on a cross. That very cross is said to be preserved. Part of it is in Rome, part of it in Paris, parts of it in Palestine, part of it in Russia. You will find large portions of it in churches and ecclesiastical museums. There is almost enough of it to build a navy. Many men, however, think it possesses some talismanic power, and they therefore take long journeys and offer costly gifts to gaze upon any one piece of it. But it is nothing; if you possessed the whole of it, it would not avail for your salvation. The wood of the cross is no better than that of any other tree that grew in the forest. Trees cannot save souls. You might visit the Holy Land, as did the Empress Helena, search for, find, possess and preserve the fragments of the cross on which Jesus died; forge the nails into ornaments, as did Constantine, and yet not be saved.

II. You may also meet with the historical circumstance. It is written that Christ died on the cross. Now you may have read that in the Holy Book, in history, poetry, fiction and philosophy, many times. You may know that crucifixion was the Roman method of capital punishment executed only upon the lowest and vilest, and therefore extremely ignominious. You may know all the particular circumstances of His death; the blackness of the heavens, the terror of the earth, the derision and contempt of men, the loneliness of the victim, and know that in this there was a great moral purpose, and yet all this knowledge is merely historical. There is no more salvation in it than in knowing that Napoleon crossed the Alps, that Columbus discovered America, the pilgrim fathers came in the Mayflower and landed on Plymouth Rock. History does not save souls.

III. You will frequently meet with the symbol of the Cross. It crowns the pinnacle of churches; it decorates altars; it is laid in the binding of Bibles and devotional books; it is sometimes worn—too often by those who are ashamed of Him who died on it—as an ornament; it is printed on banners, and armies have fought and do fight under it; it is sprinkled with jewels, and blazes on the hand of the living; it is set in flowers and laid on the casket of the dead; and yet it will not, as a symbol, avail for salvation. Souls are not saved by shadows, but by forces.

IV. You will as frequently meet with a theological cross. The cross is a divine fact. The cross of the theologian is a theory concerning the mysteries therein. Theologians gather round the cross and they fight, and, as I believe, crucify the Son of God afresh, and put him to an open shame. To-day the air is rent with the cry, "Crucify Him; He is not fit to live." Those who hold what is known as the moral theory, cry against what is known as the commercial theory, "Away with Him; He is not fit to live." And those who hold that which is burlesqued as the commercial theory, cry out, in a multitude of voices, "Away with Him; He is not fit to live." And the several hundred theorizers of the Atonement make a rabble, crying out against each other's theory, "He is not fit to live." And mind you, this is not a controversy between the bad and the good, but between good men on all sides. Bad men men have not enough interest in the cross to quarrel about it. Now, I advise you not to trouble yourself about any theories. Like Bunyan's Pilgrim, have no theories about it. Pray for the Holy

Ghost, and whatever He teaches you, learn. Let God make whatever impression of the Cross He will upon your heart so prepared. There are different saving views of the Cross. Paul gave one to the Romans, another to the Corinthians, and a different one from either to the Hebrews. Trust the Holy Ghost. He cannot err. He will lead you into all truth. The Gospel is the power of God, and not a theory of any man's or class of men. Souls are not saved by theology, but by the love of God.

I will tell you what I see in the Cross, prefacing it with the remark that I did not always see it as I do now. As our standing points shift, so our sight alters. In the man who died on the Cross for me I see,

1. God's intense hatred of sin. The feeling we entertain concerning anything is manifested in what we do to be rid of it, or what we will pay to keep it. You told the world a few years ago what you thought of slavery, and how much you hated disunion, by the thousands of sons you gave to die for your country. You tell the world to-day how much you hate popular ignorance by the money you spend to dissipate and prevent it. A mother declares how much she hates disease by her steady, daily and hourly fight to save her darling from its pains and ravages. Now, in the Cross we see how much God hates sin by the sacrifice He has made to put it away. God spared not His Son, but freely gave Him for us all. He condemned sin in the flesh.

2. We see, also, His love for the sinner. In the mother who hates and fights disease, you also see love for the child. In the battle you fought against slavery and disunion, we can see love of humanity, love of country. In your educational institutions we read not only hatred of ignorance, but love of light, progress and man. In the Cross God's love to man is manifest. Yes, God does love man. How much? Look at the Cross. "He *so* loved the world."

3. But there is more. We saw Christian under condemnation at Mount Sinai. There he learned that all sin must be

punished. We are under law, and if we have sinned, we are under its condemnation. Now, if this righteous condemnation be removed from those who believe in Christ, and if such are pardoned, then we know that Christ must have satisfied God in our behalf. God would not be righteous to forgive if He had not. Here we get into the region of dogma. It is eminently reasonable to believe that He did, though how, I do not know. There is no human analogy by which I can reach it. But what is most remarkable, the testimony of the Scriptures reaches our case readily. It assures us that He did. I believe the testimony concerning Him; believe that God is true, and go on my way freed from the curse of the law by Him who was made a curse for us.

4. In the Cross we see the spirit of a Christian life. In it we see obedience to the will of God; self-sacrificing love to God and man. The most remarkable thing about the whole of it is His loving prayer, "Father, forgive them, for they know not what they do." In that we see the spirit of a Christian life. How noble, grand, superhuman, Godlike, divine! He suffered and died like a man, at the hands of cruel and wicked men; but He breathed forgivness, like God. Even then He delighted to forgive. Now this forgiveness is the essential condition of Christian discipleship. He has taught us to pray for forgiveness "as we forgive those who trespass against us." That is the only part of His teaching that is repeated. After teaching us to pray, He added, "For if ye forgive not men their trespasses, neither will your Heavenly Father forgive you your trespasses." He again repeated it in a parable, teaching that if men who are forgiven of God do not forgive ther fellow-servants, they shall be cast into prison until they have paid the utmost farthing. Thus Pilgrim received this spirit and noble life from the Cross. It was this that brought the delightful experience of which we now speak, into his soul. His burden rolled off of itself. This was no effort on the part of Christian to get it off as heretofore. It came off as the bark of trees when the new life of spring is felt. He was filled with the

Spirit of the atonement. Love to God, which was created by a saving view of the Cross, "banished all his guilty fears." When a man's heart is full of the Spirit of Christ, the burden of sin cannot remain.

The burden rolled into a Sepulchre, "and he saw it no more." So completely does God remove the burden of sin; so abundantly does he pardon. Words cannot express the achievement.

Then was Christian glad. He wept and sang for joy. His song was offered to Christ. Its burden was, "He hath given me rest by His sorrow, and life by his death." But this is not the whole of his experience. Three shining ones ministered to him; they unitedly greeted him with the salutation, "Peace be to thee!" Then the first said to him, "Thy sins be forgiven;" the second stripped him of his rags and clothed him with a change of raiment; the third also set a mark upon his forehead and gave him a roll with a seal on it.

> "Peace be to thee," all declaring:
> One forgives him all his sin;
> One a change of raiment bearing
> Clothes without and clothes within.
>
> Then the third, his finger tracing,
> Prints a mark upon his brow;
> And a roll his hand embracing
> With a signet sealed below.

This is merely a picture of the experiences of a Christian, more or less clear, in every case. Bunyan being a Trinitarian, makes God and man, heaven and earth, meet at the Cross— man the receiver and God the minister, and to each of the persons of the God-head he assigns special work. The Father speaks forgiveness We have sinned against Him, and Him only; therefore with Him alone is pardon. The Son stript him of his rags, and gave him a change of raiment. This is the special work of Christ. He does not cover our rags with His cloak, but He takes away our rags and gives us His garment.

The Spirit did quite a number of things.

1. He set a mark in his forehead, and gave him God's spirit to bear witness with his, and assurance by their united evidence that he was a child of God.

2. He gave him a roll: That is, he wrote the law of God upon his heart. He was delegated to do the will of God as it was written of him in the volume of the Book.

This ends Christian's experiences at the Cross. Delightful, were they not? Have you had any such? Do you not lose some of the sweetest joys of life by neglecting them?

He had reason to give three leaps for joy and sing:

> "Thus far did I come laden with my sin,
> Nor could aught ease the grief that I was in,
> Till I came hither: what a place is this!
> Must here be the beginning of my bliss?
> Must here the burden fall from off my back?
> Must here the strings that bound it to me crack?
> Blest Cross! blest Sepulchre! blest rather be
> The Man that there was put to shame for me!"

With this new experience; with the spirit of the Cross; the life that sacrifices itself for the good of others, Christian proceeded. "He went on thus until he came at a bottom, when he saw, a little out of the way, three men fast asleep, with fetters upon their heels. The name of one was Simple, another Sloth, and the third Presumption." Now, being filled as he was with the spirit of Christ; being relieved of his burden; being no longer anxious for himself, he began to do good as he had opportunity. He was restored to the joy of salvation, and taught sinners the way, that they might rejoice and be glad in God. He roused them from their sleep, apprised them of their danger, but did not succeed in bringing them to their senses. Their answers are characteristic:

Simple says, "I see no danger." Men who are asleep do not, as a rule. But when there is danger, it is high time for men to wake out of sleep. The law of God, both revealed and natural, declares that punishment will follow sin as surely as shadow does substance. The law is, "Thou shalt love the Lord thy God; thou shalt love thyself; thou shalt love thy neighbor." You may say that the man who is asleep is doing no harm. But he is neglecting to do good. God demands that the law shall be fulfilled. An empty life is a wasted one. He who sows no seed in spring, will have naught in harvest. And just as we would rouse the slothful to work, so would we rouse you to concern for your salvation. "How can you escape if you neglect so great salvation?" There is danger, great and fearful danger. "You are like them that sleep on the top of a mast, for the dead sea is under you, a gulf that hath no bottom."

Sloth appears to believe in the danger, but believes also that there is plenty of time to escape it, so he said, "Yet a little more sleep." He is exactly like those who postpone the day of repentance to the day of leisure, old age, or death. Let me ask you, can the work of a life be done in the hour of death? Besides, the law is that a man shall receive according to the deeds done in the body. How can you expect to offer God a holy life, a useful life, when you only commence it in old age or dying weakness?

But Presumption saw the danger, and braved it. His maxim was, "Every vat must stand on its own bottom." That is true. Sin cannot be transferred to another. I am responsible for mine, and you for yours. We shall answer for ourselves in the judgment. I heard a presumptious man say once that he did not care for the future, he should get just what he deserved, and no more. That is just what I fear. I am afraid of what I deserve. Oh! how can I, who have sinned in thought, word, and deed, face my loving Father with a presumptious smile, and ask for my deserts. How dare I, who have sinned in ignorance and knowledge, go into His pure courts in this spirit? No, brethren, I need a Savior, and so do you.

They would none of his counsel. He was, therefore, much grieved. He noticed that they were ironed. Like every sinner, they were held in cords of their own sins. The other day I saw a convict on the street, his limbs chained to an iron ball, which held him to itself. The law had chained him to it. He would have been freed if he could; he chafed under the shame, but he was powerless. His deeds had brought him there. If you visit a convict establishment you may see men forging chains which they will have to wear. So these men forged their chains; so do the drunkard and the adulterer. Every form of sin is bondage. Sinners are in chains, waiting in darkness until the day of the Lord.

While he was musing and troubled concerning these, "he espied two men come tumbling over the wall, on the left-hand of the narrow way; and they made up apace to him. The name of the one was Formalist, and the name of the other Hypocrisy." They were born in the land of Vainglory, and came into the way in this fashion, because they thought the Wicket Gate too far round for them. They are representatives of those who profess religion for purposes of their own, and therefore have no need of repentance toward God or faith in Christ.

Formalist is one of those who deceive themselves in matters of religion. Human nature is very weak, and is grossly deceived by appearances. Many men like to keep up appearances. They buy brass and paste so that their jewels shall at least appear to be diamonds set in gold; they buy costly dress and live in large houses, that they may appear to be wealthy. This weakness men carry into religion; and so men go punctually, frequently, and soberly to the most fashionable church, and deceive themselves with the thought that they are Christians. A house does not make a home; all is not gold that glitters; a church does not make a Christian; display does not make wealth; sacrifices, incense, pilgrimages, worship, do not make life. God dwelleth with the poor and contrite; He looks on that man who is of clean hands and pure heart; who has not taken bribes or sworn deceitfully, and such as he shall stand in in Zion before Him.

Hypocrisy; an actor, represents those who profess religion that they may deceive others. But playing a part does not make a genuine character. An actor may look, dress and act like a king, but when the drama is over he may be but a sower of sedition. A man may act the part of a Christian, but when life is over, and God strips him, the real man will appear.

How foolish their delusion! "If we are in the way, we are in." It does not matter how we got in, so that we are here. The members of our family enter our houses by the doors; thieves get in some other way.

Look at the difference between these men and our Pilgrim, who came through the Wicket Gate and Interpreter's House to the Cross; and now choose ye which of them shall be your example.

LECTURE VIII.

THE HILL DIFFICULTY.

[SYNOPSIS OF CHAPTER.—Christian, with his companions, Hypocrisy and Formality, walk along till they come to a very high hill named Difficulty. The straight path lay right up it. Two other ways, which appeared to go round it, named Danger and Destruction, met at its base. These were taken by his companions—Hypocrisy taking one, and Formalist the other. Instead of going round, they led respectively to a great wood, and to a wide field, full of dark mountains, where they both perished. Christian refreshed himself at the spring at the bottom of the hill, and started. He went running, going, clambering upon his hands and knees, because of the steepness of the place. Midway up the hill he rested in a pleasant harbour, where he slept and lost his roll. Was aroused, and started on his journey with renewed vigor, hoping to reach the Palace Beautiful before nightfall. He met Distrust and Timorous, who sought to turn him back by ill reports of the journey. Christian argued that to go back was to die; to go on, only the fear of death at the worst, and therefore resolved to proceed. Here he found he had lost his roll and had to go back for it. Having found it he retraced his steps, and arrived with many discomforts and self-reproaches at the Beautiful Palace.]

WE HAVE before us a hill, steep, rugged and high, to which Christian and his companions came. There is a spring at its base, an arbour on its side, a palace at its summit. There are ways that promise to go round it, but *The Way* is straight up it. It is a difficult way, and fitly represents the passage from the Cross to the Church.

Since the world has possessed this allegory it has been claimed by Christians as the picture of their experiences. These are not all joyful; but smiles mingle with tears; nights follow the days;

storm the calm; clouds the sunshine; the waves of blessedness that flow from heaven and break on the soul, ebb back again, and a Christian is not merely left in a smooth sea, but frequently at low water. Our Pilgrim was joyful at the Cross. This soon gave place to the arduous task of climbing the difficult hill.

I say the passage from the Cross to the Church is difficult; difficult as it would be for you to climb such a hill as Bunyan had in his mind, to reach the castle at its top. It is as dangerous as the transition from boyhood to manhood, when the lad has all the passions of a man, and only the experience and strength of a child to control them. The Christian has all the powers of sinful manhood, with only the strength of Christian childhood to withstand them. I refer, of course, to such sinners as Bunyan, who came into the way of righteousness at a comparatively late period in life. Happy, indeed, are they who seek God early and find Him, so that the Divine life grows with the lower life, and from the beginning keeps it under subjection.

He has been taught in the Interpreter's House that he must go right on, though the way be not always level; now he will learn it from his own experience. Like the rest of us, he has to learn from his mistakes.

It will be well to premise that a Christian has trials peculiar to himself. Events, thoughts, affections and conduct, that have no effect on others, fill him with grief and shame. On the same principle that an artist is offended by daubs of paint which others call pictures; and a musician by noises that others call music; and a poet by jingles labelled poetry. Their sense of harmony and proportion, so abundantly educated, sees defects; feels inconsistencies so that they suffer the most exquisite misery, and misery which will neither evoke compassion nor appreciation.

"The highest suffer most,
The strongest wander farthest and more hopelessly are lost,
The mark of rank in nature is capacity for pain,
And the anguish of the singer makes the sweetness of the strain."

—14

A Christian's moral sense is so quickened, the law of God, in its refined spirituality, so deftly written in the heart by the Spirit of God, that he is sensitive to anything that offends the love of God. And what so sensitive as love? We can grieve those who love us more easily than we can any others, and we are grieved by them as we are not by others. A Christian feels to be wrong what may appear to others right. He will mourn over actions and dispositions which others treat lightly and carelessly. He is as sensitive to every degree of sin as a tender plant is to frost. This may explain some of the sorrows of pilgrims.

The Pilgrim has just left the Cross. He is possessed of the Spirit of Christ Jesus, and begins to learn the infinite tenderness of righteous sorrow. He now debates this question, "Shall I join the church?" With our Pilgrim there was no hesitation. He drank of the spring at the bottom, and then began to go up the hill, saying:

> "The hill, though high, I covet to ascend,
> The difficulty will not me offend;
> For I perceive the way to life lies here:
> Come, pluck up, heart, let's neither faint nor fear;
> Better, though difficult, the right way to go,
> Than wrong, though easy, where the end is woe."

But this is the question with many. Take into account this refined spiritual experience; take also into account that the Christian is a man in the flesh and intellect, and a babe in the spirit; and with these thoughts we may proceed to inquire why such a difficulty should exist in the mind of any to whom such a duty must be plain.

A Christian will feel a conflict between flesh and spirit, and this is a difficulty. Perhaps (this is often the case) the new life has led him to promise himself that all conflicts of this kind are over. After the first ardor has passed away he finds his old dispositions asserting themselves, and his old habits laying claim to his life. In sin he indulged the flesh, and made his intellect an important advocate thereof. He has read of the body being dead to sin; read it in devotional books and hymns, and heard from the experience of older Christians of being so free from sin that it has no dominion over their bodies, and that this is accomplished by faith. He knows again that he who sows to the flesh, shall of the flesh reap corruption. Well, he knows that he believes in Christ, but he does not find his body dead. He is in it. His carnal nature asks supremacy; it craves indulgence. The intellect, so long the ally of the flesh, reads God's word, history and biography with fleshly bias, and examples are referred to, maxims are quoted, precedents are offered. He can not make headway against such winds. He is affrighted at the inclinations of his heart, and the appetite of his flesh. He has learned that a Christian had none such. He is to be pardoned if he asks himself the question, "Am I a Christian? Ought I to join the Church?"

Let me suppose that this is really your difficulty. You may have been a drunkard, or a glutton, or even worse, and I have described your condition. What am I to say to you? I recognize that these temptations and appetites are to you a sorrow. You feel that, if carried out, they would take away the spirit you have received from God; they would destroy the peace which passeth all understanding, the unspeakable joy of your heart. You do not feel inclined to make the barter. The temptation is more than you can stand. But see you not, my brother, that your grief and resistance are proof that the life of the Spirit is within you?

I recognize, again, that you have been badly educated. No where is it promised that you will become altogether spiritual all at once. You are indeed to reckon your body dead to sin, but not to your natural appetites. God placed them there. They may be used for his glory. Let them move in the channels he has made. You are to crucify your lusts; but crucifixion is a long, slow mode of dying. Drive the nails into your lusts, but not into a solitary proper affection of the soul. You are not called to asceticism, that is cowardice; but to be a man. Be, then, a hero.

That you may join the Church is established by precedent. Paul is our precedent here. He found the flesh lusting against the spirit, and the spirit against the flesh. He fought beasts, as has every Christian. He kept his body under subjection. Paul felt as you do. Do you then as he did.

But he may find a difficulty between his spirit and the world. He will not have been a Christian a great while before he will have discovered that it is conducive to worldly prosperity. Godliness is profitable to all things having the promise of the life that now is, and that which is to come. When Christ sends the devils out of a human being, he soon gets enough of the world to buy a box of spikenard, very precious and costly. The ragged, unmanageable sinners whom He saves, are soon to be found at His feet, clothed and in their right mind. These effects influence the soul. Having received so much good, he is tempted to think there is no more good to get, shuts his eyes to the fact that there is good to do, and that these new and rich mercies are all agencies by which he can and ought to do good unto others.

He has, however, lived long for himself; his previous habits suggest that he is bound to take care for himself. He is tempted by the lust of the eye and the pride of life. At present he has not learned that it is more blessed to give than to receive. He questions whether it will be policy for him to unite with God's people. Here is a difficulty often to be met in various forms. It will be an advantage for him to do as he feels he ought, if only to keep his heart open.

There are difficulties of a marked nature between faith and doubt. The former difficulty is between spirit and flesh; this between spirit and mind—between reason and faith. The intellect is used for the purpose of the flesh, or spirit. Man reasons, imagines, and thinks at their dictation. The mind, having been long on the side of the flesh, enters into the conflict, and produces doubt concerning the very powers which have produced a new life.

The Christian reads, "the just shall live by faith." He believes, and hath the life in himself. Faith is, first of all, credence of certain historical facts. So far it is mental. It is, again, the choice of some rule of life. With a Christian, it is choosing to obey the Lord Jesus; herein it is moral. And it is conformation of the thoughts and affections to the mind of God; herein it is spiritual. A Christian may be conscious of these powers in his soul and life, and yet be tempted to doubt. And no wonder! Doubt is even consistent with faith—I had almost said necessary to it; certainly incident thereto. Personally, I thank God for my doubts, and personally, I have but little respect for the mind that has them not, and dares not grapple with them. Bunyan doubted. He doubted the being of God, and doubted his Saviour. Good men—aye, the best of men have doubted. It is not necessarily sinful. To believe without evidence is sinful, for that is to violate the law of God, written in the constitution of the human mind. It is superstition and not faith.

The genesis of Christian doubt is this: The new life makes a man more intellectual. He no sooner begins to live than he wants to know. He cannot remain ignorant. He begins to ask himself the why and the wherefore. He has been taught that to doubt is sinful, and because he cannot help doubting he believes himself sinful. He condemns himself in the thing that he allows. He began the life as a sinner, now he rises to be a theologian. This is right; he ought to be able to give a reason for the hope that is in him.

Then, again, he asks of himself and demands proofs from others concerning the verities of our holy religion, which do not apply, and because these cannot be given, his doubts deepen. Let us acknowledge at once that we cannot give the demanded proof for the things surely believed among us. Why? Because such is not forthcoming; it is absurd.

You cannot have the same kind of proof for one thing that can be given satisfactorily for another. Two and two make four. This I can prove by mathematics, in all manner of ways. Water is composed of certain gases. I cannot prove the statement by the means used to prove the other. Mathematics will not apply. I have in this instance to apply chemistry. Beecher, Simpson, Gladstone, Bright, are great orators; I cannot prove this statement by either mathematics or chemistry; but I can prove it by universal testimony, and the effect of their words. Camilla Urso is a great violinist; Arbuckle a great cornet soloist; Arabella Goddard a great pianist; Kellogg a great singer; but I cannot prove these predications by any other means than of the senses. If a man is charged with a crime, it has to be proven by testimony. History has to be proven by contemporary writings; poetry and art by other means. They cannot, however, be judged as Sterne's traveler attempted to judge them, by a stop-watch and a two-foot rule.

We are frequently asked, and the Christian asks for proofs of the things he believes, which do not apply; and because he does not ask wisely, plunges himself into unreasonable doubts and much distress. Now I cannot demonstrate that there is a God; but I can demonstrate that it is exceedingly foolish and unreasonable for any man not to believe in His existence. I cannot demonstrate that there is a future life, but I can bring forward so much presumptive evidence in favor of the doctrine, and I can demonstrate that men who refuse such evidence as conclusive, do act in the most important matters of life on so very much less, that it is unreasonable to deny, and foolish to doubt it. I cannot demonstrate that the Bible is written, as it claims to be, by holy men, inspired by God, but I can convince any convinceable man that otherwise "man would not have written it if he could, and could not if he would," and leave the burden of accounting for its existence with him. I cannot prove to the absolute exclusion of doubt that Christ came into the world to save sinners, but I can prove two things; first, that sinners are saved from sin, selfishness, and animalism by believing in Him; and I can prove that the story concerning Him as told in the New Testament, and as preached by the Churches, has revolutionized the world; that the countries without Christ are behind in civilization, and those who know His life, teaching and death, are highest in rank. I can prove that if the history we have be not true, then the fiction is the greater miracle. I can prove that the love of God, displayed in Christ, so far transcends the highest pagan conception of the relation of gods and men, as manifestly to cause every honest mind to recognize its superhuman origin. But after I have brought out all my proof to convince the intellect, I am conscious of other evidence which I cannot utter; which I can neither write or speak. It satisfies me; for it is the secret of the Lord. I know I have passed from death to life. I know that the Son of Man has come and given us an understanding that we may know Him that is true.

Much perplexity arises from this source, and as the young Christian begins the investigation of the deepest problems that can engage the human mind, it is not to be wondered that he feels the difficulty of doubt. But should such an one join the Church? I think so. There was an honest doubter among the disciples. God does not force any man's faith. If any man asks evidence He will give it. He will say to every honest doubter "Reach hither thy finger and behold my hands; and reach hither thy hand and thrust it into my side; and be not faithless, but believing." Such as the Lord instructs the Church may accept.

Every Christian will have to struggle with doubt. It may take the form already indicated, or it may be that he will doubt one or more of the accepted doctrines held by the Church to which he is attached. In such an instance the question is hardly one for the candidate to decide. It is for the Church. Can the Church receive such an one? According to Scripture, I answer, yes. "Him that is weak in the faith receive ye, but not to doubtful disputations." The practice of Churches is scriptural, although those who regard our method of receiving members as loose, had better look at home, and see if a "general assent" does not mean a strong dissent from some particular and even vital point.

A Christian will find a difficulty arising between love and selfishness. Sin is essentially selfish. Men break God's law and neglect to keep His commands, in order to gratify and please themselves. The Christian is born again, and into a mode of life in which love to God and man is to rule. He knows he has passed from death unto life, because he loves the brethren. He loves the brother, because the Father first loved him. Nor does he love in thought or in word, but in deed and in truth. Against this, the old carnal life protests. Men are unloveable and unthankful. They are stubborn, and will not readily respond to His affection. He takes the New Testament idea of a church, and sees it to be a congregation of men and women, who meet to worship God through Christ, and so cultivate the spirit of Christ. And he knows the spirit of Christ to be eminently love. He regrets that he cannot love men, that his affections grow cold. He believes in universal brotherhood as a theory; but when it comes to practice, his old nature and habits decline. He thinks he ought not to join the Church in this condition.

Herein have I sketched the difficulties which occur to men in their way from the Cross to the Church. They are not fancy pictures, but facts. Most pastors will recognize in them the the likeness of true objects.

It is now my purpose to show the manner in which these difficulties were overcome.

I said, in a previous lecture, that God is never behindhand with His remedies. I now say that He is never behindhand with His grace. He giveth grace for grace. As our day, so is our strength. His grace is sufficient for us. Strength comes before trial. Bunyan places at the foot of the hill a spring. The Pilgrim refreshes himself thereat, and attacks his difficulties in the strength thereof. Let that spring represent some means of grace; say, a season of private prayer, of quiet meditation, diligent study of the Word of God; earnest public worship—one or all of these means, that we use to obtain a supply of Divine strength.

Observe, particularly, the spring is before the journey. How true to nature! As if God, from all eternity, anticipated the need of travelers, at the foot of hills you may find the coolest, and most refreshing springs of water. Behind, beneath, in the rocks which the human eye cannot see and the mind does not imagine, God is filtering water, and, before the tourist ascends the mountain, opens a vein in its side, and lets it flow for his strength and comfort.

Let this fact of nature be a lesson in religion, and then it will correct a very unscriptural idea of worship, both public and private. We too often think, and, perhaps, teach, consciously or unconsciously, that prayer and faith are only to blot out sins. Are there not some in this condition? Do they not sin, and then go to church, or go to private prayer, for forgiveness to wash it all away? I know that there are men in this state. But, brethren, worship should always precede sin; it should be used to prevent sin. Believe me, God is more glorified in your virtue than in your penitence. You are to pray that you may not be led into temptation, but delivered from evil. There is no virtue in being happy in sin, and then going to church and calling ourselves miserable sinners. If we are *miserable* sinners, had we not better pray for grace to leave them off? You probably remember the case of King Saul; how he disobeyed the command of the Lord, and then sought to atone for his disobedience by offering a very large sacrifice? He put worship in the wrong place. He should have sought strength to keep the command. And now listen to the words of Samuel to the mistaken man, "Hath the Lord as great delight in burnt offerings and sacrifices as in obeying the voice of the Lord?" A very emphatic way of saying that he had not? It would be well to remember that God having raised up his Son Jesus, sent Him to bless you in turning away every one of you from your iniquities.

The privilege I set before you has the merit of possessing common sense. In the other method, there is neither wisdom nor goodness, but very much presumption and, frequently, very much sin. We rise in the morning, and eat our early meal to provide against exhaustion. Gymnasts practice long and well, so that in the day of trial they may accomplish their purposes with ease and success. We send our children to school during the whole of their early life, so that they may be prepared for the duties of men and women, when they become such. To-day's work is but preparation for to-morrow's want. Let us be as wise in religion as we are in other things. Let every spring in nature, every well by the wayside, every time our table is spread, every child we send to school, teach us this important lesson that grace is given so that we may conquer difficulties, the world, the flesh, doubt, and the devil—yea, that God is more glorified when we obtain from Him so much strength that these difficulties disappear.

The way was so steep and rugged that he used all manner of means to succeed, "running, going, clambering." He had to use all his strength, and exert all his faculties. There is something grandly heroic in him. He doggedly determined to keep on. So must you. How I have kept on, I do not know. I have had as many battles in the flesh as most of you; had as many doubts and questionings as you; am naturally as selfish as any of you, but here I am, by the grace of God. It has only been by persevering in the teeth of difficulties. God has fashioned all our hearts alike. He hath made of one blood all men, and therefore what is true of myself, I opine to be true of you. If we are Christians to-day, we owe it to daring, determined faith.

We need not wonder that our Christian grew tired, for we have often been weary ourselves. In this tired condition, tired of struggling with the flesh, the world, with doubts, and against a covetous self; tired of pressing on to apprehend that for which we were apprehended in Christ Jesus, we have sought rest and refreshment, and when we have turned unto the Lord, we have found it. There are times of refreshing from His presence and in His presence. This is graphically portrayed by Bunyan.

The Hill Difficulty.

"Now, about the midway to the top of the hill was a pleasant harbour, made by the Lord of the hill for the refreshing of weary travellers."

Here is a piece of English scenery. The harbor and the settle are perfectly natural. I have climbed many such hills as a child, boy and man, and found provided on them just such a retreat as is here described. I call to my mind one on Minster Hill, near one of the first churches built in Great Britain, from which I used to sit and look seaward to the German Ocean, and there invigorate my body, educate my mind and refresh my soul. Then, turning landward, look over old battle-grounds and Norman ruins, partially hid like *billet-doux* in boquets amid the cherry orchards and hop gardens of Kent. And I think the hills of Matlock, Buxton and Chatsworth, where, with almost princely munificence, such are provided. Here you may rest and inhale the perfume of the wild hyacinths, listen to a concert of birds,— the lark singing in the heavens, and the woods vocal in response,—watch a tempest playing on a distant hill, see pictures such as only the sun can paint, the river rippling, sparkling, splashing merrily at your feet, the rocks clad in fern and shrub, the hedge-rows in white blossom like the bride of summer, the banks covered with the forget-me-nots—here you may sit, think and feel thoughts too deep for tears, and forget your sorrows and weariness, till the intoxicating enchantment will lull you to sleep. I have seen many asleep in them, and have fallen asleep in such harbors myself..

I pity the man who does not enjoy such a place; but I pity the man more who thinks that such places were made to sleep in. I pity the man who cannot, and does not, find refreshment in prayer and praise and worship, but I pity more the man who is asleep in such exercises. And yet many are asleep; so much so, that they don't care to be roused. But our Pilgrim was roused. There came One to him who said, "Go to the ant, thou sluggard; consider her ways and be wise."

God, in His book, says, "Let us not sleep as do others," "Woe to them that are at ease in Zion," "Awake thou that sleepest." The enemy of our souls takes advantage of such seasons, and through the "times of refreshing" insinuates into our hearts such influences as will make us slumber. I have heard of poisonous insects making such slumbers fatal. A Christian asleep is like a Christian dead, and therefore useless.

Luther says: "The devil once held a conference with his emissaries. They came from the four quarters of the globe, to report their doings. One said that he saw a ship freighted with Christians crossing the ocean, and that he had gathered together the four winds of heaven, and blew upon it so that it was wrecked, and every one drowned. 'What of that?' cried the devil; 'their souls were all saved!' Another affirmed that he had seen a caravan of Christians journeying through a desert; that he had gathered the wild beasts of the forest, and set them on; that he saw them killed, their flesh eaten, their blood drank, and their bleached bones left on the desert sand. 'What of that?' cried the devil; 'their souls were all saved!' Then another came forward, and tremblingly said that he had tried for ten long, weary years to get one solitary Christian asleep, and had finally succeeded. Then the devil shouted, and all the sons of hell danced and yelled for joy."

If this parable contains truth, again let me ask you to beware of sleep.

Sleep is sinful to the Christian. Asleep, he cannot do the will of God. Oh, my brethren, do not let God's most precious communications to your souls produce this effect. Wait on the Lord, so that you renew your strength; mount as on wings of eagles, run and not get weary, walk and not faint.

The consequence of the sleep was—

1. He lost his roll.
2. He was filled with shame and sorrow.
3. He had to retrace his steps.
4. He had to pursue his journey in darkness.

You will be anxious to know what became of his companions who came with him to the bottom of the hill. They thought to escape the difficulties of the hill by going round it, thinking that the ways would meet. But they did not. To escape difficulty in the Christian life is to meet danger and death. This, Formalist and Hypocrisy discovered too late.

Brethren, there are difficulties in the way of righteousness, but there is neither destruction nor death. Righteousness leadeth to life. Which will you choose—the Life or the Death?

LECTURE IX.

THE PALACE BEAUTIFUL.

[SYNOPSIS OF CHAPTER.—Christian arrived at the Palace Beautiful, and was afraid to enter, in consequence of two lions which appeared in his way. He would have gone back had not Watchful the Porter told him that they were chained. He was introduced to Charity by Watchful, and then by Charity to the other members of the household, who united in giving him a very cordial welcome. They obtained from him a history of his journey, spread their table for him, and spent their time in profitable conversation. They put him to rest in a large upper chamber, where a window opened towards the sunrising; the name of the chamber was Peace. Here he slept till break of day. In the morning they had more discourse. Then they led him to the Study, and afterwards to the Armory. He stayed with them a second night. On the morrow they led him to the top of the house, from whence they shewed him the Delectable Mountains, and told him that when he reached them he would be able to see the gate of the Celestial City. They led him back to the Armory, where they armed him from head to foot for future conflicts. After which, they accompanied him to the foot of the hill to the valley of Humiliation, where they took leave of him, and gave him a loaf of bread, a bottle of wine, a cluster of raisins, and then he went on his way.]

CHRISTIAN was almost persuaded to go back when he met Mistrust and Timorous, and heard their report of the dangers of the way. But he reasoned with himself in this fashion: "If I go back to mine own country, *that* is prepared for fire and brimstone, and I shall certainly perish there. If I can get to the Celestial City, I shall certainly be in safety there. I must venture; to go back is nothing but death; to go forward is fear of death, and life everlasting beyond it. I will yet go forward." After he had made this noble resolution, he discovered that he had lost his roll; was obliged to return to the place in which he had slept, and had to tread his steps thrice over, while he needed to have trod them but once. He returned to his journey in much self-condemnation. The sun went down upon him, and, in the gloom, he said, "O thou sinful sleep! How, for thy sake, am I like to be benighted in my journey! I must walk without the sun; darkness must cover the path of my feet, and I must hear the noise of doleful creatures, because of my sinful sleep." Then the fears excited by the story of Mistrust and Timorous prevailed. "But while he was bewailing this unhappy miscarriage, he lifted up his eyes, and behold there was a very stately palace before him, the name of which was Beautiful."

This palace is intended by our Author to represent the Church of Jesus Christ. He further states its origin and design. "It was built by the Lord of the hill for the relief and security of pilgrims." Another thought is clearly revealed; the straight and narrow way of righteousness through Jesus Christ leads to the Church. From the first, the men and women who follow Christ have, as if by instinct, knit themselves together for the purposes of worship and usefulness. A power in the heart should certainly bind us as firmly together as a precept in a book, even though that book be the Bible.

Bunyan takes an Old Testament fact. The hill of Zion; her towers and palaces were called Beautiful. "Beautiful for situation, and the joy of the whole earth is Mount Zion." The temple and its worship were both beautiful. That beauty inheres in religious life, has been felt through all time. In all ages men have decorated their temples. All feel that the service of praise should be beautiful. When it is not, it fails properly to impress the mind. Worship the Lord in the *beauty* of holiness. Men are not willing to appear in Church as elsewhere. For worship, they put on their best clothes and manners. In the house of the Lord, men like to appear at their best.

The beauty of a Church does not inhere in its material possessions, however rich or brilliantly garnished, but in spiritual gifts and graces, for the Church is a spiritual combination of men. It is the family of God, named after Jesus Christ. The beauty upon it is the beauty of the Lord. God is beautiful. Oh! how great is His beauty! The fringe of a weed, the form of a blade of grass, the petal of every flower, "the meanest flower that blows," the myriad insects that fill the air on a summer night, the forest, the rill, the avalanche, the rock, the mountain, the clouds, the day, the night, the colors of light, the song of creation, declare in one voice that He hath made everything beautiful in its season.

Christ is beautiful. He is the fullness of the God-head, bodily. Such fullness, such harmony, such proportion, such gentleness, such strength of virtue, were never seen in man before, nor have been since. To those who know Him not, or whose eyes are yet unenlightened by the Holy Ghost, He is as a root out of a dry ground; there is no beauty in Him that they should desire Him. A man who does not love flowers, or who does not know flowers, will probably see no beauty in the gnarled bulbs of the gladiolus, dahlia, or lily, and will be careless and indifferent to them. But the man who loves the flowers will see, prospectively, in each ugly root a beautiful production, and in them all combined a still more beautiful garden, and take care of each in proportion to his love. They are to him very fair and dear; so is Christ to those who know and love Him. He is the Rose, the Lily, the Branch. He is the fairest among ten thousand, and the one altogether lovely. To those who can appreciate moral beauty, there is none like Him.

Now, Christians are Godlike and Christlike men, and therefore they are morally beautiful. Men of meek and quiet spirits, men of righteousness, men of purity, men of peace, men of light, and men of love, affect the world morally as does a beautiful picture, statue or song æsthetically. Such men combined make a beautiful Church. "Must not that Church be beautiful where Watchful is the Porter, Discretion governs, Prudence takes the oversight, Piety conducts the worship, and Charity endears the members one to another?" The beauty of the Lord is upon it. If any of these elements are wanting, it is inharmonious, defective, and lacks so much of beauty. The Lord desires His bride, the Church, to be beautiful.

The difficulties contemplated in joining a Church, by our Author and by others, are represented by two lions. They were chained and harmless, but Christian did not know it. They affrighted Timorous and Mistrust so much as to send them back to the City of Destruction. They brought our Pilgrim to a halt, "for he thought that nothing but death was before him." Perhaps he would have gone back, if Watchful the Porter had not relieved his fears.

The difficulties portrayed refer unquestionably, first, to the disabilities under which Non-conformists lived in Bunyan's time; and, secondly, to the many fears which persons feel at taking such a step.

To join a dissenting Church—a Congregational or a Baptist, for example—in his day, was to face the lion of the state; he was thereby prohibited from obtaining or holding any civil office. It was in every way a disadvantage and regarded as a social disgrace. It was a crime to attend any dissenting place of worship. A justice might commit for such an offense without a jury. For the third breach sentence of transportation for seven years might be passed; and should the criminal return before that time, he might suffer death. Ministers and others who would not conform to the Established Church were prohibited from going within five miles of a corporate town, or of any place where they had formerly resided. "For a time the clergy of the Church as established by law, made war on schism with so much vigor, that they had no leisure to make war on vice. The ribaldry of Etherege and Whicherly was, in the presence and under the sanction of the Church, publicly recited, by female lips, in female ears, while the author of the Pilgrim's Progress languished in a dungeon for the crime of preaching the Gospel to the poor."*

* Macaulay.
—16

John Bunyan was a Baptist; he knew what he was risking when he joined himself to the "sect everywhere spoken against." But he was too conscientious to be other than true. When on one occasion about forty souls had gathered at the village of Samsel to hear him preach, and he had announced this treasonable (?) text, "Dost thou believe on the Son of God," the door opened and a justice of the peace and a posse of constables made their appearance. For this crime they marched him to prison; for the crime of "having many meetings together to pray to God and to exhort one another," for having "the sweet, comforting presence of the Lord among them," he was sentenced by the authorities of the Church, as established by law, in these words: "You must be led back again to prison, and be there for three months following; at the three months' end, if you do not submit and go to church to hear Divine service, and leave your preaching, you must be banished the realm; and if after such a day as shall be appointed you to be gone, you shall be found in the realm, you shall stretch by the neck for it." But you have no such disabilities as these, and they are removed in England now. Right has triumphed over might, and Dissenters keep toll-gates and post-offices, collect taxes, have seats in city councils, represent the people in parliament, are made soldiers and lawyers and judges, are entrusted with secrets and business of the state, send their sons to the best public schools and national universities, and yet "'tis strange! 'tis passing strange!" the country remains.

Perhaps the matter is explainable by taking into account that there is one class of men who are seeking salvation through Christ, and another class who are seeking it through a Church. The latter have always hated the former.

This lion does not exist in this land. Should the day ever come when any one section of the Catholic Church shall have the legal right to insult the religious history of America and the other sections of the Church of Christ in this land, by calling itself "The Church of America," then the other lion will have established itself at the gate of the Palace Beautiful. But that day can never come. Even if the lion should come deprived of the teeth of the law, it would create an aristocracy on a religious foundation which I need not say is foreign to the idea of Jesus Christ. It would be an unhappy marriage for both Church and State. The parties are not congenial. God would divorce the Church for adultery, and man the State for incompatibility of temper. The sentence would be wise, with costs divided between the parties.

The other lion represents the fears which conscientious persons endure in the prospect of uniting with a Christian Church. They fear that they are not qualified; the Church will not receive them; they are not old enough, have not sufficient experience; or that they will some time or other disgrace their profession. We take no important step in life, embark in no new enterprise without such feelings. The same elements of our nature are roused when we attempt this. For the sake of those who are desirous of joining a Church, and yet may fear to do so, I may describe the process of admission, as Bunyan conceived it, and as I think it ought to be.

Watchful, the porter, allayed Christian's fears concerning the lions, and told him that they were chained, and were not there to hurt, but to discover the faith of the Pilgrims. After discovering whom he was and whither bound, the porter led him to the door of the house. Here he was met by Discretion. Watchful gave her the history he had learned from the Pilgrim. She questioned him further, and as his answers satisfied her, she introduced him to others of the household; Prudence, Piety, and Charity.

We are here taught that we are to be watchful for souls, as those who must give account to God. We are to encourage those who are found in the way of righteousness to join the Church, as did the Porter, but while we do this, exercise Discretion. Every one is not fit for church membership, not even all who apply. It would save some men to keep them out. But, in these days, when moral success is judged by arithmetic, when many, and not much, is the standard, we are likely to be careless. In building a house, you take care to sort your lumber; you do not put into it any that is unseasoned or unsound, because you know it will shrink or rot, and your house become unsafe, uncomfortable, and worthless. In like manner the admission to our churches of unprepared souls will destroy them. Two cannot walk together unless they are agreed.

With Discretion, Charity, Prudence, and Piety, he entered the Palace. Many of the members of the household met him at the threshold, saying, "Come in, thou blessed of the Lord; this house was built by the Lord of the hill, on purpose to entertain such pilgrims in." After he had received refreshment, they proposed conversation, and appointed Piety, Prudence, and Charity to have "particular discourse" with him. The story shews that Piety derived from him an account of his motives and a history of the events of the pilgrimage, with which we are acquainted. Prudence learnt the state of his affections towards the things that were behind, and Charity got to know what he had done to bring others on the way. He stood the test which each applied, and by this time supper was ready.

Now I wish you to notice one thing, particularly. In all their conversation, and they had much; in the entire examination, and it was long and searching; not a single doctrinal question was asked, nor a solitary theological dogma discussed.

It is thought and said that those of us who would waive a theological examination of those who apply for church membership, are loose and liberal; and that we have adopted our ideas because they are new; and that these views, if universally adopted, would make the door of the Church too wide. My brethren, it is not so. Our views are not new. They are as old as Pentecost. They were received from heaven, in the gift of the Holy Ghost. Neither would they make the way to the Church too broad. We have too many heartless men and women in our Churches already. They are intelligent enough to assent to a creed, and to give the technical meaning of theological terms.

The original test of Christ and his apostles was love to God and man. It has never been disannulled. Other things have been substituted for it, but it still stands, the eternal essential of Christian life—a nature like God's, the spirit of love. And so we say to those who push a creed before the candidate, brethren, it is you who make a mistake; your views are new; you have no warrant for them in the New Testament. You are working ruin to the Church, even if you do add to it daily a number of those very respectable, well-to-do people, who have no need to be born again. Moreover your practice is unwise and unphilosophical. The fellowship of the Church does not rest on the social or intellectual basis, but on the higher—the spiritual. It is therefore wrong to admit members on the face of a dead creed, if Christ demands a soul of holy love. John Bunyan is on our side, both in his allegory and in practice. His Church at Bedford was "founded on the principle, and it is still observed, now two centuries since his death, of requiring from members simply faith in Christ and holiness of life, without respect to this or that circumstance, or opinion in outward or circumstantial things," and says the latest incumbent of his pulpit, as though he had caught the mantle from the elder prophet, "On this truly catholic basis, and not on that of mere ecclesiastical organization, may the Church of the future stand." To all of which we say Amen and Amen.

But notice a more positive element in this matter. The admission of members into the Church should be the occasion of great joy. This is beautifully described in the abundant welcome which I have already read; then in the refreshments they gave him; then in their conversation until supper was ready; then the supper, the table with fat things, and wine that was well refined; and above all, the delightful talk "about the Lord of the hill; as, namely, about what he had done, and wherefore he did what he did, and why he had builded that house;" and adds our Dreamer, "By what they said I perceived He had been a great warrior, and had fought with and slain him that had the power of death, but not without great danger to himself, which made me love him the more."

> "Who can tell the joy, the bliss
> Of communion such as this!
> These have been, let others say
> At the gates of heaven to-day."

Thus they discoursed together until late at night, and after they had committed themselves to the Lord for protection, betook themselves to rest. The Pilgrim they laid in a large upper chamber, whose window opened towards the sunrising; the name of the chamber was Peace, where he slept until break of day, and then he awoke and sang—

> "Where am I now? Is this the love and care
> Of Jesus, for the men that pilgrims are,
> Thus to provide! That I should be forgiven,
> And dwell already the next door to heaven."

Compare the ideas this suggests with our formal methods. We read a confession of faith from a book, to which the candidate answers with a bookish assent. We read the terms of covenant from a book to the candidate, the Church agreeing thereto, as in duty bound, because it is in the book, responds from a book. The work is done, the books are carefully laid away for the next occasion, and the readers disperse.

Learn a lesson from the blacksmith. When he wants to unite two pieces of iron so as to make them one, he does not attempt the task if both are cold, nor does he heat one and allow the other to be cold. No! iron won't weld thus. But he heats them both to white heat, brings them together on the anvil, "strikes while the iron is hot," and so makes them one. Moral: You cannot weld a warm convert on to a cold Church. If there be joy in heaven over a sinner that repenteth, there ought to be some manifestation of it in the Church on earth.

Just now you heard me strongly object to the reception of members into our Churches on a doctrinal basis. I do not regret what I have said, but I do regret that I cannot say it in a stronger manner. But now let me state the position of doctrine. After they had admitted Christian on the basis of experience and love; on the facts of his history, motives, and purposes, then, and not till then, they led him into The Study. This is wise. A child must be born before he can be taught He must have a home and a school before he can be trained. A man must have spiritual life before he can receive spiritual things. I do not object to doctrine in itself, for I am bound as a steward of the manifold grace of God to take heed unto myself and to the doctrine, and I call you to witness that I am not ashamed to contend earnestly for the faith once delivered to the saints.

Once delivered to the saints. I am not under obligation to defend every compendium of belief that claims to be the faith. The Study is the Word of God. Bunyan never read (at least history does not record it) a work on systematic theology. He had with him in prison the Bible and Fox's Book of Martyrs. After his release he obtained a copy of "Luther on the Galatians," so old that, says he, "it was ready to fall piece from piece if I did but turn it over." This is the only theological literature that we learn of as being in his possession, and it is practical and not scientific or speculative; and yet, says the late Dr. Arnold, who echoes the sentiments of numbers in the highest places of our literature, "I hold John Bunyan to have been a man of incomparably greater genius than any of [our divines] and to have given a far truer and more edifying picture of Christianity."

If any of you were to send your sons to be practical engineers, the first lesson they would have to learn would be this: Never to take a measurement except from the standard templates. It is a fact that engines could not be made successfully if this simple rule were departed from. The old artists copied from nature. The leading scientists of to-day have always been better acquainted with nature than with books. There is a man in this country at whose feet the clergy sit, like children, to learn the ways of God. He is a one Book man; a Bible-made theologian. It is these little departures from the Bible that make our Churches so powerless to-day. In vain have we put aside the commandments of God for traditions of men. Let us learn that the truest and only needed theology is in The Book of Books. Let us keep the best of books in our hands, and our eyes continually lifted to heaven.

From the Study they took the Pilgrim to the Armory, where they shewed him all manner of things illustrative of the principle "that the just shall live by faith;" shewed him the various instruments by which holy men of old had won their several victories; then he was clad with the helmet of salvation, the breast-plate of righteousness, the girdle of truth, the sandals of peace, the shield of faith; yea, they harnessed him from head to foot with weapons offensive and defensive. Hitherto he had appeared in the robe he received at the Cross; now, that is covered with the habiliments of a warrior; he now enters a new period of his existence, in which he will have to fight his way.

A question has often been asked; one which I will now try to answer: Cannot a man be a Christian without joining the Church? I have no hesitancy in answering, yes; and what is more, I will say that some of the best Christians are outside the Churches, and they are outside in consequence. They have such high conceptions of the Christian character, such fears that they will bring a reproach upon it, that they, for these reasons, do not ally themselves with God's people. The best man, by far, that I ever knew, who lived more like Christ than any other of my acquaintance, and to whom I am more indebted for whatever aspiration I may have to follow my Lord, was not and is not a member of any religious denomination. Such as these the Church would be glad to receive.

But while I have made these admissions, I want, in my turn, to ask you a question: "Ought not such men as I have described to join a Church?" The friend to whom I have alluded, the class which I have just described, would be better, inasmuch as they would do more good in the Churches than out. To do good as ye have opportunity, is the law of Christian life. To him that knoweth to do good, and doeth it not, to him it is a sin. The Church needs them. They ought to let their light *so* shine that men may see their good works. They ought not to put their candle under a bushel. They ought to add their house to the city set on a hill, so that it cannot be hid. Can any man be a good Mason or Odd-Fellow out of the lodge? Can he be a good party politician and yet lend his influence to the other side? Will you, then, my friends, who are Christians, continue to give your influence to the world? Unconsciously, I believe, you are against us. Whosoever is not with ME is against ME. He that gathereth not with ME scattereth abroad.

After Christian had been so instructed, refreshed, and equipped, the members of the household went with him down the hill. Here they bade him farewell. He will have to go into the Valley of Humiliation alone. But they anticipated his wants; they gave him "a loaf of bread, a bottle of wine, and a cluster of raisins."

> Thus to the vale they all descend,
> Whither the Pilgrim's footsteps tend—
>   A lonely dell.
> They give him of their goodly store,
> As emblems of the love they bore,
>   And then—Farewell.

LECTURE X.

APPOLYON.

[SYNOPSIS OF CHAPTER.—*Scene:* The Valley of Humiliation, where Christian was "hard put to it." He was met here by a foul fiend, named Appolyon. He was afraid, and debated with himself whether to go back or stand his ground. He decided to stand, for he remembered that, with all his armor, he had none for his back. He therefore resolved to meet the foe. "So he went on, and Appolyon met him." "Now, the monster was hideous to behold; he was clothed with scales like a fish (and they are his pride); he had wings like a dragon, feet like a bear, and out of his belly came fire and smoke, and his mouth was as the mouth of a lion." He began his attack by a series of questions; then he claimed the Pilgrim as his lawful subject; tried to persuade him to give up his journey, on the strength of many flattering promises; and the assertion that nothing but sorrow could come to him if he persevered. This failing, he claimed him for unfaithful service; reminded him of the Slough of Despond; the wrong ways by which he had attempted to get rid of his burden; the sinful sleep; and fear of the lions. Christian remained unmoved. Appolyon therefore obstructed the way, declared himself the enemy of Christ, and began the fight. Christian stopped his darts by his shield, although they came as thick as hail. In the fight Christian lost his sword, and fell; which Appolyon seeing, fell on him, to make sure of him. While he was fetching his last blow to make an end of him, Christian nimbly reached out his hand for his sword and caught it, saying, "Rejoice not against me, O mine enemy! When I fall, I shall arise," and with that, gave him a deadly thrust, which made him give back as one that had received his mortal wound. Christian conquered. After the battle, he partook of the provision given him by the sisters of the "Palace Beautiful," and bandaged his wounds with leaves from the Tree of Life. Thus refreshed and restored, he went on his journey, with his sword drawn in his hand. "But he met with no other affront from Appolyon quite through this Valley."]

THE Pilgrim was much refreshed in the Beautiful Palace, as we have already seen; but before he left, yea, while he was anxious to depart on his journey, unequipped, unprovided, and not sufficiently instructed, the Sisters "lead him to the top of house and bid him look south; so he did; and behold, at a great distance, he saw a most pleasant mountainous country, beautified with woods, vineyards, fruits of all sorts, flowers also, with springs and fountains, very delectable to behold." This is "Immanuel's Land," the mountains are "The Delectable Mountains," from which he will be able to see the gate of the Celestial City. Fired with the prospect he recommenced his journey. He had not traveled far ere he found his way obstructed by a foul fiend named Appolyon, who objected to his pilgrimage, and endeavored to turn him back. He had to learn that a prospect and its attainment, a promise and its fulfillment, are different matters.

Any man who is determined to realize hopes and ambitions, will have to meet and overcome the everlasting NO. No effort can be made in a worthy direction without discovering this. Let a young man resolve to save money for old age. His flesh, sense of present needs, the maxims of the world, will unite against the first effort, and when it is made, join their powers to undo what is done. Take the question of slavery. Slavery is wrong. To abolish it is right. But the attempt to do so met with powerful opposition. Many arguments were used and schemes proposed, but nothing was done until hostile forces met in deadly conflict and decided the matter by force of arms. The might of right is always opposed by the powers of evil and self-interest. Intemperance is a great evil. It is right to eradicate it. But let a man who has been addicted to drunkenness, and who, in consequence has suffered in body, mind, estate, family, and society, receive the vision of a restored home and manhood, family and social position; let such an one take the usual or some unusual step to return to this, and he will be seriously opposed. Every step onward and upward will be disputed. He will be confronted by his appetites, habits, the thralldom of his character, companions and institutions, which in his reform lose the life of their existence.

Let humane men attempt to control this evil, and hostile powers will immediately arise and fight for lawlessness. All manner of opprobious epithets will be applied to the reformers; they will be derided, probably persecuted; bad motives will be attributed to them; the power of money will oppose the power of righteousness.

The farmer who conceives of a happy home on the Western prairie, will not realize his dream without conflict. With him, loneliness, lack of means, uncleared lands, miasma, tornadoes and filthy streams will contend. And it is only after years of fighting the timber, the swamp, the miasma, the mortgage, with faith, brains and patience incased in the axe, plow and drain, that he will conquer.

The Christian life is no exception to this law. A Christian has to go down into the Valley of Humiliation, and personally contend with the enemy of his soul. The conflict of a Christian is in his spirit. It is a warfare that the eye does not see. It is the true battle of life. The battles of which we read in history —Marathon, Waterloo and Bunker Hill—are but shadows of inward facts. The battles of life are fought in the soul. The Christian struggles with an evil spirit other than himself. This other than himself we call The Devil; Satan.

But is there a *devil?* A very important question to ask and decide. Bunyan believed in one; the Scriptures declare the existence of one supreme prince of devils, and hosts of evil spirits under his control. The question that I have started is interesting. We must decide it one way or the other, or our allegory will have no meaning. There are various theories and beliefs extant on this subject. I propose to discuss them under four distinct heads:—

1. The Pagan.
2. The Christian.
3. The Scriptural.
4. The Rational.

Each of these is an attempt to explain the existence of evil in our midst. Men are not all bad, nor all good, yet of the mass of men in civilized countries, if we may judge by the phenomena which comes to the surface of society, we may say that the thought of their heart is continually evil. The best of men affirm that they are frequently tempted in a most powerful manner to commit the worst of crimes. Some fall under the pressure of temptation. Others, again, make no distinction between evil and good; they call light darkness, and say to evil, "Be thou my good," thus shewing that darkness hath blinded their eyes. Crime afflicts the world like a plague. Unaccountably whole communities and countries are moved to the commission of crime. Suicide and murder become maniacal and epidemical. Under the name of religion, philosophy, science and humanity, the most revolting deeds have been committed.. Evil is incarnated, deified, worshiped; and I shall show that there is evidence to-day of "possession" in man of evil other than himself.

Now, how are we to account for this? It is agreed on all hands that evil did not originate with God. The perfectly GOOD, the absolutely HOLY, could not create evil. The thought implies a contradiction. It is unthinkable.

Man declares, by his individual efforts, by legislation, by his choice of the lesser evil, that it is foreign to him. He treats it as he does small-pox or scarlet fever. He is ever trying to banish it from himself and the world. Each man becomes vicarious to this end. It is not his normal condition. Sin is unnatural. Its results are dreaded by him.

But we know nothing of moral evil apart from personality. We cannot attribute it to anything deprived of intelligence, affection and will. If, therefore, evil is not of God—and a little thought will convince you that it is not; if man, everywhere and by every kind of effort, declares that it is foreign to him; if, therefore, we know nothing of moral evil apart from personality—we are driven to the conclusion that it emanates from a being of intelligence, affection and will: this being we call the Devil.

This diabolical power, exerted by this malevolent being, takes two forms—temptation and possession.

Pagans make this being equal to God. The system of Zoroaster makes him so, as also the religious system of the ancient Egyptians. In many Pagan countries he is worshiped now as an equal of the Supreme Being, and the phenomena of men under the absolute control of some evil spirit is not to be doubted. Says Robert Charles Caldwell:—

"I contend that it appears that certain demonstrations of the present day, as far as outward evidence of their affliction goes, display as plain signs of demonical possession as ever were displayed eighteen hundred years ago. I hold that—as far as sense can be trusted and history relied upon—several *pey-a-dis*, or devil-dancers, could be produced to-morrow in Southern India, who, as far as can be ascertained, are as truly possessed of evil agencies as was the man who was forced by the fiends within him to howl that he was not himself, but that his name was 'Legion.' Not a few of the persons I refer to are, on ordinary occasions, calm. They have their vocations, and often pursue them diligently. Sometimes they have their wives and children; they possess their inherited hut, small plantain-garden, well, and score of palmyras. They eschew bhang as a rule, and the juice of the poppy, and arrack. They are quiet, sleepy men and women, who occupy much of their time in staring over the yellow drifting sands, at the quail-flocks as they flit hither and thither, or at the gaunt, solitary wolves which skulk under the shade of thorny thickets, waiting for an unwary goat to pass by. But evening draws near; the sunset reddens over the Ghauts; the deep mellow notes of the wood-pigeons grow fainter, and then cease; fireflies twinkle out; great bats flap by lazily overhead; then comes the dull tuck of the tom-tom; the fire before the rustic devil temple is lit; the crowd gathers and waits for the priest. He is there! His lethargy has been thrown aside; the laugh of a fiend is in his mouth. He stands before the people, the oracle of the demon, the devil-possessed! About eight years ago, I was staying in Tinnevelly.

The priest appeared suddenly at the devil-temple before the expectant votaries. A caldron was over the fire, and in it was lead in a molten state. 'Behold,' calmly cried the priest, 'the demon is in me. I will prove to you all the presence within me of the omnipotent divinity.' With that, he lifted the caldron, and poured the liquid lead over his head. Horns were blown, tom-toms beaten, fresh logs of resinous wood flung into the fire, and goats duly sacrificed. The priest staggered about a little, and then fell down in a fainting fit. Three days afterwards he died in horrible agony. But his mind was clear and calm to the last. The latest words he uttered were, 'It is indeed I who am the true God!' In the midst of his fearful torture, and even in the hour of death, he believed, with the fiercest certainty of faith, that his body was the inviolate shrine of the almighty demon he adored. That demon was to him the Supreme. With that indwelling demon he identified himself. So he died, announcing his own divinity. Was that man 'possessed of an evil spirit?'

"The natives of Southern India believe that, when any one meets with an untimely end, his soul wanders about near the locality of his death, and will make deadly mischief unless it is appeased and propitiated. This propitiation, think the simple folk, can only be effected by offering to it those things in sacrifice in which its possessor, whilst he was alive, delighted. But if, notwithstanding all precautions, an outburst of cholera, or other calamity, overtakes the scene of the dead man's last moments, the misfortune is at once, as a matter of course, laid at the door of the wraith of the deceased. Something has angered it. It will not be laid. It must be a malignant devil, and nothing short of it. Beat the tom-tom louder! Let the fattest sheep be offered as a propitiation! Let the horns blare out as the priest reels about in the giddy dance, and gashes himself in his frenzy! More fire! Quicker music! Wilder bounds from the devil-dancer! Shrieks, and laughter, and sobs, and frantic shouts! And over the long, lone valley, and up the bouldered mountain-side, under the wan moon, thrills out, sad and savage and shrill, the wild, tremulous wailing of women and yells of maddened men.—'Ha, ha! I am God! God! The God is in me and speaks! Come, hasten, tell me all: I will solace you—curse you! God is in me, and I am God! Hack and slaughter! The blood of the sacrifice is sweet! Another fowl—another goat! Quick, I am athirst for blood! Obey your God!'—Such are the words which hoarsely burst from the frothy lips of the devil-dancer, as he bounds, and leaps, and gyrates, with short, sharp cries, and red eyes almost starting from their sockets. He *believes* he is possessed of the local demon, whom he continually treats just as if it were a divinity, and the people *believe* in the hallucination. They shudder, they bow, they pray, they worship. The devil-dancer is not drunk, for he has eschewed arrack. He has not been seized with epilepsy: the sequel shows that. He is not attacked with a fit of hysteria, although within an hour after he has begun his dancing, half of his audience are thoroughly hysterical. He can scarcely be mad, for the moment the dance is over he speaks sanely, and quietly, and calmly. What is it, then? You ask him. He simply answers, 'The Devil seized me, sir.' You ask the by-standers. They simply answer, 'The Devil must have seized him.'

"Of one thing I am assured—the devil-dancer never 'shams' excitement. He appears to me deliberately to work himself up to a state of ecstacy—a 'standing outside of oneself,' in its primary sense. By a powerful act of volition, he almost wholly merges, so to speak, his individuality in that of the demon he worships, as that individuality shapes itself to his own mind. He calls out, 'I am God,' when, by virtue of his entire possession by the object of his adoration, he supposes himself to be commingled with the demon-divinity, his nature interfused by its nature. Calmly he laughs at the gashes which his own sacrificial knife makes on his body; calmly, I say, for in the midst of his most frantic frenzy he is savagely calm. Whether this be devil-possession or not, I cannot help remarking that it appears to me that it would certainly have been regarded as such in New Testament times.

Let me try once more to bring the whole scene vividly before the reader.

"Night, starry and beautiful, with a broad low moon seen through palms. A still, solemn night, with few sounds to mar the silence, save the deep, muffled boom of breakers bursting on the coast, full eight miles distant. A lonely hut, a huge solitary banyan tree, grim and gloomy. All round spread interminable sands, the only vegetation on which is composed of lofty palmyras, and a few stunted thorn-trees and wild figs. In the midst of this wilderness rises, spectre-like, that aged enormous tree, the banyan, haunted by a most ruthless she-devil. Cholera is abroad in the land, and the natives know that it is *she* who has sent them the dreaded pestilence. The whole neighbourhood wakes to the determination that the malignant power must be immediately propitiated in the most solemn and effectual manner. The appointed night arrives; out of village, and hamlet, and hut pours the wild crowd of men, and women, and children. In vain the Brahmins tinkle their bells at the neighboring temple; the people know what they want, and the deity which they must reverence is supreme just now. On flows the crowd to that gloomy island in the star lit waste—that weird, hoary banyan. The circle is formed; the fire is lit; the offerings are got ready—goats and fowls, and rice and pulse and sugar, and ghee and honey, and white chaplets of oleander-blossoms and jasmine-buds. The tom-toms are beaten more loudly and rapidly, the hum of rustic converse is stilled, and a deep hush of awe-struck expectancy holds the motly assemblage. Now the low, rickety door of the hut is dashed open. The devil-dancer staggers out. Between the hut and the ebon shadow of the sacred banyan lies a strip of moonlit sand; and as he passes this, the devotees can clearly see their priest. He is a tall, haggard, pensive man, with deep-sunken eyes and matted hair. His forehead is smeared with ashes, and there are streaks of vermilion and saffron over his face. He wears a high conical cap, white, with a red tassel. A long white robe, or *angi*, shrouds him from neck to ankle. On it are worked, in red silk, representations of the goddess of small-pox, murder, and cholera. Round his ankles are massive silver bangles. In his right hand he holds a staff or spear, that jingles harshly every time the ground is struck by it. The same hand also holds a bow, which, when the strings are pulled or struck, emits a dull booming sound. In his left hand the devil-priest carries his sacrificial knife, shaped like a sickle, with quaint devices engraved on its blade. The dancer, with uncertain staggering motion, reels slowly into the centre of the crowd, and then seats himself. The assembled people show him the offerings they intend to present, but he appears wholly unconscious. He croons an Indian lay in a low, dreamy voice, with dropped eyelids and head sunken on his breast. He sways slowly to and fro, from side to side. Look! You can see his fingers twitch nervously. His head begins to wag in a strange, uncanny fashion. His sides heave and quiver, and huge drops of perspiration exude from his skin. The tom-toms are beaten faster, the pipes and reeds wail out more loudly. There is a sudden yell, a stinging, stunning cry, an ear-piercing shriek, a hideous, abominable gobble-gobble of hellish laughter, and the devil-dancer has sprung to his feet, with eyes protruding, mouth foaming, chest heaving, muscles quivering, and outstretched arms swollen and straining as if they were crucified! Now, ever and anon, the quick, sharp words are jerked out of the saliva-choked mouth—'I am God! I am the true God!' Then all around him, since he and no idol is regarded as the present diety, reeks the blood of sacrifice. The devotees crowd round to offer oblations and to solicit answers to their questions. 'Shall I die of cholera during this visitation?' asks a grey-headed farmer of the neighborhood. 'O God, bless this child, and heal it,' cries a poor mother from the adjoining hamlet, as she holds forth her diseased babe towards the gyrating priest. Shrieks, vows, imprecations, prayers, and exclamations of thankful praise, rise up, all blended together in one infernal hubbub. Above all rise the ghastly guttural laughter of the devil-dancer, and his stentorian howls— 'I am God! I am the only true God!' He cuts and hacks and hews himself, and not very unfrequently kills himself there and then. His answers to the queries put to him are generally incoherent. Sometimes he is sullenly silent, and sometimes, whilst the blood from his self-inflicted wounds mingles freely with that of his sacrifice, he is most benign, and showers his divine favors of health and prosperity all round him. Hours pass by. The trembling crowd stand rooted to the spot. Suddenly the dancer gives a great bound in the air; when he descends he is motionless. The fiendish look has vanished from his eyes. His demoniacal laughter is still. He speaks to this and that neighbor quietly and reasonably. He lays aside his garb, washes his face at the nearest rivulet, and walks soberly home a modest, well-conducted man."

What is the explanation of this? The victims say that it is devil-possession. The Scriptures say the same thing. Can it be explained on any other hypothesis?

The doctrine of an evil spirit, called by Christians the devil, has been held by them since the commencement of the Christian era. The apostles found the Jews believing in demoniacal possession, and, if we are to take the history of His teaching and miracles as true, they too believed it. It matters not that the Jews may have learned the doctrine in Persia—the fact existed. Little indeed is said in the Old Testament of the enemy of souls, but when Christ came, when the Sun of Righteousness appeared, the Prince of Darkness was exposed. You see no shadows in a dark night, but in the noonday sunshine they are to be seen everywhere. Men saw not the god of the world till He who lighteth every man who cometh into the world made his presence known.

Afterwards Manes, a convert from Persia, appeared and established the doctrine of the Manicheans, compounded Zoroaster with Christ, and wrought into the Christian the Pagan idea that God and the Devil were equal, had been so from all eternity, and were therefore entitled to equal homage. Augustine for a time believed in the doctrine, afterwards became convinced of its superficialty, abandoned it, and preached against it.

Later we find the doctrine of a personal devil the foundation of the system of witchcraft believed in by Christians of the early and middle centuries. The popular notion of this being was derived from sacred representations by monks in their mysteries, miracles and moralities. It is much the same as that which artists now indulge in, and by which we were frightened when children. He was represented as "a large, ill-formed, hairy sprite, with horns, a long tail, cloven feet, and dragon's wings." Such was the conception which Luther believed, and which gave John Bunyan the material for his artistic description. Artists' angels and demons must be taken for what they are worth. But the Christian Church has been strangely impressed with their conceptions.

It was also generally believed that there was an infinite number of inferior demons; that the earth swarmed with millions of them; that they led beautiful women astray, and increased and multiplied with fearful rapidity. The air was supposed to be full of them, and many unfortunate men and women drew them by thousands into their mouths and nostrils at every inspiration. Most persons said that the number of these demons was so great that they could not be counted, but Wierus asserted that they amounted to no more than seven millions four hundred and five thousand nine hundred and twenty-six, (it is well to be particular in these matters), and that they were divided into seventy-two companies or battalions, to each of which there was a prince or captain. They could assume any shape they pleased. They sometimes made themselves hideous, and at other times they assumed shapes of such transcendent loveliness that mortal eyes never saw beauty to compare with them.*

Coming down the centuries, we discover a great change in the opinion of man concerning the Devil, till Thomas Paine could say, with some amount of truth, "The Christian religion puts the Christian Devil above the Creator." The poets have made him a being to be admired. Macaulay, criticising the poem of Montgomery, entitled "Satan," says: "The poet, with the exception of locomotion, has failed to represent a single Satanic

---

* Mackay's Extraordinary Popular Delusions.

quality. We have yet to learn that Satan is a respectable and pious gentleman, and we would candidly advise Mr. Montgomery to alter about one hundred lines, and republish his volume under the name of Gabriel." Lamb says to Southey: "You have all your life been making a jest of the Devil. You have flattered him in prose; you have chanted him in goodly odes; you have been his jester, volunteer laureate, and self-elected court poet to Beelzebub." This is a decided change. But Milton's Satan has more profoundly impressed the Christian world. He proceeds on the principle that nothing is so much like an arch-angel as an arch-fiend; therefore his conception and representation of the god of this world are grand and awful. The Miltonic Satan has influenced theology more than the Biblical one.

But what say the Scriptures? They certainly teach the doctrine of Satan's personality and power.

Says Kitto: "We determine the personality of Satan by the same criteria that we use in determining whether Cæsar or Napoleon were personal beings, or the personification of abstract ideas, viz: by the tenor of history concerning them, and the ascription of personal attributes to them. All the forms of personal agency are made use of by the sacred writers in setting forth the character and conduct of Satan. They describe him as having power and dominion, messengers and followers. He tempts and resists; he is held accountable, charged with guilt; is to be judged, and to receive final punishment. On the supposition that it was the object of the sacred writers to teach the proper personality of Satan, they could have found no more express terms than those which they have actually used, and on the supposition that they did not intend to teach such a doctrine, their use of language incapable of communicating another idea, is wholly inexplicable."

Listen to the words of another:—

"Should any person, in compliance with popular opinion, talk in serious language of the existence, dispositions, declarations of and actions of a race of beings whom he knew to be absolutely fabulous, we surely could not praise him for candor and integrity, but must suppose him to be either exulting in irony over the credulity of those around him, or taking advantage of their weakness, with the dishonest, selfish views of an impostor. And if he himself should pretend to known connection with this imaginary system of beings, and should claim, in consequence of his connection with them, particular honors from his cotemporaries, whatever might be the dignity of his character in all other respects, nobody could hesitate for a moment to brand him as an impostor."

This is sharp language; nevertheless we think it will commend itself to your judgment.

Without citing a number of proof texts, the Scriptural doctrine of the devil may be summarized thus :—

1. He exists.
2. He is a person, an ego, with affection, intellect, and will.
3. He is a moral being. A free agent, as we are, and therefore capable of guilt, and liable to punishment.
4. He is a fallen being. He is not as he was when God created him. God created the devil, but not a devil.
5. He is malicious. He seeks to destroy the children of God, by tempting and possessing them.
6. He is a finite being. His power and influence are limited in time and degree. He can do naught without the permission of God, and no moral evil without the consent of man.
7. He is the prince of devils. Thousands upon thousands, like minded with himself, are under his dominion and do his will.
8. He has access to the souls, bodies and estates of men.

These statements convey, in a very crude manner, the teachings of the Scriptures concerning him.

The Rationalists object to the idea of a personal devil or devils. They also profess to believe in the Bible. We have a right to ask how, then, do they, with their belief, account for the statement of the Scriptures, the phenomena which we call demoniacal possession, certain cycles of crime, and the overpowering temptations of good men?

I. As to the Scripture statements.

We are told that the terms Satan, Devil, Beelzebub, the Evil One, Appolyon, etc., are mere names for "the principle of evil;" that these names are of fictitious characters, which personify to the mind this principle. But the "principle of evil" is an abstraction. It is an intellectual conception derived from and applied to certain facts. It is a phrase by which we express the substance (that which stands under) of certain facts. They existed before man could abstract the principle. They exist now, that he is possessed of the conception. The question still remains, from whom did the evil come? It is certain that it must have come from a person. Could it have come from God, who hates it, who seeks to deliver His children from it? Reason answers no. A fountain cannot send out sweet and bitter waters. Did it come from man? Man says no, by word and deed. It is his affliction, not his nature. But it may be said it arises out of man's imperfection. He is in a process of develment, and evil is incidental to his condition. But "imperfection" implies a negation. Out of nothing, nothing comes. But evil is something. We possess it, and are possessed by it. Is not the Scripture account reasonable? Evil came from an evil person, who has access to the minds and bodies of men.

II. If the plain Scripture statements are not correct, Christ has established a false doctrine. He has imposed on the world. Are you prepared to accept that conclusion?

III. If the Scripture doctrine of devils be incorrect, and the Rationalistic be true, we have this result:—

There was no evil before man.
The Devil is a personification of the principle of evil.
Therefore, man created the Devil.

This result is unfortunate for those who talk so much about the dignity and goodness of human nature.

It is unfortunate for those who, denying the doctrine, teach that man is in a process of evolution, that the race must evolve something. We need not laughingly bid them look back and say, "Behold your sires!" But we solemnly look onward and say, "Behold your offspring!" Aye, look! man that is too good and great to be imposed on by the Bible or to believe Christ; evolving fiends!

IV. The doctrine of demoniacal possession must be met by those who disbelieve in the Scriptural doctrine of devils:—

1. It is explained on physiological grounds. Those who are said to be "demoniacs were merely epileptics, hypochondriacs, or hysterical persons. Probably they were insane or lunatic." The explanation does not cover the facts. Sickness, dumbness, lunacy are sometimes, and at other times are not, connected with possession. We grant that many of the symptoms are alike, but that does not prove the cause to be the same. But how does this explanation meet the phenomena which I have brought from India, occuring at the present day, connected with Devil worship; acknowledged by the worshipers who are ignorant of the Bible, to be demoniacal possession; and which are clearly not lunacy, epilepsy, hysteria, or hypochondria?

2. It is explained on moral grounds. It is said that all the Devil there is, or Devils there are, are in man, and these are nothing but a man's lusts and passions. What is lust? If we understand it, it is man's natural appetites desiring satisfaction unlawfully. The appetites are right, for God made them. They are essential to manhood. How is it that man sends his appetites in an unlawful direction for gratification? It is unlawful to do so. It is unnatural to do so. God made the law and adapted man thereto. His highest, fullest happiness is in being natural. God could not so move him. No man is tempted of God. The All Holy is not a partaker of any man's guilt. How is it? I ask. Is not man under the control of an evil personality other than himself?

I would not mind these explanations so much if their advocates did not boast so much of enlightened reason, and pretend to give a rational explanation of the facts. To ignore phenomena is not a rational way of explaining them.

Read a few passages of Scripture, substituting lusts and passions for the Devil or Satan.—"And as he was coming, lusts and passions threw him down and tare him, and Jesus rebuked lusts and passions, and healed the child."

Jesus was led up of the Spirit into the wilderness to be tempted by the principle of evil; or to become subject to lunacy, hysteria, melancholy, or epilepsy; or He was led up of the Spirit to be tempted by lusts and passions. Then He who delighted to do the will of God from His heart—He who was the perfect man—felt within Himself great desires for gratifying His human appetites in an unlawful manner. Then Christ desired to break the law which He came to fulfill, and which He delighted to fulfill. In His heart, and therefore in the sight of God, He was a sinner. He broke the tenth commandment, longing to break the seventh and eighth Are you prepared for the conclusion? Could God have been well pleased with Him? The absurdity and impiety of such statements need no refutation.

Suppose that the views which I have given as Rationalistic were correct, what would be the practical result?

1. There is no personal devil, but by the devil is meant the principle of evil. The principle of evil is merely an abstraction. What do practical men care for an abstraction? The masses do not know what we mean by the term. The devil is revealed to metaphysicians only. Who cares to fight an abstraction? There is no heroism in knocking down a man of straw.

2. Supposing demoniacal possession to be but a physical malady, then there must be a physical cause. But has the cause been discovered? Has the riddle been solved? Is it not a fact, known to all that have studied the subject, that such diseases are frequently mental, having a mental cause? Ay! we may go deeper, and ask, is it not true that the cause is farther in the victim than the brain, and arises from the unnatural condition of the soul. It is from these latter causes that mental and moral remedies are needed and applied.

3. If demoniacal possession is lust, then one of two things is certain—either that lust is part of the original constitution of man, and therefore right, or it is foreign, and therefore wrong. If of the original constitution, there is no lust, man need

not strive against it. Wrong is right, and right, wrong. But if it be a foreign spirit moving him from righteousness, then, and only then, will he know it to be right to strive against it, and in striving, conquer it.

In this way, my friends, I have brought forward arguments in favor of the personality of Satan and devil-possession. If I have taxed your patience in doing so, my apology is, that I regard it as one of his deceitful tricks, a pleasure to him and a folly in you, to deny his existence. How pleased must he be to hear a Christian deny his existence. He gives up the fight then. He allows you to tempt him then. But how many do it? You will think me old fogyish and not liberal, and wonder why *I* should advance such views. Brethren, I will tell you. Before I studied the subject I denied his existence as loudly as any of you. But since I have read and studied the matter I cannot do so. There is a rigid dogmatism on this subject, as on all others, which I hate. There is also a looseness, a cheap liberalism on this and kindred subjects, which from my heart I despise. I despise it in myself, in books, and if I thought you had any of it I should despise it in you.

The arguments I have advanced are not answered by a curl of the lip, an incredulous smile, or by assuming that you are "advanced thinkers." They can only be answered by facts and reason. Who art thou that repliest against God?

And now, as I have composed this Lecture largely from the thoughts and words of others, I will be consistent and conclude in the eloquent language of one who, when speaking on this subject, said:

"The Bible theory is the only theory that can explain the manifest phenomena in the material and moral world. There is a God personal in His attributes and intelligent; the source of authority; the embodiment of wisdom, love, and power. There is on the other hand a being called Satan, equally individual; a creature of vast cunning and power and wickedness; the active, persistent adversary of God, and those of us who desire in our hearts to be like God. There is such a being, therefore, as Satan; and when men are commanded 'to resist evil,' it is not mere influences that they are enjoined to withstand, but the person, the evil mind and wicked heart, that directs them. Hell has its king; and all its black legions obeyed the voice that first hurled defiance at God. He lives and moves as the directing cause and mainspring of all the wickedness done under the sun. Murder, with its red hand and all its fingers dripping blood; Conflagration with her blazing torch; Rebellion that desolates; and all the lesser agents of evil—these are his children. To deny this, is to deny the Scripture; for this doctrine is as a central thread in its strongly woven woof. It can be withdrawn only in the disruption of the entire piece."*

* Rev. W. H. H. Murray.

LECTURE XI.

CONFLICTS.

[SYNOPSIS OF CHAPTER.—Christian passed out of the "Valley of Humiliation" into the "Valley of the Shadow of Death." The way to the Celestial City lay through the midst of it. It was a very solitary place. At the entrance he met two men who were going back, and who earnestly entreated him to follow their example. They described the valley as dark as pitch, full of hobgoblins, satyrs and dragons, where those who sit bound in affliction and iron continually yell and groan in intolerable misery. In the valley the path was very narrow; on the one hand a deep ditch, on the other a dangerous quag. In the middle of the valley he came to the mouth of hell. Here the battle became so fearful and intense that his sword was useless, and he had to betake himself to the weapon of all-prayer. Here he was indeed hard put to it; when he lifted his foot to take a step he knew not upon what or where it would fall. He did not know his own voice, but often mistook the whispering of fiends for it. In the darkness he was delighted to find that he was not alone, for ahead of him was a traveler singing, "Though I walk through the Valley of the Shadow of Death I will fear no evil: for thou art with me." The sun rose upon his darkness, and by its light he discovered that the rest of the vale was also dangerous, for it was full of snares and traps set for him. But he escaped them, and in the sunlight came safely to its end. Here were seated two giants with blood, bones, and ashes strewn around them; the name of the one was Pope, the other Pagan.]

HE came down from the mountain, and like our Master, to contend with devils. Every mountain suggests a valley. An attack of fever leaves the body depressed and exhausted; ships are borne across the ocean on billows; nature preserves her equilibrium by storms and calms, clouds and sunshine, ebb and flow, light and darkness. It has often been noticed in Christian experience that an occasion of joy is followed by one of corresponding depression. It is therefore quite natural for us to suppose that our Pilgrim, who has been so delightfully and richly entertained in the Palace Beautiful, will soon suffer severer fortunes. They began as soon as he had entered into the Valley of Humiliation. The descent thereto was dangerous, and although he took his steps warily, yet he caught a slip or two.

Can you not imagine him in his new armor, strong in weapons of offense and defense, and almost longing to test his skill. Let us, with the picture of the Pilgrim in our minds, tarry to think of one fact: *A Christian's life is in conflict with evil.* Just as a soldier's life is spent in battle with his country's enemies, or in defending his country from its enemies, whether foreign or domestic; so is a Christian's life spent in relation to evil. He has to attack and prevent it. I want you to think of this, for Christian living is earnest work.

In countries where the money of the people is largely spent in support of enormous armies, where the glory of a nation is written in the tale of conquest, and not in the reign of peace—they have what are called "fancy regiments." In France it was the "Imperial Guard;" in Germany it is the "Leib Garde," in England it is the "First Life Guards." They are ostensibly established for protecting the person of the reigning sovereign; but really they are institutions where men are allowed to play soldiers in time of peace, and from which they can easily withdraw in time of war. The officers buy their commissions in them, and sell out when they please. They enter for the honor, and when they have had enough of it, go out. The regiment is not supposed to go to war except in cases of great emergency. They are mere ornamental appendages to the royal chariots. They dress and talk like warriors, but in reality are not. And yet they are the proudest of the entire army, and look with contempt and scorn upon soldiers who are scarred and torn and maimed—the heroes of battles. They would be humiliated in being sent to war. In this country I have seen men playing at soldiers. They were exceedingly proud of their dress, rank and regiment. And I have seen these men called out to quell a riot, and after less than a week's endurance of military life, although they were not in any engagement, become disgusted with the rough realities of the duties they assumed. Now I want you to understand that there are no fancy regiments in God's service. None that you can enter and leave at pleasure. He needs none such. If you join the church and appear before the world a professed Christian soldier, it is expected that you will fight the devil and all evil wherever and in whatever form they may be found. Personally and collectively your sworn allegiance to the Lord, our Righteousness, binds you to give sin no quarter. It will give you none, if you are true. You should fight intemperance, pernicious literature, gambling, poverty, ignorance, unbelief, and any evil that may obstruct the progress of yourself, the Church, or the world. If we do not destroy evil it will destroy us. If a farmer does not destroy the weeds they will destroy his farm. You are not to be a dilettante Christian, but a soldier in conflict with spiritual wickedness in high places. You must fight if you would reign. As Christ was, so must you be in the world. Make yourself of no reputation, and taking the sword of the Spirit, enter the fight under the banner of thy Lord!

"There's trouble on the way;
Christian! prepare thy ready bow,
And strength, for this thy day!

"Unsheath thy glistening, trusty sword;
Thy spear bring forth with might.
Pilgrim! be valiant, for thy Lord
And God defend the right!"

Pardon this digression. Let us now follow our Author:—

"Christian was hard put to it; for he had gone but a little way before he espied a foul fiend coming over the field to meet him: his name is Appolyon. Then did Christian begin to be afraid, and to cast in his mind whether to go back or stand his ground. But he considered again that he had no armour for his back, and therefore thought that to turn the back to him might give him greater advantage with ease, to pierce him with his darts; therefore he resolved to stand his ground: for, thought he, had I no more in my mind than the saving of my life, it would be the best way to stand."

When he was come up to Christian, he beheld him with a disdainful countenance, and then began to question him:

Whence came you? and whither are you bound?

To these questions Christian was able to give a definite answer, for he knew what he had done, what he was doing, and whither he tended. He knew that he had left the City of Destruction, was in the straight, narrow way, and that he desired to reach the Celestial City. If I take a walk to the depot to-morrow, and find you there ready for a journey, it is very likely that I shall ask "where you are going." And if you replied that you did not know, or if the anticipated cars were going in the direction opposite the city you named, I think I should display some sense in doubting your sanity. To-night I ask you, as Appolyon did Christian, "Whither bound?" Do you know where you are going? Have you not heard that the way of unrighteousness leads to hell, and the way of holiness to heaven? You ought to be able to answer definitely the question. It is folly for a man not to know what he is living for. You know the old story of the preacher, who preached from the text, "Adam, where art thou?" and divided it in this way:—

First—All men are somewhere.
Secondly—Some are where they ought not to be.
Thirdly—Some will soon be where they won't like to be.

A pretty good idea of the condition of human souls. You are going somewhere. Do you know the destiny to which your life leads you?

This matter of knowing really where you are, and whither bound, you can as easily tell as the blind man who said, "Whereas I was blind, now I see;" or the Apostle who declared, that "we know we have passed from death unto life, because we love the brethren."

Satan also claimed the Pilgrim as his servant and subject.

Know ye not that ye are servants to whom ye obey? Every sinner's master is the devil, that old serpent who sinned from the beginning. When he made this claim, Christian gave good reason for leaving his service.—"The service was too hard, and the wages such as a man could not live on, for the wages of sin is death." This is the reason why you should leave off sinning. The soul that sinneth shall die. They that sow to the flesh, shall of the flesh reap corruption. The sinner hath no hope in his death. The way of the transgressor is hard, and in the end weeping, wailing, and gnashing of teeth.

Satan next makes him great promises if he will but go back. "What our country will afford, I do here promise to give thee." This is the peculiarity of the service of sin: it is all promise. It is like John's book: in the mouth very sweet, but in the midst very bitter. All that comes of leaving righteousness is riotous living, rags and beggary. There are many kinds and degrees of sin, but the greater the sinner the more disappointment and misery. Look at Lord Byron, with all that rank and wealth and genius could give him, who had given up his life to follow the pleasures of sin. Hear him in middle life, singing this mournful dirge:—

> "My days are in the yellow leaf;
>   The flowers, the fruits of love, are gone;
> The worm, the canker, and the grief,
>   Are mine alone.
>
> "The fire that on my bosom preys,
>   Is lone as some volcanic isle;
> No torch is kindled at its blaze,
>   A funeral pile!"

Such is the realization of sin's promises. Dante has told the tale in awful pictures. He makes hell to consist of the appetite that sin has created, the promise of satisfaction, and the inability to realize it.

My friends, do not believe one promise of the evil one. "Though hand join in hand, the wicked shall not go unpunished." One sin may eternally degrade you, as in the case of Reuben. The devil's promises are all lies.

Then he sought to turn him back by holding up to him the example of renegade Christians. "It is ordinary for those that have professed themselves His servants, after awhile, to give Him the slip, and return again to me."

The statement is false in design, although partly true in fact. There are some who do go back, but all do not. Perhaps the majority of those who start, hold on. It was so from the beginning. Backsliders are anticipated in the word of God. Some of you "did run well, what did hinder you?" Some of you, "I tell you, weeping, are the enemies of the Cross of Christ." "Ye have crucified the Son of God afresh, and put him to an open shame." Some of you have betrayed Him with a kiss; some have denied Him; some have cried, "Not this man, but the robber, the adulterer, the drunkard;" others, like Pilate, have given Him up to popular opinion. But there is a way of giving *the slip* out West that is peculiar. In the East you were members of Churches, in "good and regular standing." Since you have come West, you have united with no Church, and have been careless about maintaining any distinct religious character. As soon as the restraints of society were removed, and you breathed our liberty, you left the disciples and converted this liberty into license. We know your excuses— "Affairs are not managed here as there," "Preachers are not so learned, so eloquent, or so great." But are these worthy reasons for you to stand aloof from the Churches of Christ as they exist? You will not be saved by worshiping Eastern preachers, Churches, or habits; in fact, there is an old commandment forbidding it—"Thou shalt have none other Gods but me." Are these reasons worthy of those of you who have professed to love the Saviour? Are they such as to warrant you giving your influence against the powers that make for righteousness? In the East, you believed in the perseverance of the saints. If that doctrine be correct, what manner of men are ye? Either the theology is false, or you are of a reprobate mind. The cause is not the preachers or Churches of the East, but in yourselves. You are faithless to Christ, to conscience; you find it easy to forsake Him, or to follow Him at a distance. Come back to thy Master. Once more take up the Cross and follow Him, and so be His disciple.

He then claimed him on the score of past service. "Thou didst swear thy allegiance to me as thou hast to the King of Kings, yet I am willing to pass it by if thou wilt but go back."

That is one of the results of sin. We are always being urged and held back by it. In our most sacred and solemn moments the memory of past guilt lies a heavy weight on our hearts; our souls are forbidden to rise or to go forward in consequence. The sin of many years ago is like a foul weed in a garden, it now threatens to choke the Word, and make it unfruitful.

Appolyon seeks to discourage him by referring to the dangers of the way. "Thou knowest that for the most part his servants come to an ill end. How many of them have been put to shameful deaths?"

Bunyan was suffering, at the time of this writing, in Bedford jail. This must have had some influence on his mind. In his "Grace Abounding" he acknowledges this. This world is no friend to grace to help us on to God. In it we shall have tribulation and suffer persecution. The world, and what is far worse, worldly churches, have put to death those of whom the world was unworthy. There is danger of persecution and martyrdom in the way of righteousness, but not ruin. He who would save his life shall lose it.

The enemy then reminds him of the errors he has already committed. Our Pilgrim made many mistakes, all of which are known to this accuser of the brethren, and all of which are detailed to the discomforture of Christian. What Christian has not made mistakes? How frequently we have fallen into error! In our folly chosen to sin? Who is there so wise and good as not to have committed sins from the commencement of Christian life until now? And what Christian has not been accused of them to his frequent shame and disquiet?

Then Satan, completely foiled in argument, unable to move Christian from the way, declared war, saying: "I am an enemy to this Prince; I hate his person, his laws, and people. I am come out on purpose to withstand thee." Then they fought; Satan commencing by throwing a flaming dart at his breast, and following this up by throwing them as thick as hail. Appolyon wounded him in his head and hand and foot. He followed his work amain. Christian withstood as well as he could, but grew weak in consequence of his wounds. Then they closed. In the struggle Appolyon threw Christian. He had a dreadful fall. The fiend was sure of him now, and Christian despaired of his own life; but as God would have it, as the enemy was fetching his last blow, Christian reached his sword and caught it, saying, "Rejoice not against me, O mine enemy; when I fall I shall arise;" and with that, gave him a deadly thrust, which made him give back as one who had received his mortal wound. This perceiving, he made at him again, saying, "Nay, in all things we are more than conquerers through Him that loved us."

"In this combat no man can imagine—unless he had seen and heard—what yelling and hideous roaring Appolyon made in the fight: he spake like a dragon: and on the other side, what sighs and groans burst from Christian's heart. I never saw him, all the time, give so much as one pleasant look till he perceived he had wounded Appolyon with his two-edged sword: then indeed he did smile and look upward! But it was the dreadfullest sight that I ever saw."

Brethren, the enemy of our souls desires our death. He goeth about as a roaring lion, seeking whom he may devour. We must meet his attacks with the Word of God; that is the Sword of the Spirit. A Christian who is not well read in the letter of the Word is at a great disadvantage, as much so as a soldier in battle without a weapon. Job conquered by his knowledge of God's revealed will. Christ conquered by replying to all temptations, "It is written." "*Then* the devil left Him." The shield of faith will keep Satan from destroying us, but we need a weapon with which we can resist him. This weapon is the Sword of the Spirit: the Word of God.

If you visit military museums, if you go into some families, you will be shown weapons with which decisive battles were fought. The old weapons are preserved. So in God's Church. There are many of the old swords wherewith the evil one was put to flight. There should be some such in each individual's history. If "Rejoice not against me, O mine enemy; when I fall I shall arise;"—if "Nay, in all these things we are more than conquerors through Him that loved us," are the arms by which you have gained spiritual victories, preserve them in your memory, cherish them affectionately in your hearts, and when the enemy comes in as a flood, lift up these trophies of victory as a standard against him.

In England, you may wander from one valley into the other without noticing the transition. The same valley has various local names. You easily glide from one parish into another, and sometimes from one county to another. Geographically and geologically considered, the vale is one; but politically, it is many. Local traditions fix the names. The scenery is probably a little different, but essentially the valley is one. Bunyan makes the transition from the Valley of Humiliation to the Valley of the Shadow of Death as suggested by these facts.— "Now, at the end of this valley was another, called the Valley of the Shadow of Death. It is a very solitary place. The prophet Jeremiah thus describes it: 'A wilderness; a land of deserts, and of pits; a land of drought, and of the *shadow of death;* a land that no man (but a Christian) passed through, and where no man dwelt.' Now, here Christian was worse put to it than in his fight with Appolyon."

We must here resort to Bunyan's life to know what he means. Such experiences in his life owe their origin, no doubt:—

1. To the greatness of his soul.

The ripple of a rill is not to be compared to the waves of the sea; and, therefore, if we have no such turbulent seasons, it is owing to our littleness. Martin Luther, another great rugged soul, had such. God gives great battles to great hearts.

2. To his training under Mr. Gifford.

Bunyan, as we have seen, was always visionary. His intuitional powers were extraordinarily keen. His pastor might have led him with great advantage through a regular and orderly study of the Word of God; instead of this, he taught him to "attach great importance to sudden impressions, direct gleams of light, touches of isolated words, and phrases, and truths, which would bolt into the mind" without any apparent cause. This had much to do, undoubtedly, with his subsequent spiritual conflict. As you are aware, there are persons who are always feeling of their pulse, taking a diagnosis of their physical condition, reading domestic medicine, or consulting a physician. They are never well, but always under the weather. There are also others who are always looking into their hearts and lives, are acquainted with all their spiritual and moral diseases, real or fancied, and they are never robust Christians. For his own comfort, our Author looked too much within. As a rule, the less we inspect ourselves the better. Our hearts are gangrenous. To know too much of them is poison. Let us look to Jesus.

3. To ill-health.

This resulted from being put into prison. Howard mentions Bedford jail as the first that caused him to turn his attention to the condition of prisoners. Bunyan calls it a DEN. Howard, in 1789, says, "The men and women felons associate together; their night rooms are two dungeons; only one court for debtors and felons; no infirmary; no bath." "With no room for air or exercise; with little space for changing his position; with hardly a chink for seeing the face of nature, and with, at one time, as many as sixty fellow-Dissenters crammed into a space which could not with common convenience hold more than twenty—to a man, in the thirty-third year of his age, of strong physical constitution, accustomed to great activity, and permitted to pour out his soul in moving appeals and invitations all round the country, such an incarceration, viewed even on the lowest grounds, was no trifling affliction."

In this place he fell into spiritual despondency. The mind was affected thereby, and again reacted upon the body. His breastbone seemed to be broken, and says he, "I was violently seized with such weakness in my outward man, insomuch that I thought I could not live." "Live!" he cried; "I must not—die; I dare not."

Here again he thought of the torments of hell, and many other sorrows, and now he says: "I will tell you a very pretty business; I was once above all the rest in a very sad and low condition for many weeks, at which time also, I being but a young prisoner, and not acquainted with the laws, had this lain much upon my spirit; that my imprisonment might end at the gallows for aught that I could tell. Now, therefore, Satan laid hard at me, to beat me out of my heart, by suggesting this unto me: 'But how if when you come indeed to die, you should be in this condition; that is as not to savor the things of God, nor to have any evidence upon your soul for a better state hereafter?' for, indeed, at that time all the things of God were hid from my soul."

We see by this that the fear of Death was the Shadow of Death. We die many deaths in fearing one. The mere fact of physical dissolution did not seem to trouble him so much as the thought of the second death—eternal separation from God and our Lord Jesus Christ.

We must die; we have each done that which by nature banishes us from God and the glory of his face. When afflicted and trained as he, men are too likely to look to the sentence of death in themselves, rather than to Him who said, "I am the resurrection and the life, and he that believeth in me, though he were dead, yet shall he live; and whosoever liveth and believeth in me shall never die." Again I say, let us look to Jesus.

This had a moral effect on his mind. I use the word moral to describe the nature and not the character of this effect. In the Allegory he thus describes it: "There was on the right hand a very deep ditch, and on the other a very dangerous quag." In his autobiography he tells us that he was in consequence tempted to doubt the being of God and Christ, and also tempted to blaspheme. The ditch, then, is Atheism, the quag guilt.

Fear produces such effects. Fear of poverty often results in suicide. Fear of guilt exposed is an inward hell. Fear of failure saps the life of success. Fear of death hastens it. Brethren, if God should send such dark seasons into your soul; wherein you sigh bitterly and know not where your next step will land you; when your reading of the Bible, instead of bringing you comfort, adds to your torture; when you think that all the writers are pointing at you and holding you in derision; when one sentence of Scripture will more afflict you than an army of forty thousand men; I say, brethren, if God should send you such a trial, think it not strange. A foreigner coming to this country thinks everything strange, money, home-life, business, politics; and because they are strange he is uncomfortable, and weeps for home. Ye are strangers and pilgrims. This is not your rest; your citizenship is in heaven, from whence ye look for the Savior.

Although storms have been attacking the earth for centuries, and have been great blessings, yet they create fear. We see the gathering clouds; the dense, black masses of vapor marching slowly and grandly; we see the lightning flash, and hear the distant thunder; the wind rocks the forest, the heavy drops fall like an advance herald preparing the way for an army, and then we close our shutters, and some creep into the darkest room of the house until it is all over; and when over, we find that it has brought freshness and song and beauty and bread and business. We thank our Father for the storm we dreaded.

Have you ever noticed the sun at the close of a cloudless day? He sinks in a chariot of glory too bright to behold, but he leaves no beauty in his train. But the day that has been marked by storms comes to a close, and the sun sinks to his rest. In his dying light he illuminates the clouds and makes the sky gorgeous and grand. So is a life without trials. It leaves behind nothing to admire or love. So is not a life of sorrow. It leaves a life to love, to admire, to glorify, to inspire with song; to which we rear monuments, suggesting by their whiteness the purity that struggled with evil; by their direction, whither they have gone; and by our loving memories, the spirit that moved them. Out of Bunyan's trials from without and from within, came upon the world those conceptions of the way of righteousness which it has learned to love.

I must tell you that in this valley he did not know his own voice. The powers of hell breathed worldly thoughts and suggestions to his soul, with such skill that he attributed them to himself. The things he would not, he did. I must also tell you that here his sword was unadapted to the conflict. He was obliged to sheathe it and take to the weapon of ALL PRAYER. By this alone he succeeded.

There are times when we get no comfort from the Word. God wants us to come to Himself. Did you ever think that the Scriptures may and do keep souls from the highest spiritual communion? What would you think of communion of souls which always has to be carried on by letters? This is sweet when nothing else can be. But it is not comparable to those moments when with loved ones the communion is personal and complete. Brethren, there is a communion with God, with not even a Bible between either to help or to hinder. And oh! the bliss, and oh! the profit of such moments.

> "Lord, what a change within us one short hour
>   Spent in thy presence will avail to make!
>   What heavy burdens from our bosoms take!
> What parched grounds refresh, as with a shower!
> We kneel, and all around us seem to lower;
>   We rise, and all the distant and the near,
>   Stand forth in sunny outline, brave and clear;
> We kneel, how weak! we rise, how full of power!
>   Why, therefore, should we do ourselves this wrong,
>   Or others—that we are not always strong,
> That we are ever overborne with care,
>   That we should ever weak or heartless be,
>   Anxious or troubled—when with us in prayer,
>   And joy, and strength, and courage, are with THEE?"

Brethren, in sunshine or in storm—

"*Pray without ceasing.*"

There are other matters of which I would willingly speak. Of the mouth of hell; of the foul fiends who imitated his voice, and distressed him with the thought that he had blasphemed his Maker because he was tempted to do so in a subtle and powerful manner; of the comfort he felt in finding a man ahead of him in the valley singing on his way; of the daylight which broke upon him, and his discerning that though the first part of the valley was dangerous, yet this second part was even more so; and of the two giants, Pope and Pagan, who sat in a cave at the end of this doleful journey.

Not without deep meaning are they here, and therefore I must spend a few moments upon them.

Paganism is the religion of the creature without revelation. It is as sensual, as selfish, as cruel, as vain, as human nature Higher it cannot go. Vice is thought virtue. Charity, sympathy, gentleness, meekness, and all moral duties are ignored, and treachery, deceit, and guilt are practiced; with pilgrimages, sacrifices, priests, temples, superadded to expiate guilt and make up for the lack of virtue.

Giant Pope represents that powerful system of iniquity called "The Church," which held the world in darkness for centuries, and which is now the declared foe of mental and moral freedom. It is Paganism, under the name and with some of the forms of Christianity. It lowers Christ to man, instead of lifting man to Christ.

Both have persecuted New Testament righteousness.

It is a noticeable fact that men who have been tried by temptations, and by doubts—men and women who become discouraged by their weak, fallible selves—will seek infallibility. Human nature likes religion better than righteousness. It prefers the Church to Christ; the Fathers to Christ; the doctrines to Christ; worship to Christ; Paul even, to Christ. And it is natural that those who are tired with the conflicts that righteousness imposes, should seek rest.

My brethren, seek not rest in Paganism; it is not there. Giant Pagan sits like a giant to hold you, when you emerge tired and weary with conflict. Seek it not in Rome; it is not there. Pass both by, as did Christian. They are out of the way.

There is One who knows all of your battles, and to your weary souls He says:

"Come unto ME, all ye that labor and are heavy laden, and I will give you rest."

LECTURE XII.

FAITHFUL.

[SYNOPSIS OF CHAPTER.—Christian having reached the end of the valleys, and safely escaped the giants, pursued his journey. As he did so, he saw, a little ahead of him, his future companion, Faithful. He called, and begged him to halt; but Faithful would not do that. Christian therefore put to all his strength, and outran him. At this he was so much pleased, that he became incautious and fell. Faithful kindly helped him up. This done, they went on very lovingly together. They had much discourse about the City of Destruction, and their old neighbors, especially Pliable; and then of Faithful's experiences in the Way of Righteousness. He related how he had met with Wanton; with Adam the First, and his struggle to get away from him; of Moses, who beat him severely; of One who came by with holes in his hands and side, who bade him forbear; of Discontent and Shame, and of his pleasant journey through the Valley of the Shadow of Death.]

LITERARY critics have much admired the genius of Bunyan in introducing a new character just at this time. He has lately brought the original Pilgrim through such hair-breadth escapes—notably, his fight with Appolyon, and his struggles and dangers in the Valley of the Shadow of Death—that the mind requires that he should be speedily crowned with victory, or else experience relief by some new and more pleasing picture of his career. But as there are many other features in the Christian life which the allegorist has need to portray, it is impossible to bring the story to an end at present; and as our Christian does not monopolize all the experiences incident to Christian living, and as these experiences are not the same in all Christians, it becomes necessary for him to introduce another traveler. This he does with consummate skill. In the last chapter, he is but the voice of a man, singing in the valley. In this, he is brought before us, the companion of Christian, whose name is Faithful.

Their companionship began in a series of remarkable events. Faithful was ahead of Christian. When Christian came out of the valley, he saw the other, and, calling to him, requested him to stop, so that he might come up with him. But Faithful said, "No; I am upon my life, and the avenger of blood is behind me." He thought himself unsafe so long as he was not going forward. He would tarry for no one. His soul matters were between himself and God, as every man's should be. Take him for an example. Press forward to the mark of the prize of your high calling. Look not behind thee! Escape for thy life! Tarry not in all the plain! Thy soul demands thy best attention! Do not be afraid of loving thyself!

As Faithful wisely declined to halt, Christian wisely put out all his strength, and pressed forward. I say wisely. I mean it was wise for Christian to do this, but he did it in a temper. It is right that we should emulate those who are better and wiser than we, but it should be done in love. We should put forth all our strength, and keep our eyes open at the same time. In getting ahead of Faithful, he neglected to heed his feet, so he tumbled and fell.

How many do this. Let him who thinketh he standeth take heed lest he fall. We have seen young Christians sitting in judgment upon their elders, and heard them pronounce the sentence of condemnation in hard language. We have heard students condemn their tutors, and not feel a qualm of conscience or be ashamed of their ignorance. Of late we have known a worthy minister condemned by some of his brethren in the ministry, much younger than himself, and far less wise or learned, because during the late Temperance Revival he refused to put on a blue ribbon. He has been a temperance man all his life, has brought up his family on strict temperance principles, and, properly maintaining his manhood, refused to be dictated to by those who had been sober scarce a week. True, he has had to leave his

Church in consequence, and now where are his accusers? Like Christian, they vaingloriously smiled; like him, they shamefully fell.

In this city, men have lately condemned the Churches and clergy for being so slow in the temperance work (although in this instance the complaint was unnecessary and unjust), but where are the accusers? They thought themselves ahead, and are fallen. The Churches still stand, however, and the clergy are still preaching the glorious Gospel of the grace of God, by which alone a drunkard, like any other sinner, can be saved.

But Faithful came up to help him.

"Brethren, if any man be overtaken in a fault, ye which are spiritual restore such an one in the spirit of meekness, considering thyself, lest thou also be tempted." In this spirit did the one Pilgrim help the other. Let us not glory in another's fall, but let us rather glory that we restore erring brethren. This is the history of their meeting.

The Christian Church, taken as a whole, has fallen into an error which, in my humble opinion, hinders its usefulness. This particular error is the attempt to make all Christians alike. We desire to make all alike in doctrine, worship and experience. I believe in the unity of the Church, but I do not believe in the uniformity of faith, worship or experience. I believe in one Spirit, and in a diversity of operations. I believe in one Faith, one Lord, one Baptism; but I also believe in a variety of disciples. Give me the doctrines of the Fatherhood of God; the person, life, and death of Jesus Christ, His Son; the enlightenment and strength of the Holy Ghost; love to God, self, and man; and faith in the soul's immortality,— and I can have fellowship, holy and delightful, with any man, and think not of differences or minor points. Leonardo da Vinci's picture of the Last Supper ought to be studied by Christians; it ought to be the frontispiece of all our church manuals. In it there are twelve different men, each with a different expression on his face, each in an attitude peculiar to himself, revealing that they are as distinct and different in soul as in body, and yet all of them disciples, and even apostles, chosen by the Master, who knew their several idiosyncracies, and who deliberately selected them for His work, notwithstanding. Man cannot tolerate his fellow-disciples. Lord! give us more of Thy mind.

Good men and women are to-day grieving that they have not had the same religious history as others, and infer that they are not Christians because they have not. By the aid of this parable, I shall try to disabuse your minds of this folly. Experience is very much a matter of physical temperament, mental bias, local circumstance, and church connection. One star differeth from another in glory. Peter had visions. Paul was caught up into the third heaven. John leaned on the bosom of his Lord; afterwards fell at His feet as dead, and saw the innumerable multitude before the throne of God. But a sword pierced the heart of the mother of the Lord; James received his baptism of fire; walked in the way of righteousness, and ended his life without manifesting any extraordinary emotion.

But before we show wherein these Pilgrims differed, it is necessary to shew wherein they were the same. There are some things wherein all are alike. These are the things which accompany salvation.

They were alike in that they both left the City of Destruction.

Christian started first, and Faithful soon followed his example. He left that city with the same motives, reasons and purposes. It had been their home from their birth. In it were their property and friends. Here they had been held by society and pleasure. All Christians are alike in that they have left this world. They are in it, but not of it. Leaving the world means leaving a life of sin. It does not mean having nothing to do with its commercial, domestic, or political affairs. A man who leaves the world, in the Christian sense, is the better politician, merchant, husband, and parent. He renders to Cæsar the things that are Cæsar's, and is different from the rest of men in that he also renders to God the things that are God's.

They were alike in seeking to reach the Celestial City.

To reach eternal safety from a place of threatened ruin, was their mutual purpose. For this each left all he had, and started alone. Their journey had a definite end. It was clear and distinct to their minds. So is it with all Christians. We live not for the present, but future good. For we know that if the earthly house of our tabernacle were dissolved, we have a building of God—a house not made with hands—eternal in the heavens. We look for a city which hath a foundation, whose builder and maker is God, for here we have no continuing city, but we seek that which is to come. It is of no importance where you find a Christian; of what denomination, color, age—he is living for an inheritance among the saints in light. How different it is with others. After they have lived for this world, enjoyed its pleasures and honors, at the end of life are bankrupt, with nothing to live for, and nothing to die for. They have lived to a world that has promised all things, but has naught that it can pay.

They were alike in seeking the Celestial City in the same way.

Both entered the Way of Righteousness through the Wicket Gate. So do all Christians. There are some, however, who are seeking the Celestial City without reference to Christ or righteousness. They expect to reach heaven by professing religion and joining a church. Religion is not righteousness. A church is not Christ. Some religions are foolish, some unscriptural, and others wicked. But the Christian seeks to reach heaven by walking in the way of God's commandments. He leaves his sin to Christ, and commits his life to His direction. Christ is made unto him righteousness. He is made the righteousness of God in Him. They that keep His commandments shall have right to the tree of life, and shall enter through the gates into the city.

Perhaps it will be thought, as they were alike in so many particulars, that they would also be alike in all. Not so. A landscape, essentially the same, is changed according to the standing-point from which it is viewed. Its teaching is as various as men are. A poet will see in it the subject, and draw from it inspiration for song. A painter will see colors, and forms, and hues, and tints, and beauty. A scientist, laws and forces. A farmer, toil, harvest, and riches. An adventurer, money. An engineer, a level for a railroad. The same man will find it changing with his moods. This aside. It will appear different in the gleaming, and in the gloaming; different again in the storm; in the calm; in the light of the sun; in the light of the moon; in summer; in fall; in winter. So with Christian life. It is not just the same with all men. The essentials are the same, the incidentals various.

We will now consider wherein they were unlike.

Before Christian reached the Wicket Gate, he fell into the Slough of Despond; was deluded by Mr. Worldlywiseman, and was threatened with death at the foot of the Thundering Mountain.

But Faithful escaped the Slough, and had an easy time of it to the Wicket Gate. Some sinners find it easy to find Christ. To Bunyan's credit, be it said, he acknowledged this. When we consider his own sorrowful experiences, his lack of education, and the narrowness of his creed, this admission is remarkable. It would be mysterious, did we not know that Jesus Christ, formed in the heart, makes a man larger than all creeds and as expansive as all truth.

Yet he had his trials. He met with one whose name was Wanton. She had a flattering tongue, bewitching looks; she laid hard at him, and had like to have done him a mischief. In other words, he is a type of the Christian who is tempted, and had to resist temptations to licentiousness. The mental struggles of Christian are not his portion. He is assailed through the flesh. I hardly know which are the more difficult to overcome. Samson, who cared not for the Philistines, lost his power, his eyes, his liberty, and eventually his life, through the seductions of Delilah. Joseph found safety only in flight. Strong men have been brought low by her wiles. I should say the richer and more generous the nature, the more liable are we to be tempted in this manner, and the harder is it to resist. Pity it is, that she, who was made to be man's helpmeet, should have become the high priestess of iniquity, the one foul blot on Christian civilization; that she, to whom virtue is everything, and who is nothing without it, should be the chief propagator of vice, the fatal foe of both man and woman; that she should be a deep ditch wherein are buried, daily and hourly, the virtues of society; that she, like a blood-thirsty animal, should never be satisfied, but pant continually for the life blood of the soul. Know ye not that the dead are in her house, that her steps take hold on hell, and that those who go unto her never return? If she should allure and tempt thee, "Let not thine heart decline to her ways, go not astray in her path; for she hath cast down many wounded; yea, many strong men have been slain by her."

At the foot of the hill called Difficulty, he met a very aged man named Adam the First. The old man attempted to turn him out of the way, by promising him an easier life. This is a trial that did not fall to Christian. It is a dramatic representation of the world striving against the spirit. The temptation to live for carnal pleasure, the riches, follies and fashions of the world is generally very strong.

There are Christians who began their new life in poverty, and improved their worldly circumstances as soon as they walked in the way of righteousness; began to be in earnest for their earthly good not until then, but when prosperity came, neglected their spiritual concerns. Instead of putting off the old man, with all his deeds, they married his three daughters, the "Lust of the Flesh; the Lust of the Eyes; and the Pride of Life." Men do not get away from the powers of this world and worldly-mindedness without experiencing what Faithful did, "such a twitch back" that he thought the old man had taken with him a part of the flesh.

It is so hard to part with the things of the flesh; it is very hard for those who have lived for the lower nature to succeed in living for the higher. It is hard to take up the cross daily, and so be Christ's disciple. But if any man will be His disciple he must do this very thing.

—22

Lecture XII.

In going up the hill Difficulty, Christian slept and lost his roll out of his bosom in the harbour, on the side of the hill. But at about this place Faithful looked behind him and saw one coming after him, swift as the wind, who, as soon as he overtook him, knocked him down and left him for dead. The cause of his assault was the secret leaning on the part of Faithful to Adam the First. When Faithful cried for mercy, he said, "I know not how to shew mercy," and with that he knocked him down again.

In this way Faithful was made to know that the function of the law is to punish transgressors. It does not dispense mercy. Faithful's sin was of the heart, and not of word or deed. He was inclined to go with the old man, as his promises were fair, and for this, Moses, for that was the name of the man who overtook him, knocked him down.

In one sentence Bunyan speaks volumes, and observes that with Moses, it is "but a word and a blow." If then it be true that God requires truth in the inward parts, if God searcheth the hearts, if He does not look as man looks, on the outward appearance, but on the heart; if sin is sin in the heart as well as in words and deeds, then, my brethren, are we not all guilty before God? There is no difference; we have all sinned and come short of the glory of God.

And a little reflection will convince you that sin is sin, whether in the heart or on the tongue. Powder is the same in the magazine as in the gun. Murder is only the hate of the heart carried into deed. Stealing is but the covetousness of the heart carried into action. And so I might run the gamut of all the vices.

A holy God condemns every sin. His law declares in solemn tones, as it was first proclaimed from the bowers of Eden as a needed warning, and now echoed back by man in his wails and woes, the centuries downward: The *soul* that sinneth shall die.

"He doubtless had made an end of me, but that One came by and bade him forbear," says Faithful.

"Who was it that bade him forbear?" enquires Christian.

"I did not know him at first, but as he went by I perceived the holes in his hands and his side; then I concluded that He was our Lord."

In this inimitable manner, with one stroke of the pencil, our author draws the picture of our Lord and his office in saving the sinner.

You remember that it was some time after Christian was condemned at Sinai before he lost his burden at the cross. And yet so soon as he looked at the cross his burden rolled off of itself. But Faithful was not long condemned before he saw the Lord and was delivered from the blows of Moses. Please note this: the Lord did not deliver him from the law, but only from its condemnation; so does Christ save men. He delivers from the curse of the broken law, but "heaven and earth shall pass away, but not one jot or tittle of the law shall fail." There is not one law for the sinner and another for the Christian. It is equally binding on all.

Oh blessed, joyful news, that I have to preach. Christ is the end of the law for righteousness to every one that believeth. He that believeth not is condemned already, but he that believeth has the life, has passed from condemnation to life. He realizes that God is love. By faith in God's sacrifice—the Man with the holes in His hands and feet—he is made to know the tender, loving, most merciful heart of His Father, and that there is mercy with Him that He may be feared, and plenteous redemption that he may be sought unto.

Saving power pervades nature. Cut the bark of any portion of a tree, and every leaf, and branch, and root, and rootlet, will sympathize and toil till the wound is healed and the scar hidden. Let any one member of the body suffer, and the other members will unite to produce ease. Let a member of the family be sick—it may be but a very young babe—and parents, and brothers, and sisters, will deny themselves rest and comfort till health is restored. Let famines come in China and India; let war rage in Turkey—and the whole world will feel pain throbbing through its veins, and will send to the sufferers its life blood in gentle charities till the curse is removed. Let a man have a hundred sheep, and if he lose one, will he not leave the ninety and nine, and seek that which is lost? Let a planet fall, and every other one will grow dizzy, and involuntarily become a partner in its misfortune. No man, and no animal known to man, suffers, but what some one volunteers to be a Good Samaritan in the case. And shall all nature be full of remedial power—shall the universe throb with sympathy—and God, who is its Author, be denied it? No! a thousand times no! These are but indications that His Spirit fills all in all. Never can that be thought while we have the Man "with holes in His hands and side" held up as He is to the world. When a sinner can see Him to be God's sacrifice for sin, the expression of His unfathomable love to him, he becomes thoughtless of self, and is lost in an ocean of love.

> "Oh! what a load of struggle and distress
>   Falls off before the Cross! The feverish care,
>   The wish that we were other than we are,
>   The sick regrets, the yearnings numberless,
>   The thought, 'this might have been,' so apt to press
>   On the reluctant soul; even past despair,
>   Past sin itself,—all—all is turned to fair,
>   Ay, to a scheme of ordered happiness,
>   So soon as we love God, or rather know
>   That God loves us! . . . Accepting the great pledge
>   Of His concern for all our wants and woes,
>   We cease to tremble upon danger's edge;
>   While varying troubles form and burst anew,
>   Safe in a Father's arms we smile as infants do."

You will have noticed that the views which these two men had of the Cross—or rather, of the Man who died there—were not the same. No view is saving that does not penetrate the outer form and reach the spirit of everlasting love. And any view is saving that feels the heart of God throbbing with love through Christ and His Cross. Touch the hem of His garment anywhere, and we shall be made perfectly whole. There is a bridge in Austria on which the life and teachings of the Lord are to be found in *bas-relief*. In the early morning the laborers who pass it to the field, look upon the sower sowing the good seed. An hour later the mechanic sees Him at the carpenter's bench. An hour later the merchant see the merchant selling his goodly pearls, that he may possess the pearl of great price. Later, as the housewife goes to market, she looks upon the woman putting the leaven into the meal, or sweeping her house in search of the lost piece of money. Shortly after, the nurse-girls and children see Him with infants in His arms. Then when the invalid passes by, he looks on One who is healing all manner of diseases. And when a funeral procession moves slowly by, the mourners for a moment fix their eyes on Him who is raising the dead, and who declares that He is the Resurrection and the Life.

What the moral effect is I do not know, but the teaching is that as we are all in different conditions, we need a Savior adapted to them, and that Christ is so adapted. My friend, you know the kind of Saviour you need, and what you ought to be saved from. Look to Jesus from what and where you are, to what He is to thee. His power is unlimited. He is able to save to the uttermost all that come to God by Him.

Faithful's experience in the Valley of the Shadow of Death was altogether different from Christian's. He had sunshine all the way through. He recognized that Christ was with him in these lonely and dangerous places; and the sensible presence of Christ turned the darkness to light, and the grief to joy. Still the valley was not altogether uneventful, he met with some who tried to turn him back.

He met with Discontent, who told him that the valley was without honor, and to go on would disoblige his friends, besides making a fool of himself. This man made but little impression on him. But he had much harder work with SHAME.

SHAME tried to make him ashamed of being a pilgrim. He objected to religion as a pitiful, low, sneaking business; called a tender conscience an unmanly thing; and said it was slavery for a man to watch his words and ways. He also objected that few of the mighty or great were found in the way; complained that as a rule Christians were poor, assumed that they were ignorant, and oh! depth of misfortune! knew nothing of natural science, and that Christians were unfashionable. He called vices by fine names, and expressed his opinion that it was folly to seek forgiveness or to make restitution for any injury that a man may have done his neighbor.

The spirit of this man is with us to-day. He seeks now, as then, to make men ashamed of being Christians. He has great influence with some, and overthrows the faith of others. Now there are some souls (excuse the word) who are always waiting for the fashions. They will wear the ugliest clothing, walk in a crippled habit, contract disgusting vices, defy nature, and descend to positive indecency, because it is fashionable. They go to church and through a service (or rather let the service go through them) in which they have no interest, because it is fashionable. They contract debt, and never pay, because it is fashionable. They wear other people's clothing, and are, in short, incarnations of irredeemable promissory notes, because, forsooth, it is fashionable. They object to earnest, Christian work, and risk heaven because it is fashionable. Were ever poor slaves so bound? Thank God, true Christians are not fashionable. Let us not be ashamed of being out of fashion.

Others are politic. The first question they ask about anything (and they carry their habit into religion) is, "Will it pay?" and they tell lies, because it pays, and they demean themselves to ruin others, because it pays. And these are the men who try to make Christians ashamed of the life of righteousness. They would be Christians themselves if they thought it politic.

But the chief objection to Christians is their "want of understanding in all natural science." The assumption that Christians are an ignorant class of men is amusing. Well, perhaps you have noticed that Church-members, and preachers, and professors in colleges, are men of very narrow foreheads, and of an inferior quality of brain behind them. And you will have also noticed —it is patent at a glance—that sceptics and infidels are otherwise. Their foreheads are lofty and broad, and taking a crow's view of their heads, we see in a moment that they are built on the latest and most approved style of phrenological architecture. A twinkling of an eye is sufficient to convince one that they are superior men. They understand all the mysteries of the universe; if they were consulted, could suggest improvements, although it is quite possible they cannot manage their own affairs a week without blundering. But we must not expect great men to attend to little things. Sufficient is it that they are scientists, for do they not read a semi-scientific paper, written in an atheistic vein, in bed every Sunday morning? Are they not sure that Christianity is antiquated, and that a new revelation is being made?

Sarcasm aside, it is false to say or to assume that Christians lack understanding in natural science. Some of the ablest leading scientific men of to-day (and it has been so ever since the revived study of the material world) are Christians. I do not know of a solitary instance of a Christian college, of any sect, however small or humble, where natural science is not taught; in the larger colleges and universities "the chairs" are richly endowed. Nor do I know of a land outside of Christendom where natural science is taught as part of public education; nor am I aware of any of the late remarkable scientific discoveries and inventions occurring in any but Christian lands. But for Christian ministers, churches, and schools, the books which scientists write, the lectures they give, would go begging for buyers and hearers. The world cannot make us ashamed of our scientific record.

It is not our business to preach science. But it is scientific to preach the Gospel. Science cannot save men from unrighteousness. The Gospel alone is the power of God unto salvation; wherefore I am not ashamed of the Gospel of Jesus Christ. "What! ashamed of that which in the hands of a few poor individuals obtained more than a conquest over all the colossal antagonism of heathendom, whether that antagonism was royal, priestly, or philosophical! Ashamed of that which sustained itself for more than a thousand years against the combined forces of barbarism and licentiousness, and in despite of doctrinal and ecclesiastical corruptions! Ashamed of that which braved the fiercer shock, and turned into derision the vaunted enquiry of modern times, philosophical neology, the Anakim of infidelity! Ashamed of that now upheld as it is by a resplendent array of learning, genius, influence, and achievement, and against such combatants and such artillery as are now in the field! No, glorious Gospel of the blessed God, we will do thee no such wrong. Thy form has yet the majestic beauty of the skies from which it came. Thy panoply is yet effulgent as when first it was given thee from the armory of God. Sweeter and louder waxes thy voice of mercy and holiness. Every prejudice shall vanish from before thee, and thine enemies shall lick the dust. Beneath thy tread the moral wilderness shall blossom as the rose. Before thy glance the dark habitations of horrid cruelty shall disappear. Every heart shall throb to thy charm, every clime shall echo to thy praise. Under thy sway all the families of the earth shall be blessed!" We are not ashamed, again we repeat, of the Gospel of Jesus Christ.

From Faithful we learn the effect of backsliding upon the backslider. Christian learns from him of our old friend Pliable. When he returned home he was had greatly in derision; he was rocked and despised. His neighbors said, "Hang him! He is a turncoat; he was not true to his profession." God stirred up his enemies to hiss at him, and make him a proverb because he forsook the way.

Ye that have backslidden, what have you gained? If you did but know how men despise you, what they say of you, and how they feel about you! But I can tell you how they feel. They have no more respect for nor confidence in you than you have yourself. They infer that a man, untrue to God, is not likely to be true to them.

From Faithful, also we learn the effect of a Pilgrim keeping on. When Christian started, there was great talk. Many of the neighbors believed him wise and right, and one at least speedily followed him. Afterwards his whole household left that city, and sought a better. Had Christian not started, he and they had been lost. Learn this solemn lesson. You have influence and power. You are using them to the ruin or to the salvation of your friends. Oh! start this very moment, and may God grant wisdom to your neighbors and families to follow you.

In Faithful we see the advantage of serving the Lord with gladness. As we read his history, we receive the impression that he is a very cheerful Pilgrim. He is introduced singing; he had light where Christian had darkness, and escaped many of the afflictions of his companion. Fellow-Pilgrim, learn this important lesson. The clouds that hide the sun rise from the earth. The darkness that makes our pilgrimage gloomy and sorrowful comes from ourselves. Let us look away from self to the Master, always, and then we shall be filled with joy that is unspeakable, and full of glory. Serve the Lord with gladness. Rejoice always, and again I say rejoice, for—

"I say to thee, do thou repeat
To the first man thou mayest meet,
In lane, highway, or open street—

That he, and we, and all men, move
Under a canopy of love,
As broad as the blue sky above;

That doubt and trouble, fear and pain,
And anguish, all are sorrows vain;
That death itself shall not remain:

And ere thou leave them, say thou this,
Yet one word more:—They only miss
The winning of that final bliss—

Who will not count it true that love,
Blessing, not cursing, rules above,
And that in it we live and move.

And one thing further make him know,
That to believe these things are so,
This firm faith never to forego—

Despite of all which seems at strife
With blessing, and with curses rife—
That this *is* blessing, this *is* life."

LECTURE XIII.

FALSE PROFESSORS: TALKATIVE.

[SYNOPSIS OF CHAPTER.—The Pilgrims met with a man who professed to be going to the Celestial City. He was the son of Saywell, and dwelt in Prating Row. His name was Talkative. Notwithstanding his fine tongue, which he was always ready to use, he was really a very sorry fellow. "A saint abroad, and a devil at home," expressed the judgment of his neighbors concerning him. Faithful was at first much taken with him, and thought he would make an excellent Pilgrim. But by the advice of Christian, who had heard of him, he engaged him in serious conversation on the power of religion, which so exposed his hollow pretensions, that he grew angry, and declined their company.]

WE HAVE come to that part of the Pilgrim's Progress in which Bunyan introduces a number of spurious Christians. The first one is the character of whom I am to speak to-night. He gives him the very appropriate name of TALKATIVE.

But in order to discover defects of any kind in character or in substance, we must first get before our minds an ideal of perfection. There seems to be in man a sense of perfection; moral, intellectual, and physical. Whenever he sees anything that pleases him, that harmonizes with all the conditions of his mind, he pronounces it perfect, and he could not wish anything more should be added to it. If anything more be added he thinks it superfluous, and the article or character will appear overwhelmed with imperfection.

This idea has been introduced into theology, and some have gone so far as to say that every man in his own heart possesses an ideal Christ. And if you will notice, whenever we read the life of Christ and of the infinite wisdom of that life, we do not judge it by a written law, but by an inner sense of perfection which we all possess, and in which we all agree; and here is one grand argument for the Divinity of our Lord Jesus. He satisfies this idea of what we believe the Savior should be; He is presented to us in this character simply because He is perfect, and, therefore, satisfactory to our souls.

And you will notice this also—however weak a man may be, he may be almost idiotic, his intellect may be exceedingly low and his moral perceptions blunted by sin, yet that man possesses an idea of what a Christian should be. He may not be able to read the Word of God to find out what he should be; but here is another man, a professing Christian, and every defection from Christian life on his part produces a sense of imperfection in the mind of the former, looking upon it. However degraded he may be, and as I have said, however blunted his moral perceptions, the looker-on will detect the error.

Several years ago, as I have been informed, a school of physicians set themselves to work to discover what disease was, and they made a great many observations, but could come to no agreement. At last one, much wiser than the rest, said, "We have begun at the wrong end; in order to understand disease, we must first of all understand health." They then went to work and made a diagnosis of health, and when they had set up a standard of health, it was very easy to take the next step, and say that every departure from this was disease. So, if you want to make a table of distances you will first take a standard of measurement; if you want to weigh anything, you will take the article and test it by a standard of weights.

We learn what imperfection is through this sense of perfection, which we all possess; and to understand this spurious Christian, Talkative, it is necessary first of all to determine what constitutes a true Christian. This idea is set forth clearly in the chapter which I have partially read to you; to the particular paragraphs of which I need not refer, but will mention the general characteristics, that we may have in view a standard of what a real Christian is.

We should say, first, that a true Christian possesses A CONVICTION OF SIN.

Sin is that which every Christian is dealing with. It is the great problem which he is trying to solve; it is the grand obstacle the Christian is trying to overcome. Sin is that which produces in his heart a sense of weakness; sin is that which stands between him and his God; sin is that which makes him fear he may never reach the happy and holy place; sin is that which makes man shrink from death, and reel as he dreams of the pains of hell; sin is the great obstruction of the Christian life, practically and theoretically. But a conviction of sin is a very different thing from the knowledge of it. We may know that sin exists; we may have an intellectual apprehension that we and others have committed sin; but to be convicted of it is another thing entirely.

I will suppose that some one in our city, last night, went into a store and stole something; all day long that somebody has been conscious of the fact. But he is not yet convicted; the law has not touched him, though he is conscious of his act. Suppose, then, that to-night the sheriff goes and puts his hand on his shoulder and a manacle upon his wrist—that man stands at once convicted; he feels the sin, and not merely knows that he has committed it. Knowledge comes before conviction. The manacle is merely the shadow of a spiritual fact; the sheriff but a shadow of the Divine law, which in him finds a representative for the time being. In his soul the culprit stands convicted the moment the sheriff's hand falls on him.

Well, now, a Christian not only knows that he has sinned, but is convicted. He feels that the Divine law has hold of him, and that the Divine law is bringing him to punishment. He feels that he is guilty; not merely knows it—he feels it. Knowledge produces conviction, and this increased feeling in the soul concerning sin and the law is conviction. A man may say, and say from knowledge, "I am a miserable sinner;" but a man under conviction, when he comes to God's house, will not merely say, "I am a miserable sinner," but he will hang his head before high heaven, not daring to look to the skies, and out of a broken heart will cry, "God be merciful to me, a sinner!"

He not merely has a conviction of sin, but he has AN ABHORRENCE OF IT.

I do not mean to say, for a moment, that the Christian himself does not commit sin. I do not believe I ever met with a Christian who did not; I do not believe I ever met with a Christian who had attained moral perfection. There are words in use in respect to this which are suggestive. It is sometimes said that we believe that, through some pious fiction, we are free from sin. Now, there is no such thing as a fiction with God, and a Christian is not a man who does not commit sin. He does commit it. As the apostle John says, "If we say we have no sin, we deceive ourselves, and the truth is not in us." Even John Wesley preached the doctrine of sin in believers. There is, however, this difference in believers and non believers: the non believer commits sin and passes it by as of no consequence, but a Christian, when he commits sin, hates the sin and himself too. He mourns and cries out like David, "Have mercy on me, O God, according to Thy loving kindness, and according to the multitude of Thy tender mercies blot out my transgressions." The man who is not a Christian, when he sins, determines to sin again; but a Christian, if he falls, rises and fights, and strives that he may not commit it again. There is just this difference, too, between a Christian and a Moralist, or, if you like, a Pharisee: the Christian hates sin, and abhors sin in himself, but a Moralist, or Pharisee, hates and abhors sin in another. That is just the difference between the two. The Christian excuses and is lenient to sin in another, because he knows how sweet is sin, and how hard it is to fight against it; but a Moralist, a man who is so proud before God that he can cast a reproach upon his fellow beings, hates sin in another, while he encourages it in his own bosom.

Now, this is not the spirit of Christ. If you remember, there was a poor woman taken in sin, and she got into the hands of a number of that sort of men who abhor sin in others. They were all standing around her, and thought the opportunity a good one to put Christ to a test, for, according to the creed of these gentlemen, it was their duty to take up stones and literally pelt such a woman to death; and they were quite willing to do it. So they brought the Savior to her, and gave Him an insight of her condition, and then put to Him the crucial question, "What shall be done with her?" And Christ acknowledged they were acting according to law, but said, "He that is without sin among you, let him cast the first stone." The poor woman looked with shame and despair upon the ground, expecting to die; but by and by up into the face of the Lord. "Woman, where are thine accusers?" "They are all gone." "Doth no man condemn thee?" "No, Lord." "Neither do I." That is the spirit of Christ. A Christian abhors sin in himself; a Pharisee abhors it in another. A Christian is lenient to another's fault, but a Pharisee is lenient to sin only in himself and is hard upon another. That example teaches the spirit of Christ. It is Christian love, a living love and active power in the heart.

We often hear about men getting religion; and we often hear men say, in excitement, how much they enjoy religion. Because some of us have not passed through the same experience that these have, we are not to conclude that it is all fire and excitement, and that there is nothing genuine in it. My friends, that is not true; religon is a power in the heart, transforming the life. How do we know? Just as we know that we live and feel. A man feels pain, yet he cannot make an intellectual analysis of it, nor prove that he is in pain. The next time you are in suffering, try to prove, by some metaphysical process that a logician would accept, that you are in pain, and I defy you to do it; you can only state the fact. An excess of pain in the body produces its effects upon the face and upon the form. Then, again, there is excessive sorrow, not a physical effect at all, but a mental one, yet that affects the physical being also, because the physical and spiritual senses are united. On the other hand, there is joy in the heart, and it lights up the features and enlivens the life. Then there is the power of love, which transforms everything to its nature and object. Now, what is Christianity? What is religion? What is the religion of the Lord Jesus Christ in the soul? It is not a mere theory in the head, but a power in the spirit. I say, what is it? I shall have to repeat myself here, but I do not mind it. It is love. Christianity is love—love to God—love to man.

It is necessary to distinguish this from several things. For instance, this love of God must be distinguished from love of doctrines concerning God. A man may really love Christian doctrine; he may love theology; he may love heterodox theology, or orthodox theology; he may have a creed which commends itself to his reasoning faculties, to his mind; it is convincing to him and satisfying, and he may love it very much, and yet he may not love God. For instance, a learned man may love the science of theology; he may see wonders in it, and yet may not love a fellow-being. All professors of theology are not Christians. We all may love doctrines concerning God, and yet not love Him.

Then again, love of man must be distinguished from an abstract love of righteousness. There are men and women in this world who say that they do love righteousness so much. They tell us so, and it is a very good thing to love righteousness, but not good to love it for its own sake. There are a great many righteous men who are no good to the church. You can find no fault with them; they never did any good and never will; they are in this world just a round naught; there is nothing loving about them; nothing fruitful in them; they are simply nonentities; they do no particular harm, and they do no particular good. Love of man does not mean love of abstract righteousness. I tell you I am rather afraid of men and women who love righteousness, when they love righteousness more than man.

Then we must distingnish this love of man also from abstract humanity. It is the fashion now-a-days to write God with a little g, and humanity with a big H. Men love Comptism, Sociology, and talk incessantly of the science of humanity; it is all humanity—over and over again, humanity. This love of abstract humanity has done no good in the world that I know of in the way of ameliorating the vices and sorrows of men. I have yet to see a hospital built by men who love humanity; I have yet to see an orphan asylum established by these professed lovers of humanity. Many a professor of this humanity passes by the beggar at his own door and fails to wipe away an orphan's tear in his own city.

We are not here to love abstract good, abstract righteousness, or abstract humanity.

What, then, does love to God mean? It means this: Love the man that is next you; love the man that is here; put it in scripture language, "Love your *neighbor* as yourself."

But some one will say, "You don't know *my* neighbor, sir. The men and women around us here in the city are exceedingly low, depraved, very dirty, very drunken, vicious; I have no objection at all to putting a dollar in the collection for those poor heathen out yonder, to support one man in a million of such; I like that; I like the gospel to fly abroad, and hope it will prevail; we take the missionary papers; oh yes, I love the gospel." Who told you to love the gospel? Neither God nor Christ wants you to love the gospel. Christ says, if you see a bleeding man lying on the roadside where you pass along, bind up his wounds and give him what he needs, whether a brother or an enemy. That man is your neighbor, because he needs you, and God has sent you to help him. Let's away with such stuff as loving abstract good, abstract humanity. Love God, and your neighbor as yourself.

It is this love, if you remember, which is the fulfillment of the law. Love fulfills the law simply because it is the spirit of the law. Love any one in life, and there is no wrong you can do to that one; love not, and all vice may creep out of such a condition.

But then, a true Christian has not merely this conviction and abhorrence of sin; he does not merely possess this power of love in the heart, but it issues in a life of practical benevolence.

To repeat what James wrote, "Pure religion and undefiled before God and the Father is this: To visit the fatherless and widows in their affliction, and keep oneself unspotted from the world." If the description of the Judgment that our Lord has given be true, we may see the whole thing revealed there. The whole thing depends upon our practical benevolence. If in that great day the Lord shall say to us, "You fed the hungry man, you clothed that ragged child, you visited the sick and afflicted, and attended to the wants of the needy," He will also say, "Come ye blessed of my Father."

And I think I know something about this "doing it unto me," for I have had friends in my house of late, and among many things that have come to my house, with the friends, were kind expressions of love; some little books and little toys for my little ones; and when those little ones took one thing after another and brought it to me, I felt that I knew something of what the Savior will feel in that day when he shall say, "Inasmuch as ye did it to these, my little ones, ye did it unto me."

The needy are God's little ones—all these men and women around us living in sin, and neglected, by whom? Ah, we know by whom, and they are Christ's little ones. And the whole judgment will turn upon what we have done for them. There is no Christian life apart from this practical benevolence. Do not think you can enter heaven because you have entered the Church. You cannot; it is impossible. Unless you will give up your substance to feed the poor, and take up your cross daily and follow Christ, ye cannot so much as enter the kingdom of heaven; ye cannot become His disciples.

We have now before our minds, in a very brief and imperfect way, an ideal Christian. Let us now look at this man Talkative's mistake.

He supposed that Christian life consisted in knowing and then talking of religious matters. His whole life was made up of this: hearing of religious things and talking of them. But we know great talkers are not always great doers, and this was the result discovered by the neighbors of this man—that although willing enough always to talk on the subject of religion, it was rather distasteful to him to enter upon its duties.

Can a man be a talker of religious matters, and at the same time not be a Christian man? We think he can be. We think that a man may be a theologian, and yet not a Christian. A man may speculate upon the great doctrines of religion; upon the being of God; the immortality of the soul; the future state; the trinity; the unity; the essence of God; "man's free will, foreknowledge absolute"—he may speculate famously on these things, and yet not be a good Christian. Yea, a man may spend twelve or thirteen dollars to get a Bagster's Bible, and may go round with it under his arm, saying, "See my interest in the subject;" he may be able to trace all the references in it from Genesis to Revelation; be able to repeat chapter after chapter of the Holy Word by heart, and yet not be a Christian. Religious knowledge is not religious life.

A man may work miracles, and not be a Christian. A man may be a preacher of the Gospel, and yet not be a Christian. Our dear Lord has said, "Many will say unto me in that day, Lord, Lord, have we not prophesied in thy name, and in thy name cast out devils, and done many wonderful works? And then will I say, Depart from me, I never knew you." Now, that is fearful to think about, but it is a fact. A man may be a theologian, and a man may work miracles, and a man may preach the Gospel, and yet may not be a Christian. Did not the apostle Paul tremble before the merely supposed fact that he might be in that condition, "Lest by any means, when I have preached to others, I myself should be a castaway?" A man is not a Christian because he is able to preach Christianity. It is ten thousand times easier to preach than to live it. It is life, my brethren, that will tell in the other world.

Let us hear Paul again: "Though I speak with the tongues of men and angels (that is, with the eloquence of earth and even heaven), and have not charity (that is, love—this love to God and man of which I have been talking, this power in the heart, and this practical benevolence in the life), yet with all powers of speech, and without that power of love, I am become but sounding brass and a tinkling cymbal. Then, though I have the gift of prophecy (of preaching), and understand all mysteries (endowed with powerful intellect), and all knowledge, and though I have all faith, so that I could remove mountains, and have not charity, I am nothing; and though I bestow all my goods to feed the poor, and give my body to be burned (as a martyr to the truth, to the abstract truth, or to the telling of it), and have not charity, it profiteth me nothing." Nothing!

You sometimes see a band preparing to play, and you see one man tightening up a drum, pulling the strings here and there, and striking it with a stick. Before the band begins he will strike once or twice, just to give the time; there is no music in that. Then a man will take the cymbals on his hands and clap them together, merely to show the others that he is ready; but there is no music in drum and cymbals by themselves. But presently the band starts up, and there is a volume of congruent sound, a filling up of all the parts—the deep-toned bass, the shrill tenor, the mellow alto; and then the drum gives force and vivacity, and the cymbals lend charm and vigor to the whole. Useless by themselves, they are delightful and grand when mixed with melody. So that talking by itself means nothing; but mixed with good works, with a pure love in the heart of him who speaks, and true adoration for God and service for his fellow-creature, what he says puts power and vigor and life into the music he makes in his journey to the skies.

To illustrate this a little further: Cannot a sick man lecture on health? Oh! yes; he may be a thorough invalid, and yet lecture well and profitably on that subject. I notice a man can talk about riches, and at the same time be exceedingly poor; he can talk about gold, and have none; he may talk about economy, and yet not practice it in his own household. A man may talk about things he does not possess. So a man may talk about religion, and yet not have one spark of it in his soul. I believe it is better to have the gold than to talk about it. Is it not? I do not know myself, but I think it is. It is very much better to have health than to lecture about it; much better to be a practical economist than merely theoretical upon the subject; and it is much better to have the love of God in our souls than to write volumes or preach sermons upon it—much better to serve man in his need than to have beautiful theories concerning humanity, the truth of which we can never test.

A very interesting question arises here. Who makes such men, and how are such men as Talkative produced? Let me come to the point at once: I say preachers help to make such men as Talkative, and they do it in this way, by preaching an impracticable religion. We preach so many things that men cannot do. We preach about the mysteries of the Gospel, and so much upon purely abstract questions. Do, do, do! So it is all the way through the New Testament. I preach good works. I say the New Testament insists upon good works. You cannot get to heaven without good works. It is folly to try; you cannot, my friends. "Christ has purified us unto Himself that we might be a peculiar people, zealous of good works," Paul wrote to Titus. "All scripture is given by inspiration of God, and is profitable for doctrine, for reproof, for correction, for instruction in the way of righteousness, that the man of God may be perfect, thoroughly furnished unto all good works," he wrote to Timothy. You cannot get away from them—good works. I preach them. I would that I could produce more of them. But here is the mistake: we preach upon remote, abstract questions, instead of insisting upon the practical power of Christianity.

Let us see how it was in the primitive Church. The apostles preached; those who had money gave to those who had nothing, and the converts had all things in common. The apostles went about, not merely preaching of the mysteries of the kingdom of God, but healing all manner of diseases, feeding the hungry, giving feet to the lame, raising the dead, and being powerful in all sorts of good works.

But then, too, it is not altogether the preacher's fault. Men become "talkative" by often resisting the truth. You are here to-night, my dear friend; you have been here several Sabbath evenings since it has been my pleasure to preach these sermons upon the Pilgrim's Progress. You have had warm feelings, which, if followed out faithfully, would have led to your profession of the Lord Jesus Christ. Have you not had your duty so impressed on your mind that you felt it was the right thing to go and seek out some in need, to help them? I assume that you have felt thus, yet you have not confessed Christ, you have not rendered that human aid which you felt it your duty to give, and what is the result? Active habits develop character; passive impressions harden the heart, and you are here to-night harder than you were at the beginning of these lectures, less inclined to truth, less inclined to good works, and more insensible than you were when I began to preach these discourses.

To illustrate: The physician goes about among the sick every day and sees the aspect of suffering until he grows hardened. The undertaker, at a funeral, knows he should look solemn, when, perhaps, he does not feel so, and finds it requires some effort to appear mournful; but give him a year's practice and training in his duties, and you will find him always ready for a funeral. His life becomes hardened to his calling. Even philanthropists; I mean Board-of-Director-Philanthropists, may become hardened to the facts they deal with, until what they began from a spirit of love, is carried on in a hard sense of cold duty. Thus you see the effect of passive impressions. It is only an active life that can save us; a passive life must necessarily harden us, and here we come to the philosophy of that shrewd saying, "gospel-hardened sinners."

However, these hardened souls, the calloused subjects of passive impressions, make fine critics. Why, we can all tell how a Christian ought to live; we can all criticise Christians; and we can all criticise a sermon. We may not be able to preach one, but we can criticise one. That is frequently done.

We might illustrate this topic in many ways; but enough.

The talkative Christian neglects the culture of his soul; neglects to work the truth into himself by habit. Let us see how the Master would save us from this talkative condition of religion. He says if any man would know the doctrine let him do the will. Christianity is a practical thing; a life of practical benevolence. It must be wrought into the soul. We must go about doing good. If we would be Christ-like, we must follow the Master. But this Talkative neglects the culture of his soul. For instance, he is quite willing to talk of the mysteries and histories and the doctrines of religion, and things that have perplexed him; but he does it for the sake of discussion, and not for the sake of his soul. That is a mistake. We must use spiritual things as we do food for the body, not simply to enjoy, but to impart strength. We buy and read books and attend lectures for the cultivation of the intellect, but not for that alone, for the object of that cultivation is that we may apply it. So with our aesthetic nature; we look upon things of beauty and bring to our homes bits of music and sweet song; and gaze upon lovely pictures and landscapes to cultivate the sense and refine and heighten the tone of being; and so in spiritual things. It is a sense of the good we are to get which brings us to church to sing hymns and bow our heads in prayer, relate experiences and read the Bible; we wish to cultivate ourselves, but the thing must not stop here. The Christian does not live to himself; no man does; nor does he die to himself, let him try as he may. The Christian cultivates his soul that he may save other souls. You cultivate your garden and your farm that they may produce—not for the mere sake of the cultivation, that would be labor in vain; and when we cultivate and nothing grows, we feel that our time is lost. You are looking for results. So it is with the Christian; he lives for Christ, and he dies to win eternal life.

The doctrine I have been preaching is this: You cannot be saved unless you save others. Without attempting to save others, you are merely like TALKATIVE.

LECTURE XIV.

VANITY FAIR.

[SYNOPSIS OF CHAPTER.—When the Pilgrims had rid themselves of Talkative, and before they entered the town of Vanity, where a great fair was kept all the year round, Evangelist met them and gave them good and timely counsel. The way to the Celestial City lay right through this fair. As the Pilgrims entered it the people were much excited on account of their demeanor, speech, and clothing. They thought them fools, outlandish and crazy. They then grew angry, because Christian and Faithful thought lightly of the goods they had for sale. When asked what they would buy, these men replied, "We buy the truth." This produced a riot. Then they made prisoners of the Pilgrims, charged them with being the cause of the riot, and had them before Lord Hategood, who, with a jury and witnesses like-minded with himself, sentenced Faithful to death. After much cruelty, they burned him to ashes at the stake. As Faithful died, the Dreamer saw, standing behind the multitude, a chariot and a couple of horses waiting for him. They took him through the clouds, the nearest way to the Celestial Gate.]

THIS chapter commences with another illustration of the doctrine on which I have so frequently insisted, that God prepares men beforehand for the trials on which they are to enter; and that it is Christian wisdom not to wait until we have sinned before we seek God, but to seek Him before we sin. Prevention is better than cure. As I have already said, there is something in the Christian's life very much better than being forgiven, and that is being approved of God. There is a passage in Scripture which teaches us to be approved of God, but we are apt to forget the truth there taught, and make prayer and faith the all-sufficient offices of Christian duty, to the neglect of right conduct; we may thus even make God the minister of sin. Some of us have frequently sinned much, that grace might abound. Too many of us fall into this error.

Bunyan now brings his Pilgrims into Vanity Fair; but before they enter and are brought in contact with its hostility and persecution, they meet their good friend Evangelist, who gives them much good instruction; tells them to be faithful unto death, and informs them of the manner in which they must pass through this fair, if they would please God and benefit men. This, you see, is the preparation before the trial comes, and teaches us the method of Divine grace, for God gives His grace prospectively—God is always beforehand. He is able not only to lift us up, but to make us stand. He puts on us the whole armor, that we may stand in the evil day, and having done all, to stand.

Vanity Fair is said by critics to be one of the finest pictures in the whole book. It is a representation of the fleshly side of this world. If you like, an incarnation of the carnality abounding in the world, by which Christians are all more or less tempted. I do not mean to say, nor will I teach, that this is a fair picture of the entire world in which we dwell, but it is a true picture of the carnal side of it.

It is a fine picture, and in order that you may understand it, it is necessary that I should give you a description of what Bunyan had in his mind when he drew the picture.

Practically you know nothing of what he refers to. You may know something from reading, but not from actual experience, of the model in Bunyan's mind of his Vanity Fair. You have your fairs in this country, but generally they are associated with churches. I would not say that they were ever connected with anything like gambling, thimble-rigging, and grab-bags, or, indeed, anything of that kind; such things would be condemned in saloons, and are therefore not tolerated in churches, and so let us say nothing more about the matter.

But you have in this country some very good honest fairs in connection with the churches, for the *honest, cheap* sale of fancy articles, which bring in considerable revenue. All those things are pleasant enough to see. You have also your agricultural fairs—by the way, an important means of developing agricultural prosperity. Such fairs are, indeed, very healthful in their present condition, promotive of the spirit of agriculture, in which this country must abound, and in producing a spirit of emulation, move men to do their best.

But centuries and centuries ago, when civilization was not quite so extensive as now—in its very dawn—churches were built and dedicated to some patron saint, who took (or rather, was said to take) the church and the community in which it stood under his or her particular control and care. Once a year feasts were held in those communities in honor of their respective saints. In those days, merchants, traveling in caravans, would go the round of these festivals, and offer for sale articles of luxury or necessity, enough to supply the people for a year. The merchants took advantage of the large concourse of people gathered on such occasions, and of the chance of their having accumulated means to supply their wants at the annual fair. But as trade developed and commerce extended, stores, or shops, as they are called in the old country, were established in every village, town, and city, and so the necessity for itinerant merchants passed away. Like many others, the institution has survived the occasion which gave it birth, and the feasts or fairs are kept up to this day. They have, however, degenerated from fairs for trade into mere fairs for pleasure; and the description which Bunyan here gives of the old English fair, as it now exists, is actually true. As Bunyan says, there are a number of rows of booths at this fair for the sale of fancy goods. You will also see booths adorned with glittering toys, not merely to tempt the passer-by, but enable the proprietor to get possession of pennies by some sort of trick or artifice. There is very little of honest value offered at such places. As you pass along, you will see, on this side, a quack doctor, who is improving his opportunity to abuse the physicians of the neighborhood, and who offers instead, his own prescription and nostrums as a sure cure for all diseases. On that side is a shooting-gallery. Here is some tawdry show, and over there you hear someone singing a bawdy song. At night all is glitter, but the silver is nothing but tin, and the glittering gold nothing but tinsel. It is, in fact, all vanity, and nothing but vanity. The whole stock at these fairs is often absolutely worthless, and yet they continue. They have become a disastrous source of moral corruption, besides carrying away from the neighborhood where they are held the vainly spent earnings of the people. Acts of Parliament are continually being passed to curtail these institutions. Many such fairs have become illegal in the larger towns and cities of Great Britain. In many places, however, they are still kept up, in order to promote, as is said, the old English spirit; and many a young man, and many a young woman, date their ruin from attending these fairs. If you compare the articles of merchandise there, they are mostly lighter than vanity; and so Bunyan takes this institution as a model for his picture of the carnal world. These fairs in England have become so offensive that, in some places, the whole people are crying out against them. Their allurements are a type of the perils which beset the path of a Christian.

We are in the world, my brethren, but not of it, and we are continually in danger of being overpowered and ruined by the world. But you may say, is not this strange that we should be in peril from the very circumstances of our existence? Nevertheless, it is so. There is a ship about to cross the ocean. She starts from the shore beset with dangers from the very tide on which she expects to be borne into her destined haven; the winds on which she depends to make her voyage may be the means of her destruction. Men cannot control the winds or the waves, but with skill and good seamanship they can control the ship in the midst of them. Soul and body are intricately connected. There are dangers to the soul arising from the appetites which God has planted in our bodies for their benefit. Nay, by the necessities of our existence here, our souls may be lost. As a ship gains her harbor, often with sails rent, masts swept away, helm gone, and pilot lost, so may a Christian, after the buffetings of life, enters heaven in discouragement and distress, and on the very verge of despair.

This picture of Bunyan's is a fruitful theme for study. I lay it down as a principle, that nothing that is essentially of this world can possibly satisfy the craving of the soul of man. For instance, you can epitomize it all into what is called gold. If you have money you can have much of this world; you can buy friends as well as houses and lands; you can draw to yourself pleasures from all quarters.

Taking money, then, as the very best thing this world can produce, let us now see how very unsatisfactory it is, and how worthless to the human soul. Mind you, I do not mean to say that you should not get all the money you can honestly, but you should possess your money, and not let your money possess you. Here is all the difference in the world. One man will have gold as he has the fever—that is, it will have him; and the cure in this case often is severe. He must use his gold or it will abuse him.

How vain is money! Yet we are all trying to get it—all trying to save a little. I will suppose you are in need of some one to occupy a place of important trust; a person is recommended to you, in whose favor it is first remarked that he is very rich, and endowed with all the worldly advantages of culture and polish which riches can bestow. Suppose even that his connections, too, are rich, and hold high social and civil position in consequence of their wealth; and when it is all told as a recommendation to your choice, what then? Why, you ask, but what of his moral character? "O well," perhaps is the reply, "of that there is less to say—young men, you know, will be young men." But that, you answer, is not satisfactory. I want a man that I can trust in matters very important. You say he is very rich; but that is nothing at all. I want a good character. And when you have found a flaw in the character of the applicant, all the gold of a mine would not fit him for your purpose. So here is an illustration of the vanity of gold; there is a standard which it can never reach.

Well, suppose a man comes to your office to-morrow, to borrow money; what do you enquire? And by the by, I heard a gentleman say, not many weeks ago, that when a person of a particular nationality (I am sorry that nationality was not my own) came to him to borrow, he never asked a question as to his security—the nationality made everything all right. But suppose, again, that a man is reputed to be very rich, while at the same time you know that he is immoral and leads a life that ought to be a shame to any man—it may not, indeed, be publicly known, but the fact has been privately wafted to your ears—do you not take that fact into consideration before trusting money in his hands? Do you not require the name and character of honesty before you are satisfied? Here, then, is still further illustration that gold is not equal to character. It is not.

Then think how many men who have been rich grow suddenly poor. Then, again, how many are poor in the midst of their riches. Often a man and wife, after twenty years of increasing wealth, sit down and look back over the course, not merely of increasing wealth, but of increasing trials, until they sigh for that sweet early time when their life began together in a cottage. Their lofty mansion has not brought them happiness, but only increasing care; and it is a fact, as a general rule, the more gold a man has, the less is he satisfied, for the truth is, God never intended the human soul to be fed on anything so perishable. He never intended that its mighty craving should be satisfied with dust. And when a man is stripped of all the things for which he has toiled his life long, and stands at last a bankrupt before his God and his fellow-man—when character is gone, and gold is gone—which does he feel the loss of more? Which do his friends think the more worthy? In the loss of character, there was a loss of that which gold could never buy; his condition is pitiable, not for the loss of his gold, but because he has lost his righteousness, and stands worse than poor before heaven and earth.

I say, if we compare gold with character, it is utterly worthless; it is vanity of vanity. When men come to die, what do they pride themselves in? That they leave the world reputed rich men? No; they know they have to leave all that behind them. They cannot carry riches with them; gold is valueless in the regions whither they go. But if they have laid up treasures in heaven, then they are rich toward God and toward the coming kingdom.

Then how different is the standard of value in Vanity Fair from that of sober reason. In the fair you will pay for a mere tinsel imitation of a good article more than you would have to pay at an honest shop for the honest gold. Rubbish there will cost you more than the value of a good thing in fair trade. The day after the fair every little boy blows a trumpet, or snaps a flimsy whip, or sports a gilded watch-chain; but in a day or two the trumpets are broken, whips untwisted, and the gilded watch-chains rusted and thrown away. Everybody is disgusted; worthless baubles have cost more than articles of value would have done at an ordinary jeweller's, for the articles thus bought would have had some intrinsic worth and lasting value, whereas the money expended on the trifles of the fair was utterly thrown away. So with men and women who prefer this world, and this world's pleasures, and this world's goods, to those of eternity. We buy baubles for a passing pleasure, and then throw the toys away. Ah, if we could get the dead to speak, they would tell us where true value lies; they would tell us that the things of this world are vain compared with those of the higher and better world. These trifles we have but for a moment; but the things that are not seen endure forever.

Let us view for a moment the conduct of these pilgrims at this fair. They excited a good deal of astonishment as they passed along, for they were altogether different from the crowd. For instance, there was a great deal of difference in their dress, and in their language, too, for it is said that these men spoke the language of Canaan. They were evidently foreigners and strangers—pilgrims, just as all Christians in this world really are.

But some one may say, I do not notice that there is so very much difference between church-members and the world. Well, my dear friends, I do not suppose you do. There are many things to be considered at this point. In the first place, church-members are not necessarily Christians; yet there are some Christians in this world of ours, and in our churches, too, and we cannot help but know them. You know them—do you not?—the moment you see them. They may not make a very loud noise. They may not be very conspicuous in any sense. Yet you see the distinction which Bunyan expresses in this picture, and which may be characterized by the much-used theological phrase, "In the world, but not of it." These men were in the fair, but they were not of the fair. But how can a man be in the world, and not of it?

I remember, about five years ago, when I landed at Baltimore, it was on a Sunday morning, and, like a good Christian, I went to church on Sunday morning. I had been taught to go to church on Sunday morning. But I find Christians here do not go to church on Sunday morning; they are so tired. But that aside. I came, a foreigner, to this land. True, I looked like an American, and spoke the English language almost as well as an American, and one might think there could be nothing remarkable about such a foreigner as myself on the wharf or in the city of Baltimore. But I remember the first thing I tried to do was to pass a piece of English money, and I brought out a sovereign and gave it to a man, who handed me the change in what was, at that time, to me, most disgusting—a number of dirty bills. My shining, ringing gold, with the head of the queen on it, reduced to that! I felt my nationality rise against it, and demanded something better, but could not get it. The spirit of John Bull was in me strong; I did not like the case at all. Then, I suppose, there was something so peculiar about my dress, though, indeed, I dressed much as I do now. But I got into a street-car, where I knew nothing about the regulations; knew nothing about making change; knew nothing about the way Americans do things; how they get into cars, or how they get out of them. I know there must have been something peculiar about me, for a lady (I believe that is the word to use) burst out laughing when she saw my awkwardness. The driver of the car spoke English, but I could not understand him. I could not understand the preacher whom I heard, though he spoke English just as I claimed to do; I *could not* understand him. The idioms, the allusions, the illustrations, were all perfectly foreign to me. Of the American people I met that day, none of their habits were familiar. I came further West, and sat down at a table; but I did not know when or how to begin, for everything was done so differently from my training. For a long time I could not count your money; I may have been many times duped, I do not know. For a long time I could not "catch the hang" of any of your ways. I made myself conspicuous frequently, no doubt, being a stranger. Everybody seemed staring, everybody laughing, for, you see, I was in this country, but not of it—simply a foreigner and a pilgrim. Absolutely there was not very much difference in the mere appearance, but in education of thought and feeling the difference was radical. I remember getting on the cars at Columbus, where a man remarked to me, "Sir, this republican form of government is the best on earth." "No, sir," said I, promptly; "Queen Victoria is the best monarch, and a monarchy the best form of government." Well, I do not think so now, but if I had had my way then, I think I should have brought over the Prince of Wales, and made him king of the land.

Let me explain further what it is to be in the world, and yet not of it The man who loves righteousness—the righteousness of Jesus Christ—differs from a man who is righteous, only according to the law of this world, by the whole principle of love. The former, when reviled, reviles not again. He abides by the rule, that "What ye would men should do to you, do ye even so to them." Now, that is a height to which the world can never rise. The highest righteousness that the law of this world can attain to is this: exact from every man what he owes you, and whoever injures you, injure him again. Everything above that is Divine. Then there is a difference in the language of the Christian from that of the man of the world, just as there is between the language of a poet and a historian; between the language of a philosopher and of an ignoramus. The ignoramus cannot understand the philosopher. The difference is vast between the Christian and the worldly man. For instance, here is a man who cannot sing—cannot sing a note—and he goes to the piano, strikes the keys, after studying the score before him; strikes one and then another note, mechanically; by calculation he hits each note and chord; there is no music in his playing. But here is another, who, after having glanced at the same score a moment, will at once give natural expression to what is written, and produce the most exquisite music. And just like the difference between the mechanical performer and the true musician, is that between the worldly man and the Christian. The Christian makes music on his way to the skies. He draws his minstrelsy from heaven, which lifts his soul up into a sphere of peace as he passes through a troubled and antagonistic world. There is the difference. The man of this world says, "Let me live for this world alone; let me get all the pleasure I can." The young man goes out in the world, crying, "I will get all the pleasures I can; I will get all the riches I can, and what I get I will keep." But what says the young Christian? "I will live above these pleasures, and improve my mind and heart. Instead of seeking to gather fame and repute, I will seek rather to gather men to Christ. I will live so as to enlighten men;" and whatever he acquires, he acquires with the hope of doing good, and when he gets old, if he has much of this world's goods, it is only that he may use them for his Master, to help bring his Master's love to his fellow-men. The Christian does not live for himself. This is not his country. His citizenship is in heaven, from whence also he looks for the coming of his Lord.

There is one point in this subject to which I want to call your especial attention. These Pilgrims in Vanity Fair did not talk religion—they lived it. Men saw by their lives that they were sincere and worthy to be followed. If I should give this congregation any advice, it would be this: Don't talk religion. It is a very easy thing to do. All you have to do is to buy a devotional book, commit a few phrases to memory, and let them gush out whenever you have an opportunity. But do not talk; just live; do your duty. You, fathers, when you go home tonight, let your children know a father's love. Mothers, bring

—26

your dear ones to a knowledge of the Savior. Live, young man, that God may crown you. Live each so that those who come after you shall you blessed; that when laid in your coffin those who gather around you shall shed tears that you are gone. Live your life. Let your light shine; be always shining and bright and holy, that men may see your good works and glorify your Father in heaven.

Let us see now how these Pilgrims endured persecution. In the first place it is fashionable to say that Christians themselves have committed a vast deal of persecution. Scientists are continually throwing it in our teeth that Calvin burnt Servetus at the stake. Poor old Calvin—poor old Servitus. That the church did also stop a scientist from proclaiming that the earth rolled round the sun, instead of the sun rolling round the earth, is too true. The Church did really persecute that poor man. Poor man—poorer Church! But is that all that the Church has done? How strange it is! The Church has persecuted scientists—I wonder that there is one left. Wonderfully strange, is it not? We have these two remarkable instances against us, and we need not snatch the weapons and render railing for railing, and abuse for abuse. But may I say, that having read somewhat extensively of scientific literature myself, I find this prevalent spirit throughout it, that though Christians nowadays may not be particularly wicked, yet they are all *fools*. Well, we can bear it. You must not suppose that I have anything against science. Christians have persecuted scientists, they say, and they have had hard work to reach their present place in the face of the opposition of the Christian Church. That I do not believe. There are more scientists in the Christian Church and in the Christian world to-day than anywhere else on the globe. And where there is no Bible truth, there you will find no science. Well, look at these Christians under persecution. It is the tendency of human nature always to persecute, and the lower will always persecute the higher; ignorance will persecute learning; weakness will always pick at strength; light cannot agree with darkness; oil will not mix with water; the Spirit of Christ cannot commingle with the world; God and the world are antagonistic. And here is an argument against a state Church. In some parts of christendom there are state Churches, and I give it as my conviction that they are a curse. Men are talking about a state Church for America. When that day comes it will be a dark day for this land. The true Church and this world are antagonistic; the churches have been so mixing with the world that they have brought to themselves much of the spirit of the world; and often instead of houses of God being built for sinful men to worship in, we see pretentious edifices erected for the religious comfort and convenience of those who are altogether superior to the ordinary race of men. This is all wrong. So the flesh lusteth against the spirit, and the spirit against the flesh, and the men of the flesh will always, as they have done, persecute the men of the spirit. There is nothing that this world, taking the word in its fleshly sense, hates as it does the spirit of our Lord Jesus Christ. So these men suffered persecution. First of all they put the Pilgrims in a cage. I have never seen a fair without some men taken to the cage for drunkenness. The cage is simply a place of confinement where the culprit's feet are made fast in the stocks, and he is thus exposed to public ridicule and public torment, for sometimes twenty-four hours. In such a position they can neither stand nor lie down. So these Pilgrims were put in the cage because they condemned the life of Vanity Fair.

Faithful was tried for opposing the laws of this world, and for open and avowed hostility to the great fair. The accommodating jury brought him in guilty and worthy of death, and then the persecutors brought him forth, all the while under forms of law, abused him, and at last burned him to ashes at the stake. And thus came Faithful to his end.

Here we see how a good man dies, and we see an illustration too, of the way the good have been persecuted. The reader of history will see too how the blood of the martyrs became the seed of the Church, and how over against the spirit of persecution rose higher and higher the spirit of devotion.

Lecture XIV.

My brethren, if we want to see what the death of a Christian is, we must look here. Study the picture. We see the life fast ebbing away; the strength failing; the last struggle, the last groan; the eye is fixed, the spirit gone—and that we call death. But lift the veil. The Christian has died, and what has become him? He has gone into God's presence—into the Celestial City; he has gone into a more perfect condition; gone from the sight of men into the presence of his Lord. Heaven is not so far away; it is only just across the river, that is all. Only a little higher up, to our Father's house. It is not millions and millions of miles away, but here all around us, influencing us, its inhabitants ministering to us and shaping the means of our salvation. Faithful was taken the nearest way. He had finished his course; he had fought the good fight; he had passed through the pangs of martyrdom, and he proved faithful unto death. There was the glorious dying of a Christian.

But what must dying be to that man who has not proved faithful to his Christian profession? What will it be to him who fails in the hour of temptation—who is a good man until he gets into Vanity Fair, and then turns aside to buy the gilded baubles of its vain merchandise, and, having persuaded himself that he could purchase an enduring monument with this world's gold, at last on his death-bed finds himself a beggar? What must death be to the man who has once tasted of his Lord's love, and sold that love for thirty pieces of silver, as the traitorous Judas did? Ah, when his last hour comes, the feeling of that deed, like the murder of his own soul, will rise to drown him in despair.

But the faithful Christian, having passed through all the storms of life and resisted the lures of Vanity Fair, swifter than the wind, than light, than thought, is caught up instantly to meet his Lord, where his Lord has gone to prepare the way.

My friends, let us be faithful unto death. It is not he who lives a good life for a little while, but he that endureth to the end that shall be saved. Remember we are not yet out of Vanity Fair. Bear in mind the answer of these Pilgrims, "We buy the truth; we sell it not." Buy the truth about yourselves; buy the truth about the world; buy the truth about God and about Christ; buy the truth about hell and about heaven; buy the truth about righteousness and a good life; buy the truth, accept no gilt; buy the truth, and if an evil life leads to hell, as you dread ruin, flee from that hell. Take the path to heaven, and take the first step to-night; repent of your sins, believe on the Lord Jesus Christ, and thou shalt be saved. Get the Spirit of your Master, who went about doing good. Love God and love your fellow-men, and be faithful to this love even unto death.

LECTURE XV.

THE HILL LUCRE.

[SYNOPSIS OF CHAPTER.—Christian set out alone from Vanity Fair. His influence and that of Faithful had been so powerful that many were inclined to go with him. One, named Hopeful, was true to his desires, and became Christian's companion. They had not gone far before they fell in with Mr. By-ends, of the town of Fairspeech, and, shortly afterwards, with Mr. Hold-the-world, Mr. Save-all, and Mr. Money-love. As these men made gold their god, and were willing to go to the Celestial City "in silver slippers" only, the companionship soon ended. The Pilgrims were tempted out of the way by one Demas, who owned a silver-mine in the hill Lucre. By him they were invited to turn aside, and dig for treasure. They resisted; but when By-ends and his friends came up, they greedily accepted. As the mine was dangerous, and had previously destroyed many, they were lost, and by the Dreamer seen no more. Christian and Hopeful then came to a pillar somewhat in the form of a woman, and read on her forehead the solemn words, "Remember Lot's wife."]

THE central idea of this Lecture finds its expression in the hill Lucre, in which was a silver-mine, to which the Christians were tempted to turn, that they might find treasure. All that precedes that scene belongs to it, as well as all that follows it; and it will be a very interesting study, I think, to see the kind of men who resisted the temptation, and the quality of those who succumbed to it. We shall also be able to see, possibly, the worldly result of such a temptation as that which Demas held out to the Pilgrims. There is something else in the Lecture, notwithstanding. We have here the introduction of a new character, called by our Author, Hopeful. Faithful has ended his life by martyrdom in Vanity Fair, and has taken the short road to the Celestial City. This Hopeful is a Pilgrim, who has come from Vanity Fair. Here is one thing that we must pay particular attention to: he was instructed; in fact, he was persuaded to go on a pilgrimage by the manner of life and spirit of the men whom he saw in Vanity Fair. This is something that we may talk about for a moment.

Last Sunday night I gave you this advice: do not talk religion. If you have any, let it be felt; if you have any, it will take care of itself. You know, when the sun shines in spring, it produces all manner of flowers. It clothes all nature with beauty. It speaks with no voice, and makes no sound; but the light of the sun, with all that is genial and blessed in it, moves in silence, and earth feels it and responds. So let it be with our religion. Certainly that is the religion of Christ when He says, "Let thy light so shine that men may see thy good works, and glorify thy Father which is in heaven." Just live the life, and let the influence of its light emanate from you.

Then we are taught also the influence of a good man's death; not merely of a good man's life, but of his death. Faithful perished in Vanity Fair, and Hopeful arose to be the companion of our original Pilgrim. He tells Christian that there are many other men of Vanity Fair of a like mind with himself, persuaded by the death of Faithful to go on a pilgrimage. We see the illustration of this effect nearly every day of our lives. The death of one is the life of many. All the life we know anything about in this world of ours is based upon death. Things have to die in order to keep the living alive. If we go to history, it has passed into an axiom now (a proverb which no one will gainsay, I suppose), that "the blood of the martyrs was the seed of the Church." And now, frequently, the good pastor has to die before the congregation is converted. The mother dies, and then the children determine to follow her to heaven. The father dies, and then his sons and daughters make the same resolution. The Sunday-school teacher dies, and then the scholars determine to follow him to the higher and better world. I know it was so in my own case, and I think it is true in life generally, that men think seriously of religion when a good man dies; and so the death of one, in that way, becomes the life of many.

But Bunyan may mean still another thing. He may intend to show the influence, at different times and at different points in the Christian's journey, of different Christian graces. Faithful, for instance, exhibited the grace of faith, fortitude, obedience, firmness. He was faithful unto death against all the bitterness of opposition. Now we have Hopeful, in whom, probably, the presence of faith was not quite so prominent as in his stronger companion, but in whom the beautiful gift of hope bloomed into life immortal. And here we have something that is perfectly true to life and character. We find a Christian at one period of his life exhibiting a particular grace—perhaps that of patience; at another time, he may show forth the virtue of hope; and, under other circumstances, still a different grace, until, one after another, the whole round of graces, succeeding to view, culminate in him, and he stands forth at last like his Master, an embodiment of love. Just as the pure light contains all color, while itself has none, so a Christian life contains all the graces, combined so equally that, like light, it is not valued till lost. This accords with Scripture: "He giveth grace for grace; He giveth grace according to our need." Sometimes we need that of fortitude, and sometimes that of hope; sometimes we need one, and sometimes another. It depends upon the condition of our pilgrimage as to the kind of grace the Christian will exhibit to the world.

Now to return to what we said before about the influence of Christian life. Remember that the only Bible the worldly man reads is the Christian man. Generally the only Bible the church-member reads is the pastor of his church; and generally the only Bible a worldly man reads is a Christian life. This is as it should be. "Ye are our epistles (Paul might have said, 'Ye are our Bibles'), read and known of all men." Our Christian example may do our Master's cause harm, or help on His blessed kingdom.

These Pilgrims journeyed together in a very happy condition, meeting with others upon the road, and with incidents of which we need not speak, until they came to the blessed plain called the Plain of Ease.

As travelers in a desert, who, after having toiled under a scorching sun all day, come at eventide to an oasis or well of water, shaded by palm-trees, and there find refreshment and take their ease, so Christians, now and then in their experience, come to particular spots that seem perfectly easy and perfectly delightful. They, too, find just such sweet places of rest. They meet with much trouble; much that goes against the flesh, and are weary and thirsty walking over paths scorched and dry, till sometimes they wonder whether, after all, it is worth the while to lead a Christian life, instead of going aside after carnal things, and obeying the maxims of the world; and just then they come upon some little blessed spot like this, in which they tempt themselves to turn from the way and take their ease. I say, there are such seasons in the Christian's life, as every Christian will testify. And there is danger in these seasons.

We are apt to suppose, too often, that the danger in Christian life arises from persecution and trial; but those periods are not nearly so dangerous—because they are not nearly so deceptive—as these periods of delusive peace, by Bunyan so fitly described as the "delicate plain called Ease." When there is a calm upon the sea, there is much more danger to the ship than when there is a storm. The ship can outride the storm, but the question is, can she outlive the calm? When there is a great calm in business; when a man and his clerks have to fold their arms and sit down all day long, waiting for a customer, and, when the customer comes, use all their arts not to let him go—I tell you, there is a great deal of danger in that condition. Bankruptcy seems to be the end of that. But when all are exceedingly busy—all have something to do—the danger is not so threatening as in a time of ease.

There is peculiar danger, then, in these restful seasons of Christian life. Let us now consider how well-timed were the temptations that assailed these Pilgrims at this part of their journey. Just as they began to feel happy in the sense of rest—in that blissful frame of mind—they came to a hill called Lucre. A hill, you will notice, described as a little out of the way—a point I wish you to be particular in observing. Just a little out of the way, Bunyan says, there was a silver-mine, and Demas was standing just a little out of the way, inviting them to approach this silver-mine, and dig for treasure. How well-timed was all this! They had tasted the delights of ease, and were now tempted to turn aside, only just a little out of the way, and easily make themselves rich.

Satan is never behindhand. When our Lord was hungry, it was then the tempter bade him command the stones to be made bread; and when the woman saw the fruit was of a kind to be desired to make one wise, it was then the serpent insinuated that the day she ate thereof she should not die; and when God had struck Job till nothing was left but his wife and his sores, it was then the wife said to him, "Curse God and die;" when, if ever a man could have cursed, it was then. The temptation came so well-timed that I wonder the good man had power to resist it. Just mind this, then, if you please, that temptation to sin will assail you at the very moment of your greatest liability to yield. It is when you are hungry that you will be tempted to make bread in an unlawful way; when you want to be wise, some snare will waylay you; and when you feel yourself stripped of all you hold most dear, Satan will urge you to deny God.

The temptation of Demas amounts to this: to go a little out of the way of righteousness for silver—to sacrifice righteousness for money. That is putting it in plain language; and is just what Bunyan meant. It is an old temptation, but it is also a new one. It is as old as the time when man first weighed his piece of silver, and it is with us fresh and new to day. Men have been tempted, and have succumbed; and men are still tempted, and still succumb to the temptation of Demas—to go a little out of the way of righteousness, and sacrifice conscience and right for riches. Do you ask for examples? Go into politics—not that I believe there is more corruption in political life than in any other, but I go there because when instances of the sort I refer to occur, they acquire public notoriety, and you are all more or less acquainted with them. In the history of this, and every other country, there have been men who professed godliness while they sold their country to a party; men, too, have been of this sort who have sold their country to a corporation; there have been men who, after taking upon themselves the duty of protecting their country, sold it for a few pieces of silver, into the hands of its enemies: as Judas sold his Lord, in the hope of being made rich ; so they have sold their trust for the love of filthy lucre.

Go again into business life, and there you will find much of what I refer to; not more there than anywhere else, but it exists, and this temptation is very great there. I go into a number of houses in the course of my family visitations—not that I am a great family visitor, I am not—but I do go into houses sometimes, and I hear people say, "You know, Mr. N., it does not do to send children to the store; you had better go yourself, for they will put anything into the hands of a child, and don't serve children as they do adults." Now, is it right to give a child ten cents' worth less than to a man or woman ? When a man does that, it is not merely ten cents' worth of crime he is committing, but he is incurring the weight of the whole moral law. It is the unrighteousness in the deed that tells—and that is, a man has gone a little out of the way of righteousness for silver. The silver may be only ten cents' worth, yet for that the man has robbed himself of character and the sense of a good conscience, by taking advantage of a little child.

There is another way in which the thing is done ; one business-man will give you to understand that it is not perfectly safe to trade with another business-man. While he probably will not say a single word, he will arch his eyebrows, and shut his mouth, and shrug his shoulders; you know a man can be slandered by an arched eyebrow just as he can by the tongue. He don't speak openly, but he gives the impression that you had better be careful of that man, for he will overreach you if he possibly can. Then some men do tell lies in business. It has passed into a proverb that *business is business;* and men say, everything is fair in war, in love, and in business. I wish I could alter that proverb, and say, business is righteousness. Business should be righteousness, and if a religious man, a member of the church, professor of godliness, does these things, that man is then just what Mr. By-ends describes himself—making a stalking-horse of religion to get through the world with. Men make a cloak of religion, and think to cover their acts, and conscience dies; but God will judge them for the deeds done in the body.

But then this disposition is not confined to business; it goes into the pulpit—it does, really. Bunyan tells us of Mr. Two-tongues, who, in order to please his people, says one thing and lives another. Then, again, the whole argument of Mr. By-ends, and Mr. Money-love, and Mr. Hold-the-world, amounts to this: That a man who is a preacher may alter his principles in order to please the people, if they require it. Some pressure is made upon the preacher, and he is expected to keep back a truth which his people may not very well like, under the threat that he cannot otherwise get a living among them. On the other hand, there are preachers who claim that they have outgrown the churches to which they minister, and that they can no longer, consistently with their consciences and advanced thought, preach the form of theology upon which those churches are based; yet because they get a good salary will still stand there, a living pulpit-lie—nothing more or less. Out upon such! It is wickedness in high places; and if men don't despise such false prophets, they ought to do so. A just God will judge them. If a man has outgrown his church, let him get out of it; let him put on a coat that will fit him, and no longer stalk about in a borrowed garb, not his own.

We want more honesty; we want more men like John Bunyan; we may not agree with all he has said or done, but we must admire the honesty of the man. I cannot understand how a man can stand up, for instance, in a Methodist pulpit to preach Universalism, instead of getting out of it into a Universalist pulpit. I cannot understand how a man can profess Trinitarianism, and yet stand in a Unitarian church and deny it. The world is wide; God will take care of His truth, and He will take care of an honest man, anywhere.

Well, we must hasten on. Let us now look at the application of this lesson to the general immorality of the world. Look, for instance, at immoral literature; there is money in it—yes, there is money in immoral literature. I remember going into a large stationery store—not in this city, I am happy to say—and I found on a table there a large collection of immoral books. I saw a young man come into that store and buy one of those books—such as I pray God you young men and women may never see or know. I said to the clerk, "Do you sell that sort of literature?" "Yes," said he—"Anything you want?" "Oh! no, I thank you, I am not here to buy, I merely ask for information. Is the proprietor in?" "He will be soon." "Is he a member of a church?" "Oh! yes, sir, he is a member of a church, and superintendent of the Sunday-school." "Indeed! And sells that kind of literature?" "Yes, sir." "Why?" "There is more profit on that sort of book than on anything we sell, sir. Buckle's "Civilization," Gibbons' "Decline and Fall," "Shakspeare?"—Well, sir, we sell twenty dollars' worth of that reading where we sell five of the standard sort." "And a superintendent of a Sunday-school is selling that sort of stuff?" "Oh! yes." Now is not that shameful? Yet if I have the right of it, I am told that one of the most immoral manufacturers of this country is sustained by professing Christians. I am told that a firm of professing Christians are employed in the manufacture of burglar's tools. I say, is not all this shameful? It is making a stalking-horse of religion to get through the world on. That, as Bunyan describes it, is rowing one way, and looking another.

Again, we hear of the Blue Ribbon movement against the great liquor interest, and they give us figures upon figures to show the crime and immorality it creates. There is much of it. The subject is discussed in all manner of forms and shapes, as respects the saloon-keeper, the brewer, and the distiller. Do you think the saloon-keeper really means to make drunkards? Do you think he designs to increase the tide of vice in this or any other city? Why, there is not one who has such an idea in his head. Well, if you go back to the brewer, does he intend to increase the immorality of the country? No. Go the distiller— he thinks of nothing of the kind. Go to the Christian merchant who deals in the corn which he knows is going to be employed in this way—has he any intention of increasing the prevailing immorality? Oh, no; certainly not. Where, then, is the secret of the evil that is done? Ah, the good old Book tells us: "The love of money is the root of all evil." The saloon-keeper goes into the business because there is money in it; the brewer goes into it because there is money in it; and the corn-dealer goes into it because there is money in it. I do not know so much of this country, but I know something of the country from which I came, and I know that there, some of the principal brewers are prominent members of Christian churches. I know something of their zeal in support of church work in the city of London. I know some of them have written pious and devotional books, and are personally considered most estimable men; at the same time, I know their love of money is such that they love it more than they love men. But we must leave them to God; we cannot judge them. We must not attempt to do it; to a man's own Master must he stand or fall. We must bespeak charity for all men; only I do say this, that the tendency there manifest is clearly this, to go a little out of the way of righteousness for the sake of the silver that may be found in the hill called Lucre.

I said I did not know so much about this country, yet since I have been here, I have learned a little that I did not know before. When I first arrived, comparing this country, in the light of this chapter which we are now considering, with the land where it was written, I thought there could be no such tendency to make religion a stalking-horse here as I had seen there. There, if you were to go into the churches on a Sabbath, you would see many a man who went to church simply to get customers; but I could not think any one would do it here.

Yet I learned that, in the first city where I was a pastor, a man came to my church who had just come to the place to begin business; and, after he had been there two weeks, a gentleman called upon him, and said he, "Look here; I want to say to you that if you want to succeed in business in this town, you had better join such-and-such a church." I remember in the last place where I preached, a gentleman, coming to the village to establish a dry-goods business, also came to our church, and seeing that we had already two dry-goods men in the congregation, went off till he found one where they had none, and there he afterwards attended. I have heard since I have been in this city that a gentleman—a dentist—came to this church a short time, and went away again; and when asked the reason of his change, said, "They have too many teeth there." I did not suppose men would do it. I did not think that in this country, where men are so much more independent, and where society is not burdened with so many old institutions, such events could occur. But after all, human nature is much the same everywhere, and if men can get money by religion, they are apt to think they may as well get it that way as any other. Many have sold their Lord, many have parted with a good conscience, for the sake of a good purse.

Let us look a moment at the person of a man who succumbed to the temptation—By-ends. He said, if you remember, that he was for religion in good weather; he did not believe in going against wind and tide. He was not a man of principles, but a man of fancies; a man who was most zealous of religion if only she went in silver slippers (you see the figure)—if there was only something to be got by it—most zealous for religion when she went in silver slippers. There are some men in the world who have no principle. It is said that the highest form of animal life is that which results in the vertebrate; that is, backbone. A good subject to think about, particularly in these days.

Those animals that have not backbone are like mere animated pieces of mush; and there are some men who have not yet risen to the condition of backbone, and who are nothing but animated mush. Do anything you like with them, shape them after any fancy, they will do whatever pays the best, and risk their very soul for filthy lucre. They persuade themselves that it is wisdom, and they reason that they have the Bible on their side. These men would neither die for themselves, nor for other persons; nor would they live to save their souls, or to save anything for their fellow-men. They make the centre of life themselves; they move the earth to contribute to themselves, and they prostitute the treasures of heaven to same purpose. They make themselves rich in things temporal, while they are starving in things eternal.

Well, these men came up in view of Demas, who invited them to a hill called Lucre. It was an exceedingly dangerous place, as Bunyan describes it; and of those who yielded to the temptation and obeyed the invitation, he says they were never seen any more. What became of them, we do not know. Not seeing them any more, afforded Bunyan an opportunity to impress the fact upon the minds of the survivors, and so he brings them to a view of something exceedingly startling, which was a statue, apparently in the form of a woman; and they lifted their eyes to it and saw some hieroglyphics upon it, which they could not at first decipher, but finally read upon the woman's salted brow the words, "Remember Lot's wife." This, you know, is the only text from the Old Testament taken by our Lord, who bade His disciples in all time to remember Lot's wife.

Let us try and recall her for a moment. She was a woman who lived in Sodom, in the full enjoyment of all its pleasures. Sodom was threatened with destruction, she was warned by an angel to flee from the city, and with her husband at her side she set out on a flight for safety; but when she was nearly across the plain, near the little city of Zoar, she turned around to look back towards the spot where her treasures and pleasures were—and the pitiless hell pelted her to death, and crusted her with its salted fire. Where she turned to look back there she stood, dead, a monument for all time to all those who look back from a spiritual life to a carnal one.

I have read in some Commentator that Josephus says this pillar still remains; while from other works I learn that there is nothing standing there resembling it but the stones into which the story has been read. And some do say that one of them was the pillar into which Lot's wife was changed. Be that as it may, the monument may not stand on the shore of the Dead sea, but it stands where it can never crumble away—in God's word—a great lesson in history, written for our learning, in the Eternal Word of God. God has petrified the woman who looked back from a flight to save her soul.

In crossing the ocean, as you draw near the shore you will find huge rocks looming from the sea, on which stand light-houses. What does that mean? It means that some time or other a party of human beings, on a voyage of profit or pleasure, struck upon the rocks in the darkness, and went down to death; and to save others from a similar fate, at each of those places where such a catastrophe has occurred, a light-house has been built to mark the danger. Those light-houses are the true monuments of those who have perished, and when through the awful night of storm a gleam is caught from those beacons, the mariner knows he is in a region of peril, and in haste turns his ship in another direction, to save himself and his charge. So it is with the Christian. He knows from the statue in the Word of God, with the awful inscription upon it, the fate of one who looked back when she was in the act of saving her life, and where she stood to look back, there she died. He heeds the lesson of our Lord, and "remembers Lot's wife."

Gold is a good thing. Riches are good. It is our duty to get as much as we possibly can—to be as rich as we can in this world, because it is better for a good man to have gold than for a bad one. But the evil is in going out of the way of righteousness to get it; the evil is in doing injury to another to get it; sacrificing our conscience in the strife for it; bankrupting our souls for its sake. There is the danger. And after all, suppose we have accumulated all we can, until we fancy we have enough to satisfy, and we say to our soul: "Soul, thou hast many goods, I will pull down these barns and I will build greater, for I have not wherewithal to bestow my goods. Soul, take thine ease; eat, drink, and be merry." Yet, at last, within us will arise a voice, pealing from the inmost depths—Thou fool! thou fool; a voice at which the dead will shudder in their hollow sepulchres; the dying with their last breath will echo it; the life just beginning to live will whisper it; all nature will thunder it, reverberating throughout earth's remotest hills and caverns; the still, small voice will arise in might, and gathering strength like a whisper in a microphone, burst like the shriek of a giant: Thou fool! this night thy soul shall be required of thee—thy soul! and then whose will be the things with which thou hast promised to entertain that soul forever?

Men are kept out of heaven, not so much by their sins, as by their loving earth. Some men have to be converted twenty or forty times before they are decent. Other men have to become bankrupt before they are Christians; have their homes broken up, their children, wife, and friends stolen away and laid in the grave, before they come to think seriously of that world where there is no death, and where there is no sorrow.

The whole thing comes to this: Will you have a good conscience, or not? Keep a good conscience; it is the voice of God. Do not smother it; let it speak. It is the personal revelation of the Almighty to you. It is the whisper of heaven to guide your life. Do not sell conscience! it is the spirit of your Saviour; the Spirit of your Lord within you. Every time it warns you, hearken to its wisdom, for it may save your soul. "Remember Lot's wife." While in the very act of being saved, she looked back to sinful Sodom; her heart went after her perishing treasures; and she perished because she loved them, and and not the things that are substantial and spiritual, eternal and abiding.

LECTURE XVI.

DOUBTING CASTLE AND GIANT DESPAIR.

[SYNOPSIS OF CHAPTER.—Their path lay alongside a beautiful river. Here the Pilgrims walked with great delight. From it they wandered into By-path Meadow. It appeared to run parallel with their way, but, as they afterwards sorrowfully discovered, it diverged slightly at every step, and so before they were aware, they had gone far astray. Night came on; in the darkness they attempted to retrace their steps, but failed. Worn and weary, they lay down to rest. In the morning Giant Despair saw them asleep in his grounds. He, therefore, made them his prisoners, and cast them into the dungeon of Doubting Castle, where they were kept a week without light or food. The giant frequently beat them, and often urged them to make an end of themselves. At the end of the week they began to pray, and then Christian remembered that he had a key in his bosom which would unlock any of the doors in Doubting Castle. They applied it to the door of the dungeon; it opened, and then to the outer doors and gates of the prison. They all flew open, and so they made their escape.]

BUNYAN now brings his Pilgrims through a new experience; the experience of doubt.

The just live by faith. We live a life of faith upon the Son of God. We do not seek things that are seen, but things that are not seen. We embrace the promises of God, the pleasures and blessings of the life of a Christian, by the exercise of faith. This being the case, doubt is frequently exceedingly lively, and always extremely liable. The state of faith always supposes the opposite state of doubt, and what we find to-day, or might infer from known facts, is a marked truth in Christian history. Throughout the history of the Christian Church, there have been men who doubted the doctrines which were commonly received among us, and have expressed their doubts to the world.

We are all apt to suppose that the things which take place to-day, if bad, are worse than any that ever before occurred; if they are exceedingly good, and we are pleased with them, we think nothing so worthy has ever appeared before. There are a great many Christian men and women who, seeing the prevalence of scepticism to-day, do say that it is a worse form of doubt than has ever before existed on the earth. Well, I do not believe them; I have an honest doubt about that. I believe that the questioning that exists in the world to-day is more honest, more intellectual, and of a much better kind in its fibre and in its intention, than any kind of doubt that the world has ever before known. I do not believe that the things of to-day are worse than they have ever been; I think they are better. Good men are better than they used to be, and bad men are better than they were. The world is progressing, and men are better and have truer conceptions of good.

Nevertheless, we have a more imposing form of scepticism to-day. Doubt is more popular than it was, and there seems to be a kind of aristocracy of doubt—if I may use such a term—which gives it a pretense of a little more than really belongs to it. We begin to gauge a man's brain by his capacity for doubting; and it is looked upon as hardly an evidence of sanity or strength of intellectual fibre to believe the ordinary, simple facts of Christ's life, or the doctrines of religion.

The most extraordinary thing in the world—and, I think, the most sublimely ridiculous—is a doubter's smile. After he has been talking with you, and discovers that he cannot convince you that what he thinks is right, the sublime manner in which he will smile upon you, the extreme pity with which he will regard you (as if he felt that he ought to be a missionary to bring you into larger sympathy with the views of more advanced thinkers)—I may say it would be quite sublime, if it were not sometimes a little too ridiculous.

There are three kinds of doubt, it appears to me, in the world to-day.

There is, first, Philosophical doubt pertaining to the doctrines of religion. There are a number of men—and some of them of the very finest intellects in the world—who belong to this class of doubters. They are sceptical concerning the fundamentals of all religon. They do not take the Christian religion into court any more than any other, but arraign them all. Hence, they call in question the very being of God. Then they will doubt the immortality of the soul, and with that, also, the future of rewards and punishments. Not merely do they doubt, but some also deny; and they give reasons for their doubts and for their denials. We have a great deal of this form of doubt abroad, and it is formidable in proportion to its honesty.

Then we have Rationalistic doubt. The difference between the Rationalist and the Orthodox thinker is this: Both agree, I think, in receiving the Bible as the Word of God, but the Orthodox will say every word written therein is the word of God. The Rationalist says, on the other hand, these writings of man contain the word of God, and he makes it his business to go through the Word, separating the wheat from the chaff, and what he calls the word of God from the word of man—the mind of God, if you will, from the mind of man. Then he will take all the good that there may be in other religions, and bring it together into a systematized form of theology, conforming all to his faith; and whatever there may be in the Christian religion that does not suit his reason, he will cast aside as being unwarranted to his faith. It is simply the exercise—I think, frequently the undue exercise—of reason, sometimes at the expense of faith. Still, we have it in the world, and I think it is doing the Church of God very much good service. It has its faults, while at the same time it is doing a vast amount of good. We want a great deal of Rationalism; we want to be rational in our faith and religion, too; we want to commend it to every man's conscience in the sight of God.

Then there is the Spiritual form of doubt, but not nearly so prevalent now-a-days as it used to be. This kind of doubt seems to be indigenous to the Calvinistic theology, and that type of religious life which makes sensation, or, if you like, spiritual feeling, the grand fact of religion. Persons who are Calvinistic in their creed, and persons who rely upon their creed —let their feelings be excitable or pacific—are very apt to drop into this form; and when they put it into words it takes this shape, "Am I elect or reprobate? Was I ever converted? Have I not been a hypocrite all these years? Shall I ever reach my journey's end? Shall I be received into heaven?" I often find these questions among elderly people; good old men and women who have been fighting the Lord's battles year after year, and are just ready to lay off their armor and put on their crown, but because they have been brought up in a stern theology, they question their own salvation. To tell the truth, there is not a great liability to this kind of doubt throughout the world at the present time. We are too apt to take it for granted that, if any one be saved, we are of the saved ones, we are the elect. Theology has shifted its battle-ground from where it used to be a few years since, and this spirit of doubt has, therefore, no extensive range. I wish men were more spiritually-minded; I wish I were myself. Still, we must take things as they are.

Let us consider a little the effect of doubt upon the mind. Taking the chapter I have read as our text, I think I may say, in the first place, that religious lack of belief, whether philosophical, rationalistic, or spiritual, is a result, and sometimes a form, of idleness. The Christian life, as laid down by the Lord Jesus Christ, should be a useful life. A man should go about doing good; relieving the necessities of men; showing by his works that he is a child of the Father who is in heaven. The apostles insisted that we should show our faith by our works. And let me say this, the ideal Christian life is one of usefulness, and the Christian becomes useful only as he believes in the Lord Jesus Christ. Now, I know a great many say they believe on the Lord Jesus Christ, and yet are not useful. They come to church, but do not work for it, and are of no use to the world; they do not go about doing good. Oh! but, they say, if any come to us we always relieve them. And yet, that is not going about doing good. Go, and give medicine to the sick, bread to the hungry, a cup of cold water, in the name of your Master; go, and clothe the naked, visit those in prisons, and teach the ignorant; go, and do that. That is the Christian life, and no man is living a Christian life who does not do that. He cannot do it by proxy, or leave others to do it for him; but does it himself, as the Lord has commanded, and no man is Christ's disciple who does not do His bidding. I do not care whether he is a member of the church or not; I do not care whether "elect" or not; I do not care whether he thinks his name is formally written in heaven as he has signed it on the church-roll—no man is a Christian who does not follow his Lord in doing good. The ideal life, then, is one of usefulness; but doubt makes us useless. If a man does not believe in what he does, or in what he is required to do, he cannot do it. It is not the men of doubt, but the men of broad, deep faith, who are doing good in this world.

There came a time in the progress of the world when it was necessary to provide a relief for the over-populated regions of Europe—a relief needed then, and needed centuries afterwards; and there was a man who watched the moon and the stars—a man of intellectual power and far-reaching thought, who came forth with the declaration that there was another world waiting to be discovered, all ready for the people who had become much too numerous for their old abode, and he asked that he might be sent thither that he might find it. But his country doubted, and the world doubted. There was a gathering of the savans of the world, who looked upon his plans, and pronounced them chimerical—they doubted. By and by, however, the faith of the man triumphed; for it is through faith that we triumph in all things worthy; and after awhile he was permitted to set sail, and in due course of time discovered this new world of ours. It was that man of all the world who had faith, and not the millions left behind, the doubters, that discovered America.

It is said now that men have lost confidence; times are so hard and money so tight; but I notice as I go about that it is not the men who have lost confidence who are keeping up this city and county and state and country, but it is the men who believe in man; it is those who exercise commercial faith that keep things going, though they go never so slowly. And it is not the man of doubt but the man of faith who keeps things moving, morally as well as physically.

Again, doubt is a state of misery. Bunyan has described it, and he brings his illustration from his own experience. That good man, John Bunyan, the orthodox Calvinist, rigid, but great enlightener of the world, the man at whose feet the wisest have sat, receiving from his hand the water of life—that man had doubts. Is it sinful to doubt? Certainly not; so doubt is honest it is not sinful; but doubt may be wicked, just as coming to church may be wicked, or praying may be wicked. It all depends upon the man, his motives and circumstances. But this man Bunyan was tossed about by his doubts, and cast into the deepest possible misery. You can read the story of it in his "Sinner Saved" and in his "Holy War." There were various kinds of doubt injected into his soul which made him miserable and wretched.

Now why should a state of doubt produce misery? I assume the fact, first, that it does, without attempting to prove it. And now why should a state of uncertainty produce misery? I hold, though of course I may be mistaken, that man has certain innate religious ideas—intuitions they are called by some—and one of these intuitions is the soul's instinct of a future life; and another truth which I hold as written on every man's being, is the moral law. Every man knows just how every other man should act to him, whether he himself acts rightly toward that other man or not. Every man knows what right is. This I call the first revelation God has given to man, and God has knitted that revelation into every man's being; it is in his bones, in his blood, in his brain, in his soul—it is all over him, and you cannot find a man anywhere, until he has been spoiled by civilization, who does not intuitively believe in a God. I do not say he will have correct ideas about God, but he will believe in the existence of a being outside of himself, on whom he depends and to whom he is amenable. He believes in the immortality of his soul—always desires another life. Again, he believes in his responsibility for his conduct, and in future rewards and punishments resulting.

Then there is another thing that the natural man everywhere believes in—he believes in a Christ. Every man has in his soul an ideal Christ; every man expects a Christ, a Savior, some one to deliver him; and those who reject Jesus of Nazareth and the Christ in whom we believe, still expect one. Read the history of Spiritualism, say during three or four years past. Now and then you will find there expressed the prophecy that some one is about to be born who is going to deliver this world out of all its wretchedness, and place it in a state of peace and happiness. Read Ecclesiastical history, and you will find that in every century some one has come forward to pronounce a prophecy that Christ would appear. All are looking for a Savior. And not only do men have an ideal Christ, but they all expect a Savior who will come to help and bless them, individually.

Now, then, if such ideas as these be native to man's belief, if you should destroy such innate ideas, you would leave the man in a state of incompleteness and wretchedness—he would no longer be himself. You may deny the fact that there is a God, and say there is nothing but the desire for one. You may deny the immortality of the soul, but will still wish that your soul was immortal. You may deny that God sent His Son, and that he appeared in human flesh for man's salvation; still man will pray that a Savior may come, and long for a Christ to deliver him from the thralldom of his sins. You may deny the future of rewards and punishments, and still a man's inmost soul will feel that there is a ruling principle of justice in this universe, in which he must believe. You may deny it all, and what have you done for man? So far as he believes you he must be unhappy. It is said that insane persons never weep, they feel great misery, but can never shed a tear, the natural relief for misery. So with those who, born with all these cravings after God and immortality and the desire for righteousness intuitive in the soul, if they become deprived of the natural bent to which their own instincts would lead them. A state of doubt, then, is a state of misery; and it cannot be otherwise.

So miserable were these Pilgrims here that they actually contemplated suicide. And, if you remember, Giant Despair himself advised them to lay violent hands upon themselves, either by pistol, poison, or the rope. However, in this case, the Giant failed to persuade his victims.

I do not know whether Bunyan himself knew it, but it appears he did. It is, however, a fact, for the proof of which I refer you to the works of leading Atheists, and if chapter and verse be required by any one, I will be happy to furnish them. Most of them defend, and many of them advocate suicide. This is but a natural result of despair. When a man doubts the great facts of life, what is there to live for? Doubt God, and what is there to live for? Say there is no eternity, and what is time worth? Life is not worth the living if there be no God, and if there be no immortality. And so very naturally these men advocate suicide. If I believed as they do, I think I should take my life in my hand and go out from my despair into the blackness of darkness forever; for life is a mockery if there be no future, and if there be no God for to love us, through all our mistakes.

Let me now recall to you the circumstances which led them into this condition of doubt and despair. You notice the chapter commences with a delightful description of a river, and the Pilgrims walking in the path by its side. For my part I really don't know anything more pleasing than to walk by the the side of an English stream; all graceful flowers are growing there, and luxuriant fruits hanging above your head. I say I know nothing more delightful. As I have read this chapter my thought has gone home again to the scenes of my boyhood, and the reminiscence has been exceedingly grateful. There are sweet experiences, when rightly used, in the life of every Christian; delightful seasons in which we seem to be walking in green pastures and beside still waters; when Christian life appears to be all sunshine, all flowers and joy and fruit. There are some of those precious seasons in every Christian life. But mark this, they do not last long. We are sometimes sorry they do not tarry with us; yet it is no doubt a good thing for us that they do not. As these Pilgrims passed on through this delightful part of their journey they found that the river and their path began to diverge, and as they went on their way apart from the river, they were obliged to leave the flowers and fruits and pleasing shade, while their path became every moment rougher and less inviting, and at last they grew extremely tired. They did not like to go away from the river, and they cast about to see if they could not find a compromise.

I have been teaching you all along that the path of the Pilgrims was, in the main, a path of ruggedness and self-denial. These Pilgrims, soon wearying of the unwelcome revival of trial, sought to return to their late delights, and looking over a stile, to which they came in their way, they discovered another path stretching away through a beautiful green meadow, and apparently running parallel with their own, and they thought to themselves to take this new path, which looked so easy, and leave the old one, now grown so hard.

How many of us do that? Christians go to their church meetings sometimes, and find peculiar seasons of refreshing, and the place seems a little heaven below.

> "Once they sing, and once they pray,
> And so they keep the holy day."

And their hearts keep up an echo to the strain:—

> "My willing soul would stay
> In such a frame as this,
> And sit and sing herself away
> To everlasting bliss."

But you will notice that such satisfying experiences as these lie right in the path of righteousness, not out of it. There is great temptation to the soul, in recalling such experiences, to be seduced from the way of righteousness, in hope of securing a renewal of pleasure Let me tell you, then, that, as a rule, you will find the Christian life antagonistic and agonistic; against flesh and blood. It means' to row against wind and tide; it is to go against the natural selfishness of the spirit of man; it is against man's pocket, against man's pride, against man's worldliness, and against the maxims of this world; and since its loving, Christ-like spirit is only to be found where Christ's love is shed in the hearts of His followers, those who leave the path of righteousness, in undue longing for pleasure, will find—and find in bitterness—that, though it is not hostile to the world, the world is hostile to it. Sweet, then, is pleasure when it comes in the path of duty, but out of that path it is dangerous.

Let me show you, by one or two illustrations, of this going astray. There are those who substitute worship for duty. Do you not know it is a very easy thing to go aside on Sunday, and, as it is called, "worship God?" Let the choir sing to you, and criticise it; let the preacher preach to you, and criticise him; sit in displeasure, and go away in disparagement; or be pleased, and retire to talk of the excellence of the sermon and the melodious singing. It is easy. Ah, good man, he has been to Church, and he thinks he is a Christian! But that is not being a Christian. As well might a man, after eating a hearty breakfast of his wife's preparing, stalk down town saying to himself, "I am a good financier." Ask his wife; she knows. A man comes here to the public service, takes part in worship, and says, "I am a good Christian." Ask God; He knows. Let me tell you, my friend, if you come to worship your Maker, forgetting your brother, forgetting a little child whose daily prayer for bread you might have answered—if you come here forgetting those, the love of God does not dwell in you. Do not forget them for worship. I notice some people think they exhibit considerable interest in the Sunday-school because, once a year, they go to the Sunday-school picnic, and after that, all the year round, never come in to take a class. I do not think they are very much interested in the Sunday-school. I think they make a very poor display of Christian interest. Going to a picnic does not bring you into the Sunday-school, but, on the contrary, taking a class and teaching it so faithfully that you are so worn out you cannot go to a picnic—that would help the school along. Here, then, is the first mistake: leaving righteousness for pleasure.

And now, another thing: In going aside, they fall in with Egotism and Self-Confidence. When these Pilgrims got out of the way, they saw a man named Self-Confidence before them, and they asked him where he was going; he said to the Celestial City; so they took it for granted that they must be in the right way. Some men are very confident they are on the way to the Celestial City, when they are not going there at all. We are apt to be untrue to ourselves; cover up our sins; disguise our shortcomings. He that doeth not the Master's will goes astray, and in duty neglected, danger begins. There is danger in obeying one's self-confidence and trusting to one's own notions, instead of abiding strictly by the will of God and the declarations of Christ.

Then, how these Pilgrims got into doubt, appears to have been: First, through tasting religious pleasure; then, in hope of renewing the pleasure in going astray from the Path of Righteousness; and then finding themselves in the wrong path, continuing in it through self-conceit and egotism.

Now, then, for the way out of this condition of doubt and despair.

One way is mentioned by Bunyan, and that is by prayer. These Pilgrims began praying on Saturday night, and kept on praying until the break of day; all night long through the darkness they continued in prayer. But some one will say, I do not believe in prayer. Well, that proves you have never been at sea; because if you had ever been in a storm at sea, you would believe in prayer. Now, let us understand each other about this matter of prayer. You say you do not believe in it, but, perhaps, you do not understand what prayer is. Perhaps you reply, I have not thought it worth while to think about it. Well, I tell you frankly, on the whole, I myself do not believe in many prevalent theories concerning prayer, yet I believe in prayer, and I may tell you that you are not true to your own nature if you have no faith in prayer. The soul, with the tongue of its native instinct, cries out for God, and will pray. Who are you to gainsay it? Look at the dying man, with his feet on the threshold of eternity, hear him pray; see the storm-tossed mariner, how he calls on God for safety; behold the mother stooping over her sick babe, hows she prays; the widow and the orphan, alone, crying for their heavenly Father's care; ah, look at the sinner afraid to die, and hear his voice of agony; see the savage bowing before his strange god—and tell me if the voice of nature does not call out for prayer? It does so, and if you have not prayed, you will pray sometime, and you had better do so now.

The way out, according to Bunyan, is by prayer. There was a man who last winter went to Mr. Moody. He had previously sought comfort for the troubles of his soul from many of the leading pastors of Chicago, but they could not satisfy him. His doubts lingered; and finally he sank into despair, and was in danger of being a castaway. At length his friends persuaded him to see Moody, to whom he was at first averse, as not being a man of sufficient culture to help him. He went to Moody, however, and made known his case; and when the Evangelist heard it, he said: "My friend, I can't do anything for you; yours is such a case as only the Almighty God can save," and down he went on his knees and began to pray; and the man felt the force of what was said, and soon fell on his knees also; and there by Moody's side his doubts were dissipated, and he saw the light.

I do not know whether you have read the life of that remarkable man, Charles Kingsley, a man as different from Moody as you could possibly conceive another man to be. When he sent out "Alton Locke," the religious world cried against it, but the author was in earnest, and, after the outcry, a letter was received from one of the most notorious Atheists of England, and one of the most intellectual thinkers, saying that when he read the book—though he had gone through many apologies for Christianity without conviction—when he read that simple story, he felt that here was a man who was living near to God. Communion with Kingsley led him to prayer, and in prayer that man found the peace which all should seek and all must desire.

While these Pilgrims were praying, Christian suddenly cried out to Hopeful, "What a fool am I to be lying here in this dungeon, when I have a key in my pocket that will unlock all and any of these doors." "Pull it out," said Hopeful, "and try it." And he pulled it out, and with it they unlocked the first door, and then the next, and at last the outer door, and so fled away, though Giant Despair did his best to bring them back again. This was the key of promise. Every prayer is based upon promise, or it is no prayer at all. Every prayer brings the promises in sight.

> "Prayer makes the darkest clouds withdraw;
> Prayer climbs the ladder Jacob saw."

Prayer pierces earth and reaches heaven. It brings the love of the Father to the child, when the child is relying upon the Father's promise.

But, you may say, "That does not suit me at all, for I do not believe in prayer." Let me ask you again, have you ever tried it? "Why, no, certainly I have never tried a thing which I regard as absurd." But I say it is absurd, foolish, and wicked for you to say prayer is absurd when you have never tried it. Suppose you are sick and call a physician, and he looks at your symptoms and prescribes for you, and you ask him, "What's that you are going to give me?" and he tells you the name of the medicine—would you say to the physician, "I sent for you to prescribe for me, but I do not believe in the medicine you advise?" Says the physician, "Have you ever tried it?" "Oh, no," say you, "I have not tried it, for I do not believe in it." What an absurdity! If the physician should say, "I am your physician, and I tell you it is adapted to your case, and if you take it you will get well," would you not finally take his advice and the medicine? Trust entirely to your physician; do just as he tells you. It would be foolish in the extreme to refuse his remedy because you did not believe in it, when you had not tried it.

God says to us in his Book, Ask and ye shall receive, seek and ye shall find, knock and it shall be opened unto you; try Me and prove Me, and see if I will not open the windows of heaven and pour upon you such a blessing as you shall not have room to contain.

But they not only prayed, they continued in prayer. There was a poor woman who went to an unjust man and cried for deliverance from her oppressor, but the man would not hear her, until finally she prevailed through her importunity; then, says Christ, "Will not God avenge His own elect who cry day and night unto Him? I tell you He will avenge them, though He bear long with them." Then there was a man who became dissatisfied with himself, and looked back over a life of deception, wrong, and devices to make favor with men, until he found out at last that to make true favor with men he must first be in favor with God. He knelt by the brook Jabbok, and all night long wrestled and prayed for a blessing; when it was slipping from his grasp he held it tightly, crying out, "I will not let thee go until I find the secret of the universal blessing; I will not release thee until this change is wrought." And so prayer prevailed and Jacob was converted into Israel; the man of deception to a man who prevailed with God.

Try it, my friend, make the experiment. God does hear and God does answer prayer; not anything and everything we like to bring before Him; not in our own way, but always in His own way; all we ask in submission to His holy will.

Prayer will dissipate doubt. Prayer will bring us to lean upon God. Prayer will bring life and strength to our souls, and enable us to live the life of faith upon the Son of God. And not only faith in Christ, but what does Christ say? Have faith in God. We must not forget the Father in the Son. We must not forget God in Christ. Christ leads us up to God—brings the wandering spirit back to God—lifts the fallen up to God. Believe in God the Father. All things are possible that are not sinful with God; and all these things are possible to him that believeth.

Are any of you, my friends, in doubt? Young man, are you in doubt—in doubt about the realities of the Christian life—of the facts of the holy life; of Christ; of the common belief among us? Are you in uncertainty? What shall I say to you?

I remember reading of a Man who went about healing all manner of diseases, and there was a poor afflicted woman who heard of this Man. She believed in His mission and His power, but she went her own way about being cured. She sought no introduction—used no formality. There was no hypocrisy or pretension about her. She simply said to herself, I believe in His power; I believe in the efficacy of His touch, and if I can but just touch the hem of His garment, though I am such a poor and miserable creature, I feel that I shall be healed. I know His willingness to heal—yet I will not intrude. I am very poor and very wretched. And so she watched Him as he came from the house of the dead, whom He had been raising to life, and the crowd pressed around Him. His disciples were trying to defend Him from the multitude. She brought herself in His way, and with the tip of her finger touched the hem of His robe as He passed, and she was immediately made whole.

Young man, if you have doubts, seek the Savior, but seek Him in your own way. Pray in your own way. Do not pray as we tell you. Pray in your own way. Wrestle into faith. Do anything that will drive darkness, despair, and doubt from your soul. Rest not in unbelief; act upon the one or two things that you do believe; be true to yourself all the way, and remember that many men have reached the eternal yes through the everlasting no. Live a life of faith, and do not attempt, for it is impossible, to live a life of doubt. A man must believe. Do you now believe? If you believe in God and Christ ever so feebly, be this your first prayer, "Lord, I believe, help thou mine unbelief." It has been answered; God grant that it may be in your case.

LECTURE XVII.

THE DELECTABLE MOUNTAINS.

[SYNOPSIS OF CHAPTER.—From Doubting Castle to the Delectable Mountains, in Immanuel's Land, the Pilgrims came. Here they were met by the shepherds Knowledge, Experience, Watchful and Sincere, who shewed them some wonders, notably: The scene from Mount Error, where they were apprised of the effect of false doctrines; next, the scene from Mount Caution, where they saw the effect of doubt; then the By-way to Hell from that advanced stage of pilgrimage; and, lastly, Mount Clear, from whence they had a prospect of the Celestial City. They left, singing.]

YOU will have noticed, as we have proceeded with these Lectures, that the better part, the brighter and more joyous experiences of these Pilgrims, are reserved for the latter end of their journey. It is quite true that they have been in many severe conflicts and trials, but it is also a fact that the increased joy counterbalances the increasing sorrow.

We are now brought to a very advanced stage of the Pilgrims' journey. Here we have a very beautiful pastoral scene, where the Christians are represented as enjoying themselves in a hallowed and blessed spot.

Now, we may adopt it as a principle, and I think make ourselves certain, that the further we go in any right course of life, the better it is for us; the happier we are in it, and the easier it is to progress. I have heard parents say that, though they have had much trouble and sorrow and anxiety with their children who have passed out of their hands into life, yet, as counterbalancing that increased sorrow, they have also great joy in seeing them taking their part in the world as men and women. Parents say, "We never were so happy as in having our children every night under our roof; and now, when they have grown up and have gone out for themselves, we spend anxious nights wondering where they are, whether they are safe, morally and physically;" and yet, then we hear them acknowledge, "When we see our son a man in body, intellect, and character, fighting the battles of life as a man should; and when we see our daughter a woman, with all the beauty of virtue resting upon her, out in life, ornamented with a meek and quiet spirit, bringing home again the sweet memory of days not long passed away—we find ourselves happier far than when we heard their infant prattle, so full of music to our ears." And so it is in everything. You see a pupil in music; she begins with a great deal of hard work, and progresses with effort still harder. The master first sets her to learn the fingering of the instrument; then he gives her a harder score. As she goes on, her progress is still a series of hard beginnings. By and by, when she has mastered the instrument and mastered the score, and become independent of both, as she strikes the keys she puts music into the instrument exceeding her utmost expectation, and that which was a synonym for toil is now the term for joy. Here is a boy whom we send to school. While the teacher is trying to teach him the elements of education, he is thinking, perhaps, only of tops, and marbles, and jack-knives. When you ask him about his lesson, he makes many blunders; his mind is running on a dog-fight, or a boy-fight, or something of that kind, and it is simply misery to him to be cooped up in school all day long. But you keep him at it, and in a few years you will find that same boy in a corner reading "Robinson Crusoe," and you cannot get him away from the book, for he has progressed to the point of enjoying that most charming of all books for boys; and so, you see, in this case also, that to him at last his greatest sorrow has become a source of the greatest pleasure. Now, it is just so in Christian life. It is a much harder thing to begin it than to continue. The difficulties that inhere in it pass away, and we become strong as we grow, and as we go on, joy comes to the soul.

And here I will add what, perhaps, some young people may not at once believe, that old people are much more beautiful than young ones. It is a fact, however. Spring is exceedingly beautiful, with its flowers and perfume; summer is grand, with all its multitudinous growth and splendid efflorescence; but the fall of the year, with the halo of age upon it! with ripening harvests! with all the trees dying in beauty!—is the sweetest sight Nature has to give us! A young man is wonderfully beautiful. There is something divine about a well-developed, well-balanced, strong young man; but he is nothing to the old man, with a hoary head, found in the way of righteousness, surrounded by a corona of years and virtues, ripening into Christian glory. A maiden, just passing into womanhood, is beautiful; but she is naught compared with the loveliness of the holy mother brooding over her children, about whom hovers a sacred beauty, without which no home can be complete. It is God's plan to give us more beauty and more joy as we progress in any right and useful way. Then, let me encourage those who find the beginning arduous; let me encourage them by promising that, the further they go, the better it will be, and the joys of their religious experience they will find to arise out of their trials and conflicts.

I saw a man, yesterday, carrying a heavy burden on his shoulders. He was a colored man, and he was met by another colored man, whom I heard say to him, "Sam, you seem always to have a heavy load on your back; I pity you." Sam looked at him a moment, and said, "Yes, that's so, but that is the way I get my living." My fancy followed him as he went home on Saturday night with the fruits of his heavy burdens: the food and clothing, and, perhaps, a picture for his children and a book for his wife. I thought of the contrast as I walked along, and, entering upon the public square, saw a number of men standing about the corners, with their hands in their pockets, whose only occupation the whole day long was to keep the stores from falling. They were not getting their living, because they had no heavy loads to carry. Most of the enjoyments of life, one way or another, come from the burdens we carry. It is so in practical affairs, and it is not less so in religious experience.

Again, these Pilgrims are represented as meeting some shepherds in the Delectable Mountains. These shepherds are, undoubtedly, a true allegory of the qualities developed in the soul at a certain stage of Christian experience, but we may make another practical application by considering them as a figure of the proper qualifications of Christian ministers. These shepherds are represented as tending their flocks. The common figure of the Christian ministers in the churches of the day is a shepherd; a pastor. We may, therefore, regard this as Bunyan's lesson of what a Christian minister should be. The names of these shepherds are Experience, Knowledge, Watchful, and Sincere. Undoubtedly it is the duty of a Christian minister, in order to save the souls entrusted to him, to lead, guide, and instruct them.

The physician and the attorney must be qualified to do their service to the bodies and estates of men, and it is none the less important for a minister of the Gospel to be duly qualified to fulfil his responsibilities. If you read the Old Testament you will find the expression, "The priest's lips should keep knowledge." Read through the New Testament and you will find it is the same thing. Paul advises Timothy not to lay hands on a man suddenly, nor put a novice, that is an ignorant young convert, into the office of the bishopric, lest he fall into condemnation of the devil—in other words he says, don't put an ignorant, untried man, at any cost, into the Christian ministry. When you look at it for a moment you see the reason, for he is a man who has in his hands, it might almost be said, the eternal welfare of immortal souls. Such a man must not be ignorant. People should demand knowledge in their ministers, and men should be in no hurry to rush into the Christian ministry. I began to preach when I was fifteen years of age, but I wish I had not begun until I was thirty; for I have an idea that no man is fully grown until he arrives at those years. At any rate, Christ waited—although we are told he grew daily in wisdom and in stature, and in favor with God and man; although he could put and answer questions with the doctors in the temple, yet Christ waited until he was thirty years of age before he began to preach the gospel. Paul went for three years into Arabia before he was qualified to preach; and Moses was qualified with an Egyptian education and long training before he was chosen to lead the people from bondage to the promised land. God needs no man's ignorance. God is not the author of confusion and has no work for the hands of the ignorant. Too much learning there cannot be in a Christian minister, if he would be fully equipped and prepared for his great work. He must possess knowledge, but what kind of knowledge?

There was a time when the Christian minister was the depositary of all knowledge in his parish; all matters pertaining to literature and science, as well as theology, were referred to him. But now, since mental growth has become so rife amongst us, a minister's work has become more clearly defined, and it will become still more clearly so as society moves along. The minister will have his separate work in his own separate department, and others will have theirs; he will no longer be looked upon as a walking encyclopedia of all the learning of the community. Yet he will need knowledge. And first—if I may be allowed to premise, I am not at all my own ideal of a Christian minister; He must know that he has passed from death to life.

It must be clearly defined in his own mind that God is good and Christ is precious. He must have the witness of the Spirit with his spirit that he is a child of God. He must know that he loves men, and has passed from death to life.

Again, he should know a great deal of the Word of God. An old Puritan divine said there were just three qualifications for a complete Christian minister.

First. A good set of brains in his head.

Second. A good knowledge of the Word of God.

Third. The grace of God in his heart.

But he not only needs to be learned in the written Word. He must also know human nature; he needs to study men, and the only way in which he can do that well is to work among men. The best college to which you can put a preacher is the ordinary vocation of life. Paul learned much as a tent-maker; Christ was a carpenter's son. Let him go among men and study them and understand them, if he can.

I had a deacon in one of the churches over which I presided, who was very wise, or at least he so impressed me, in his own conceit. He came into my study one day and saw a work upon Mental Philosophy lying upon my table, and he had an idea that a Christian should read nothing but the Word of God, or, as he phrased it, "The Werd"—I cannot pronounce it just as he did—just a little cant and slang attached to that style of thing that is simply detestable to me. Well, he said, "What do you do with such a book as that, now?" "Why," I said, "I read it." "But what does a preacher want to read that for?" And he took it up and looked at the title—I think he could scarcely spell it. He remarked again: "All you want is to study the Word." "Well, now, my friend," said I, "you are a farmer, are you not?" "Yes," he said, "I am." "What is your soil?" I asked. "Well," he replied, "limestone; a good deal of limestone in it." "What is it good for?" "Well, it is a capital soil to feed sheep on and for raising some kinds of grass." "Ah," said I, "it appears you know about your land, you have been studying something else yourself beside the seed you sow on it; therefore you see I am no more foolish than you, for as you have been studying your soil, so I am studying mine; this work informs me in respect to the soil where I expect to plant my seed, and it is just as necessary for me to understand my soil as for you to understand yours; for I suppose you would not sow any kind of seed on your limestone, and so I am not going to cast any sort of seed on my stony hearts, this way and that, without regard to where it may light, or what good it may do." Whoever studies the subject must come to the conclusion that it is absolutely necessary for a preacher of the Gospel to study men, and to become well acquainted with other men; it is well to apply the advice of the old philosopher, "Know thyself."

They know men and speak for them best whose own hearts have taught them the lessons of human love and trial. I used to think I was particularly tender and sympathizing with the bereaved, but there came a time when death entered my own house; took away my fairest flower and laid her in the cold grave. After that my ministry to the afflicted seemed a different thing, for whereas before I only felt for them, I now felt with them. O! it is good for preachers to be tried, and if I have learned anything in life beside what I have acquired from study, it has been in the hours of trial common to all men. While they have been bitter they have called forth a song.

Then the shepherds were not merely men of knowledge and experience, but they were also watchful. They watched their flocks. They were men who could give an account, and were very careful of those whom God had entrusted to them. Watchfulness in connection with a preacher is generally understood to mean that he is good family visitor, and no doubt it is often supposed that if he is not a good visitor he is not very much of a pastor, and does not fulfil this requisite qualification of watchfulness; accordingly there are preachers, and I believe religious men, too, who visit from house to house industriously, seeking to become what is called acquainted with their people. Yet you cannot know a people by family visiting, where you are taken politely into the coldest and primmest room of the house, to wait until the friends are dressed and ready to "receive" you, and where people do not show their interior life, but only their *veneer*. They do not tell you their trials, except some few that must come to the surface; you cannot know a people in that way. You cannot know a people except in trials, when your friendship and assistance are welcome.

In this connection let me remark that there is no good in preaching in the abstract; none at all. The sermons I preached at a former parish would not fit you, and the sermons which are being preached in New York, to-night, would be of no use whatever here. Suppose a lawyer, before a jury, should take up an old plea, made in an old case before some other jury, ten or twelve years ago, and use it again in the trial pending. There is a specimen of a good plea in the abstract. Or, imagine him applying one of Demosthenes' orations to a Fourth of July celebration. A good thing in the abstract, you will say, but not suited to the occasion. Watchfulness, then, requires special study of the Word of God in its application to the special case. There is no good of family visiting in the abstract, any more than there is in abstract preaching.

Then there is another word in Bunyan's description of the shepherds expressive of a very essential qualification in a preacher of the Gospel—that is, *Sincere*. The word has a history. It comes from the potteries. When in olden times men tested the quality of pottery, they used to rap it with their knuckles, and if there was a crack or flaw in the article, that crack or flaw would spoil the music of its ring; but if there was no crack or flaw, and the article was whole, it would ring out a sweet, whole tone—sincere, sincere—and keep on ringing to show that it was true. It is necessary, when we preachers are rapped by the knuckles of trial, that we, too, should ring out sincere. Oh, it is necessary for men to be true, and especially preachers of the Gospel. It ought to be remembered that it is the life that preaches, and not the tongue; honest manhood and true purpose, with love for souls, and not mere talk in the pulpit, however eloquent that talk may be.

These shepherds took our Pilgrims to see the wonders of the Delectable Mountains. First of all, Christian and his companion were led to the top of a hill called Error. This hill was steep on the further side, though easy to climb. They looked down to the bottom, and there beheld a number of people, dashed to pieces by falling off the precipice. Bunyan then gives examples of those who have fallen over there by getting into the error of denying the resurrection of the body. This part of the Allegory is intended to illustrate the natural result of religious error.

The very first error of religious men in our days, I think, is this, that it does not matter at all what a man believes, so he does right. You may go on doing right, it is said, and no matter what you believe; the sort of notions you may have in your head are of no consequence whatever.

—31

Lecture XVII.

That seems to be the prevalent error in the Christian churches of to-day. But the error is unmistakable and serious, because all that a man does is built upon his beliefs; built upon something spiritual, which convinces him and guides his motives. If a man is inaccurate in his thinking, that man, by that inaccurate thinking, will run into folly, and folly will very soon lead him into sin. I have no doubt, indeed, but the Christian church has imposed, and still does impose upon men, a number of doctrines not necessary for salvation; but I say this, that no man can think correctly, and therefore live correctly, who does not receive into his heart correct and true doctrine. You might just as well say that it does not matter what a man eats, so long as he works well, as to say that it is no matter what he believes, so that he lives well. Much depends upon what a man eats. Mistakes are fatal, though time may be required to prove them. So, suppose we go out to gather mushrooms. "Mr. N.," you say, "is this a mushroom or a fungus?" "Oh, no matter; you eat it. If you relish it, it is mushroom; and if it kills you, it is fungus." I know it has killed others, but then it does not matter what a man eats, so that he lives. Do you not see that his life depends on what he eats and drinks? Read history. All sin has had its beginning somewhere or other in false doctrine. Take Rome: when she began to fall, she began first in her doctrines of religion. Take the history of any nation, and it is the same; of the old Grecian philosophers, and it is the same. Instead of building on eternal principles, they left them, and by degrees became corrupt, till Socrates came asking for the truth, and they gave him hemlock. The history of all the world, I say, tells the same tale. And we know what error is by the fruit it bears; a good tree cannot bring forth bad fruit. My advice is, take heed to the Word and the doctrine, and be careless about neither.

Then the Pilgrims are taken to the Hill of Caution, where they are given a kind of retrospect; they look far off and see a number of men walking up and down among the tombs. They perceive that those men are blind and stumble about, and cannot get out from among the tombs. Christian asks the shepherds what this means, and is told that these men went out of the way because it was rough, and were thus led aside into Doubting Castle, and finally taken by Giant Despair, after having their eyes put out, to live among the tombs. They were literally the blind leading the blind; they could not see, and thus were an illustration of the result of shirking; for it leads to doubt, and he who encourages doubt, loses at last the capacity of belief. When a man has arrived at that point, there is no telling where he will go. He can no longer tell right from wrong—seems not to have the moral grip to get and keep the truth to himself. So there are a number of men who are accustomed to praise reason at the expense of faith; they are going to believe nothing, they say, but that which they can prove by reason; it is not intellectual, they say, to believe; forgetting that doubt itself is belief of a negative kind. What are the facts in the case? Read the history of men who eschew faith in the ordinary doctrines of the Christian Church, and what will you find? Take Lord Herbert of Cherbury, one of the first English Deists; he wrote a book to prove that revelation was unnecessary, and that Christianity was not a revelation. Read his life and you will find that, after he had written his book to prove revelation unnecessary, and that Christianity is not a revelation, he doubted whether he ought to publish it. He can best tell how his doubts were overcome:

"Being thus doubtful, in my chamber, one fair day in the summer, my casement being open toward the south, the sun shining clear, and no wind stirring, I took my book, *De Veritate*, in my hand, and kneeling on my knees, devoutly said these words:—

'O thou Eternal God, author of the light which now shines upon me, and giver of all inward illuminations, I do beseech Thee of thy infinite goodness, to pardon a greater request than a sinner ought to make. I am not satisfied enough whether I shall publish this book, *De Veritate*; if it be for Thy glory I beseech Thee give me some sign from heaven; if not, I shall suppress it.'

"I had no sooner spoken these words, but a loud though gentle voice came from the heavens—for it was like nothing on earth—which did so comfort and cheer me, that I took my petition as granted, and that I had the sign I demanded; whereupon also I resolved to print my book. This, how strange soever it may seem, I protest before the Eternal God is true; neither am I in any way superstitiously deceived therein, since I did not only clearly hear the noise, but in the serenest sky that I ever saw, being without a cloud, did, to my thinking, see the place from whence it came."*

As Dr. Vaughan says: "The noteworthy aspect of the affair is, that a book which denies the existence of an eternal revelation, which tells us it would be superfluous if given, is made to come to us attested by such a revelation! We are expected to believe in a work which denies the supernatural, because its author has been assured of its truth by means of the supernatural. Lord Herbert is an existence of such importance that a revelation has been made to him, but the great heart and soul of humanity in all past time, has not been an existence important enough to have been so favored."

If your mind is in the habit of doubting, there is nothing you may not be led to believe. So when men give up the Scripture there is no telling into what they may drift. Foolish and ridiculous, you know, to believe the truths contained in the Scriptures!

There are men who scoff at the idea of a spiritual religion, and yet are very curious about spiritualism, and hold doubtful communications with spirits, to all appearances from below, while denying communication by means of prayer with the Father of spirits above. Spiritualism is a grand fact. There can be no Bible if spiritualism is untrue, but when men reject the spiritualism of the Bible, do they get a better? Certainly not. Read the works of Andrew Jackson Davis, and you will find in his "Great Harmonia" how he has informed the world

---

* Life of Edward Lord Herbert, pp. 279, 280.

that the Bible and the teachings of Christian churches are all antiquated, and that he comes to bring a new revelation from on high of a new order of things speedily to be ushered in. We read how the seer has had the life of the inhabitants of the planets revealed to him. He says their thoughts are so lustrous that you can read them on their faces. He says, again, that they are much nobler in their mental powers than the inhabitants of our world, yet they are obliged to go on all-fours. This is the end to which we are led by this boastful prophet of a new order. Such stuff as this is sent out as the great new revelation to overturn the old. Christ is nothing, and the work of the Church is nothing. Men who deny the fundamentals of religion buy such books, and read and believe them too. There are large numbers who ignore the argument from design, as we call it, by which we infer that this world was made by an intelligent and holy Being. Very many of these men are not only quite industrious and intellectual, but some are very honest indeed; and you may see them go to a sandhill, take out an old piece of pottery, and discourse very learnedly to the effect that the piece of pottery indicates the existence of a pre-historic race. They then look upon this vast universe, with its rolling spheres of light in order, and see no design; then turning to an old pot, swear that there is an Indian behind it. The extent to which men go, if they shut their eyes to the light, is surprising. The very light within them becomes darkness.

You have heard me say many things in this connection since I have preached to you, especially since we arrived at the topic of Doubting Castle and Giant Despair. And, perhaps, you think I am rather hard on this class, but, brethren, there are no men with whom I sympathize more than with the man who doubts— none; and I will tell you why: From my earliest associations I have been brought up with doubt; I was cradled in it; my relatives were doubters and sceptics and infidels. When I was but a lad I was set among about twenty of them, heard their teachings, and was in early life influenced by them. At last one of them came to his dying bed; the first one to be sent for by him was the lad into whose heart he had tried to infuse his own darkness. When I saw him, after he had realized that he was about to die, he took my hand in his, and said, "God forgive me, for trying to make you doubt. Pray for me;" and, young as I was—not more than thirteen then—I knelt before the sceptic, prayed as well as I could, and a day or two afterwards walked with those who carried him to his grave. I have seen young men begin by doubting and at last sink into lives of sensuality and sin; for it is an inevitable principle that incorrect thinking will lead to corrupt living; it cannot be otherwise. If a man call error truth, and truth error, he has made a fatal mistake, from which he will have hard work to rise. It is no playing matter. Beware! If any of you are troubled with doubts yourselves, remember the advice of Maurice: "Do not take the shadow of a superstition from any man till you have the substance of a faith to give him." That very superstition may be the only thing that keeps him to true life. Do not take it away, or his blood may be on your soul. If you have any honest doubts, go and solve them, but corrupt no one.

After their visit to Mount Caution, they are taken by the shepherds to the side of a hill, where a door is opened, and are bade to look in. They there see the doom of hypocrites—those who professed themselves Christians when they were not—whose exemplars, the Dreamer tells us, they also saw: Judas, who sold his Redeemer for silver, and Ananias and Sapphira, who betrayed the Holy Ghost by keeping back part of the price. And here the Pilgrims ask these significant questions: "Did not these persons look like Christians?" "Did they not for a long time keep in the way?" "They did." "Then how far may a man go in this way, and yet be lost?" They see that there is a by-way to hell, and they are told that some keep in the way as far as these mountains, and even further. When we come to the last chapter, the Dreamer will show us a door to hell even from the gates of heaven.

There are some Christians who know they have lost their spiritual life, and that they have but a name to live, while they are dead. They may appear to be full and rich in the wealth of life, but strip them of the veiling flesh, and they are poor, miserable, blind and naked; they are gaunt and bony skeletons. You who have lost your life know well what I mean. You know the aching void, that the world can never fill; you know the soul's longing for a retaste of what it once enjoyed; you know the peace you found in prayer, and the hope in faith; and now all is bitter. You feel, better than I can tell, the meaning of this lesson. There are some that have sold their Lord; there are those that have kept back part of the price, and there are those who have sold their birthright for a mess of pottage, who, for a little of this world, have given up their hope of heaven.

From this mournful spectacle the Pilgrims are led at last to the mount called Clear, and here the shepherds bid them look through a spy-glass, to see if they can see the Celestial City. At the Palace Beautiful they had been promised they should catch a glimpse of the Celestial City at these mountains. They take the telescope, and look and see the gate. They see something of a city, but all as through a glass darkly, just as in this world heaven must seem.

Brethren, there are not many Mount Clears in the Christian experience. Yet there are some. They are those seasons when we look through faith to the promised land, and get its picture upon our souls. A telescope, made of bits of glass in a tube, opens to us in the skies visions of worlds of beauty far away; and so the heart, through the promises of God, looks forward and sees a holier, better world for man. The vision may not be clear, but something is seen, and that makes its impression upon the soul, whereby the thought of heaven becomes surer and more glorious.

Such is our prospect, my brethren. On these Delectable Mountains see how much is taught; how much is learned. Let us learn the terrible lessons, but let us not learn them at the expense of the love that teaches—

> "There is a better world, O so bright!
> Where sin and woe are done away, O so bright!
> Where glory fills the balmy air,
> And angels with bright wings are there,
> And harps of gold and mansions fair, O so bright!"

There is that land of perfect rest; perfect joy; perfect beauty; perfect love! Let us lift our eyes to the promise of God, and view the land that is not very far off.

LECTURE XVIII.

THE ENCHANTED GROUND.

[SYNOPSIS OF CHAPTER.—The shepherds of the Delectable Mountains took leave of the Pilgrims by severally giving them a note of the way, bidding them beware of the flatterer, of sleeping on Enchanted Ground, and by wishing them God speed. On their way to the Enchanted Ground they met with Ignorance, of the town of Conceit. In leaving him behind they entered a dark lane, where they saw Turnaway, who had been bound in cords by devils. Then Christian told of one Little Faith who had been robbed in these regions by Faint-Heart, Mistrust, and Guilt. A Flatterer enticed them from the way until they were caught in a net, from which they were delivered by a Shining One. They met with Atheist, who derided them, but without effect. Then Hopeful related his experience for the benefit of Christian.]

THE chapter of the Pilgrim's Progress, which I have partially read, is so long that, in the Lecture, as in the reading, I am obliged to omit that part which relates to Ignorance. I do this with the less diffidence, because the next chapter is devoted chiefly to him. Accordingly, without further introduction, I will enter at once upon the parables here presented to us by Bunyan.

The Pilgrims are now nearing the Enchanted Ground, which will be more particularly explained. The first parable we meet with refers to a character of the name of TURNAWAY. Now, our Lord has told us that if any man put his hand to the plow and look back, the same is not worthy of the kingdom of God; and, again, He has taught us in one of His great parables that the kingdom of heaven is like a room swept and garnished, and then left vacant, occupied soon after by seven devils, each worse than any that had been in the room before; whereby we learn that to undertake and fall away, to sweep, garnish and leave exposed to new impurities, makes the second state worse than the first. Such are Christ's teachings, and such we find in experience.

We have known men who began the Christian life and ran well for a while; but a time came when something evil seemed to possess them, and they became worse than they ever were before they made a profession of religion. The philosophy of this I do not understand, and, therefore, shall not attempt to explain, but simply note the fact.

We have read of a character in this book named Pliable, who went but a little way with Christian, and finding the way difficult, returned. When Faithful is introduced, he informs us that this same Pliable, after his turning, became despised; that men derided him, and chaffed him, till they made his life miserable, calling him renegade, and coward, and traitor to his profession. So this person whom Bunyan styles *Turnaway* appears bound with cords, and thus bound, the Pilgrims see him borne away by the very demons he has himself admitted to his company, unto eternal punishment.

What is the lesson here? What are the cords by which the sinner is bound? The sinner is bound by the cords of his own sins. By them he is bound hand and foot, and cast into outer darkness, where there is weeping, wailing, and gnashing of teeth. Think of it, ye careless Christians. Your deeds are making habits, and habits are making character, and character creates destiny. Certainly this is the case with men who turn their backs upon Christ. They begin with some small thing; perhaps, at first, neglect of private prayer, or neglect of the Bible, or neglect of self-instruction; or, it may be, with finding excuses for sin. Perhaps they neglect the public means of grace until, at last, they are found with those who keep not holy day, but walk in the paths of unrighteousness; or they may go on ignoring their downward progress, plunging deeper into sinful pleasure, till at last they sink into a state of indifference, and where they sink they perish. You know as well as I, that such is the natural history of sin. When the Pilgrims looked again upon this man whom they thought they knew, they saw written upon his back the words, "Wanton professor and damnable apostate." The real spiritual, literal fact in such a case is, that those words appear all over—in the flesh, in the blood, in the life and in the very soul of every ruined creature who sells The Christ.

The next parable in the chapter represents a man trying to get to heaven with very little faith. He gets tired on his way, and lies down to rest. There is this to notice about him, he came from the town of Sincere; was, in fact, quite a sincere man, but his misfortune was to have but little faith. Now, a little faith is better than none, but much faith is better than a little. A man with little faith will be sure to have more trouble than a man with a great deal. You know how much more embarrassment the man meets who has but little money than he who has much. You know how much heavier burdens appear to the man with little strength than to a man who is robust, muscular and strong; and you know how many more difficulties the man with little learning finds, how many more knotty and numerous problems throng about him than another who has drunk deeply at what the poet calls "the Pierian spring." A little learning is better than none, a little money is better than none, and a little strength is better than utter weakness, but much of these is better than a little. If you have ever been much upon the water, you know how hard it is to ride in a little boat; the skiff is small, and you must sit just so, plumb in the middle, turning neither to one side nor the other, lest you tip the boat over. You hardly dare to move a muscle, or even to breathe hard, for fear of capsizing. On the other hand, when you are on a great boat, a large ship—say, one of those glorious monsters that plow the deep, superior to wind and tide—you walk the deck, you recline in the cabin, you leap and play, and do whatever you please to your heart's content. And as it is much easier and much safer every way to cross the Atlantic in a big ship than a skiff, so it is far better to make the voyage to heaven with a great deal of faith than to attempt it with a little, although a little faith is better than none. Still, it behooves us to pray the apostle's prayer, "Lord, increase our faith." The trouble is, we are too much afraid of believing. There is much truth in the statement of Barnum's—not original with him, however—"that more men are duped by believing nothing than by believing too much."

The dangers of "Little Faith" are illustrated by Bunyan in this way: The poor fellow is met by three brothers, Faint-Heart, Mistrust, and Guilt. Faint-Heart demands his purse, Mistrust runs up and grabs it, and Guilt knocks him down with a club. The idea is clearly this, that if you have but little faith it will manifest itself in a faint heart, in mistrusting the things pertaining to the kingdom of God, until at last you are led into actual guilt. This was the case with Peter; he had but little faith, while he thought he had a great deal, and when he was brought into trial he mistrusted, and finally denied his Lord and Master with curses. At last he was stricken down with his own guilt.

Brethren, let us strive to get more faith. Let us believe that though heaven and earth shall pass away, yet not one jot or tittle of God's Word shall fail. And let us fully trust the Eternal Word.

There came upon the Pilgrims a man dressed in a very white robe, but whose flesh proved to be very black. This person flattered them very much, and by this means succeeded in enticing them out of the path leading to the Celestial City into a by-way, and so beguiled them that they had at last turned right about and were again facing the City of Destruction. All this was accomplished by flattery. Ah, beware of flatterers. "He that flattereth with his lips," says the good old Book, "layeth a snare for the feet of his neighbor." And yet how we like it.

Do you not like to be flattered? Is it not as sweet as honey and the honey-comb? Who can stand it? When one man wants to succeed with another, all he needs to do is to use a little flattery. It is like oil, only it goes a longer way, destroying all friction, and making things go so easy. How much is it used in business?

I met with a man last summer who always smiles. By the way, let me whisper in your ear, beware of the perpetual smiler. This man was always smiling, and I have since learned that that smile had duped hundreds. It was fatal to all it charmed. Remember that the man who flatters you is always on the lookout for himself. In the nature of the case it must be so, for he would not care to flatter you unless in his own interest. But the reason the Pilgrims came to fall so easy a prey to the flatterer was that they had at that point left off doing their Christian duty, and had fallen into a discussion of abstract questions in Theology. The circumstance of the fate of Little Faith, which had just appeared to them, was the occasion of their discussion. They had fallen into theological hair-splitting. They began to talk and talk and talk about certain terms and conditions in which they had found themselves, and in which it seemed to them Little Faith was found. They had left off doing their duty, to discuss abstract Theology. Now, Theology is a very good thing in its way, but it never ought to be allowed to take the place of Christian duty. It is much more divine and Christianlike to give a hungry man a loaf of bread than it is to stand in this or any other pulpit for an hour, splitting a Theological hair. It is more Christ-like to clothe the naked than to prove by the Bible, or any other book, that the righteousness of Christ is a sufficient robe to cover an unrighteous life, or even a defective one. Abstractions are profitless; they are the burden of schools of divinity and systems of Theology. The Lord Jesus Christ never bids us leave off mercy to begin discussing this question or that, but to go on in practical good living until the spirit of Christ is formed in the heart.

They were flattered out of the way, and were then chastened. A Shining One came to them with a whip, and scourged them. "Whom the Lord loveth he chasteneth, and he scourgeth every one whom he receiveth." They had been led out of the way into the net; they were brought out of that net with chastening, and again led in the way of righteousness. It would be good for us all if we received more chastening; too often we need to be whipped to our work.

We now come to the Enchanted Ground. As soon as the Pilgrims reached this part of their journey, they began to feel exceedingly languid, and an almost uncontrolable desire to sleep. They consulted with one another as to the advisability of lying down for repose.

What does this mean? It means that while the religion of Jesus Christ always benefits a man, his weakness is apt to pervert it. We are told that there was once a man who dwelt among the tombs in such an outcast condition that everybody was afraid of him. He was possessed of demons, whose name was Legion. We are told that after Jesus Christ had cast out the demons from the man, he came out from the tombs and sat at the feet of Jesus, clothed and in his right mind. This great change was due to Christ.

There are some of you men and women here to-night, who, in some way, either directly, or indirectly, owe the coats and dresses you now wear to Christ—owe the food you eat to Christ. But for Christ you would be ragged and hungry. You all owe your enjoyments, comforts and luxuries to Christ; owe it to the fact that your fathers and mothers, or the society around you from your childhood up, were subject to Christian influences. You would have no music in your homes, no music in your souls, but for the refinement of those influences. And yet how often it will turn out, and how natural it appears to be, that when we are elevated in the social scale by the grace of Christ, and have reached an easier grade of circumstances, we then want to take our religion easy. As soon as we begin to wear broadcloth, we begin to feel a sneaking distaste for poor folks, and seek to get among the rich, refined, and cultured. We are tempted to call that Christianity, when in fact it is nothing more nor less than absolute, abominable selfishness, with not a vestige of Christianity about it. Only that man is a Christian who does his Lord's will. Remember that he who knows his Master's will and does it not, the same shall be beaten with many stripes. You have seen such instances. Men have been lifted into a better state of things by the Christian religion, and then turn about and will have nothing to do with it—nothing practically.

There comes a time in the life of most Christians when they begin to think they ought to leave off work; they think they have done enough and may take their ease. They say, "I have been working in the cause of Christ for many years; I have held this position and that; I have given so much to the poor, or I have done this, that, or the other thing. Now let some one else take my place while I step aside and rest."

Let me tell you, my friends, the time to quit work will never come. You have no right to quit. When the breath goes out of your body, may you, with your Lord's permission, leave off work in this world, and then you will leave off in this world only to begin in another. Never, never shall we pay all the debt we owe. This is the Enchanted Ground; getting into those spiritual and social conditions when we think we have no more to do because we have done so very much, or are too great to work for Christ and man.

But there is another lesson in the chapter. These Christian Pilgrims met with a person whose name was Atheist, who sought to turn them out of the way of righteousness. And I want to call your attention now to the arguments employed by the Atheist. He asked the Pilgrims whither they were going, and when they told him, he used a very common argument with his class—HE LAUGHED. When they enquired the cause of his laughter, he said he laughed to see them so ignorant. "To see," he said, "what ignorant persons you are, to go so tedious a journey, and yet like to have nothing for your trouble."

This is the last time I shall have a chance during these Lectures to say anything about the Atheist; I shall, therefore, speak a parting word. If there are before me any of that class, let me say to them, in all kindness, pray do not brag of your reason, and of your fondness for testing everything by reason, until you have come to the conclusion to give up laughing at religion; and when you give up laughing, I wish to remind you that the largest half of your argument is gone. I have never yet met with an Atheist—and I have met with many more than I can see people here to-night; I have had as large a congregation of Atheists as this to preach to, and I always preach to them when I have a chance and my health permits; always—I never met with an Atheist yet with whom ridicule was not one, and the principal one, of his stock arguments. Shall I prove it? Read Leslie Stephen, read Clifford, read Morely—in my opinion, the most advanced and most intelligent Atheists of the day. Some of you may say, we do not know them. Never mind; take my word for it—the most advanced, perhaps, and most intelligent of their class, and yet they cannot keep this fashion of ridicule from their writings. Read Ingersoll, and when you have eliminated the ridicule from his Lectures, what is there left? I frequently meet with this argument against the Bible and Christianity: "Absurd! Nonsense! No man of thought thinks thus to-day. No man of any intelligence would entertain such opinions now. Religion is only fit for women and children—that's all!" I say, I meet with just such arguments as that. Strong arguments, you may say, perhaps, with very proper irony. No, they are not arguments at all, and yet they are aimed at some weak souls, upon whom they tell, and make them shrink into themselves in meekness and in fear. I say this to the whole school of infidels, they have no right to claim to be led by reason so long as they resort to ridicule. Any fool can laugh. Do not pretend to reason while you deride. Do not think it any answer to say, "Pshaw!" "Absurd!" "Nonsense!" for it is no answer at all. If the Christian Church is the monster of iniquity it is represented to be, some stronger weapon should be used, in the name and for the sake of man.

Then, again, another stock argument of the Atheist is, that he has gone all over the question of Christian evidence, and knows more about it than Christians themselves. This trick is quite popular. They say, "We have looked into these things; we have studied this subject; we have sifted it all through, and there is nothing in it." They assume—and I can give you chapter and verse for it from their works, and I can quote language from their lips, too—they assume that they are the embodiment of all the knowledge on the subject. I readily grant that there are a number of Christians, so called, who never look into the question of Christian evidence at all, for all they seek is to be taken by the easiest stages out of hell to heaven; that is all they care for. They never study the Christian religion, nor do they live a Christian life. There are many of them in our churches, and many of them all over the land, getting first-class seats in first-class churches, with the expectation of getting reserved seats at the Judgment day. And I readily grant that there are a number of Atheists who have given more attention to Christian evidence than multitudes who bear the name of Christian. But that, as a class, Atheists have given more attention to the investigation of the subject than Christians, as a class, I absolutely and without qualification deny. And I make another statement—Atheists are not capable of giving more attention to the subject than Christians are. Again, that Atheists are not desirous of making more investigation than Christians are. And yet another; Christians, as a class, are more honest in the matter of investigation than are Atheists. And I will go further and say, no attempt has yet been made to undermine the Christian religion and disprove the truth of the Bible, but has been well answered, and more than answered; so that in every crisis of the Church, as is well known to the philosophical and historical reader, the infidel has been obliged to change his ground. Yet if infidelity is true, how is it that it is not the same thing from age to age? Christianity is the same. It never changes. It was love to God and man when it commenced —is now, and ever shall be. Infidelity is not the same, but day by day, and hour by hour, its votaries are obliged to make concessions to us, and to give ground. If you are at all acquainted with the history of these matters, you will know it as well as I. But I hear men—who never read the Bible, nor any book or writing on the side of Christian evidence whatever, but who get an Atheistic paper once a week—say that they are well acquainted with Christian evidence, and it is *nil*. Now that is nonsense; is it not? But that is not all. Half of the infidelity of the day is not the result of reading, not the result of sincere and honest thinking, but of mere wayward captiousness.

During the progress of these Lectures I have, perhaps, said some harsh things; some that were sarcastic concerning infidelity in its various forms, as it has been indicated to us in the chapters of Bunyan. Perhaps I may seem to have spoken harshly about science. I have nothing to take back. I have not uttered a thing that I have not believed to be true, and I take back nothing. But why have I thus spoken? Because I love science. I love the truth always, and no scientific fact has ever yet been given to the world, and brought to my knowledge, but it has seemed like a gleam of light from the face of the Father to my soul. I love the light that science sheds; I am glad in its welfare, and glory in its progress; and that is the reason I would be merciless in my assaults upon the spirit of a science, falsely so called.

Again, I love logic. I love debate, but hate assumption with all my heart. A thing can be reasoned out, if we reason fairly; and so I have no words too scathing for the false logic so often applied to these questions.

I say again, I love the truth. I would rather be with true things in hell than to be with false things in heaven; and if the truth, as I find it, shall lead my steps to hell, I shall take those steps undaunted and without fear. I love the truth, and I hold to this position: that whatever is palpable—universally palpable—though it may not be exactly demonstrable, is yet for all practical purposes true, for the mind of man cannot keep alive clinging to a lie. Lies are shifting sands; the soul cannot abide in them. They are not germane to the spirit, for it is made for truth. A lie will not fit to it; the soul shakes it off, and hurls it away as its foe.

Hence, I repeat, I love the truth and everything pertaining to it, and with all the strength of my soul I hate Atheism, because I believe it to be the blackest lie that ever foisted itself upon man.

Then there is another reason why I think and feel as I do. I love man—not much, perhaps—I say it not boastingly, but I say it because I trust I have something of the spirit of my Master, who died for men. I say I love man—by that I do not mean abstract humanity, but man—the men and women who are nigh me. I do love them, sunk in sin though they may be, brutalized as they seem, they yet bear the image of God, that image which declares that they and we are brothers.

And now here I throw down a challenge: If you will find me a message sweeter to the human ear, more elevating to the soul of man, than this message of the Gospel; find me a work to do more ennobling than this Christian work; find me a life humbler and yet more sublime than the Christian life; here, before man and God, I declare that if you will find it I will give up teaching the Gospel and preach that message instead. I will give up this work I am trying to do and do that; I will give up this life and take upon me the other; find it for me, and I will do it. I say this deliberately—I count the cost—show it me, and I will make the change to-night, or as soon as it can be revealed to me.

There were six or seven hundred drunkards in this city that now are sober. Yet three weeks ago they were wretched, miserable drunkards. I met a drunkard's little boy some few weeks ago, on the street, and said I, "Johnny, will you come to Sunday-school?" He looked at his rags, and said, "Please, sir, papa would not like me to, looking this way." Only a week or two ago I saw him again, and he ran up to me eagerly, saying, "Mr. N., father says I may go to Sunday-school next Sunday."

I saw a man take the temperance pledge, and as I looked at his wasted and squalid form, I said to him, "Sir, your wife will be glad to-night." Brushing a tear from his cheek, he replied: "Ah, she will have cause to." I saw that man again, clothed and in his right mind, and his wife was beside him, proud and happy. If nothing else has been done, at least these men have been made sober. I do not claim it to be a perfect work— nothing of the kind. But what there is of it is good—very good. And what I want to get at now is, Who started it? Did the Atheists of this city, who love truth and liberty and reason so much, meet together and say, What can we do for such men? No, they did not. Did the professional theologians assemble, men who spend their time in splitting hairs and laying down stiff dogmas, in this form, "This is pure doctrine, and you must receive it or be damned;" did they meet and begin it? No; they did not. But those who did begin the work were a few Christian men, who joined their heads and hearts and said to each other, Cannot we do something by our love of God and man, to save these poor souls from sin and misery? And they thought they could, and they tried, and did it. Men are sober in this city to-night who were not sober then. Homes and wives and children are happy and bright to-night that were dark and wretched then. Disparage it as you may, the work is good, and who began it? That's the question. It rose out of the very genius and spirit of the Christian religion. It was the duty of the Christian, and the Christian only thought to do it. And so I say, show me a grander work than this, and I will go and do it. If there is a better life to live, tell me, and I will try and live it. If the good old Book be untrue, prove it a lie, and I will take up the truth, if I can find it anywhere, and abandon the lie. But let us have no more to do with vain assertions or ridicule.

Now there is a fair challenge; will you take it? Ah, but says some one, "You won't be convinced." Why not? "It is not to your interest; you are a preacher." Friend, I am as independent as any man living; I do not depend upon the Gospel for my living; I have lived hard and worked hard in ways that would be acknowledged so, and I can do it again, and will do it forever, rather than teach a lie. I am willing to sacrifice whatever there may be to sacrifice in my position. Give me a better life, I say, and I will live it, though it cost me life itself. Give me a higher calling; nobler duties; a sweeter spirit than Christ's, if you can. But what have you to give? Nothing but mockery. "O you won't be convinced, you say to me, because you don't want to be." But, my friends, I have asked you to show me something to make me want to. It is not hard to convince a man who wants to be convinced; and if you have the material to persuade, use it. You say you have truth on your side; why not prove it? It would be a good thing for your cause to convert me. Do you say this is nonsense? I say the blame lies with those who provoke it.

What has the Atheist to give a dying world when he takes away religion? What will he say to the mother who buries her babe; to the widow and the orphan? What has he to say to the soul bowed down with grief, or in the article of death? What will he say to the weak, struggling with their own weakness—that life is but a mixture of good and ill, with no real distinction except that made by fanatics? Will you corrupt the world or save it; pour darkness on it or let in the light; bid it live by faith, or cover it with the pall of infidelity?

This chapter teems with lessons. I would like to add another lecture to the series, and devote it entirely to the single subject of this man Hopeful's experience. Let me run hastily over it. We have had the experiences of Christian and Faithful; now we come to the experience of Hopeful. Hopeful gives an account of his Christian experience; he says that he once loved sin, as we find we all do, for sin is pleasurable. Oh! the dirty, beastly drunkard, some say; but, hold there—he cannot be beastly exactly, for whoever saw a beast drunk? Pray do not insult beasts like that; for poor unfortunate man alone seeks pleasure in unlawful ways. But ridicule him not, for he is God's child and your brother. Your Savior died for him, and stands with longing arms to receive him to Himself.

Well, Hopeful loved sin, and then he was moved at last by fear. Shall I tell you how he was convinced of his sin first of all? It was by seeing the consistent life of Christian and Faithful as they passed through Vanity Fair: it was thus they convinced him of a better life than that he was leading. If you want to know the strongest argument you can use to lead men out of darkness, just let them look into a life of light as into a mirror, and see their own foul lives reflected back upon themselves, and they will be convinced, self-convinced of sin. The best Christian argument in the world is the Christian life—such a life perhaps as your dear old mothers led, and as many mothers now are leading.

Hopeful was convinced by the life of Christian and Faithful. An awful dread of hell and judgment fell upon him, which was not unreasonable, for that man only has entirely lost his senses who has entirely lost fear. Then he set about reforming himself—left off his evil practices; but yet oppressed with dread, felt with a shudder that he was not saved. For reformation is not salvation; reformation is not regeneration; they are very different things. He argued with himself in this way: "Suppose I should be obedient from this day to the day of my death, still, what is to become of my past disobedience? Suppose I have run into a merchant's debt, and owe a hundred pounds (or, as we may say here, a hundred dollars); and suppose I mean henceforth to pay as I go, still there stands the old debt against me, for which (as was the case in Bunyan's day) the merchant can cast me into prison any day he likes." Such was the reasoning of Hopeful. He said to himself, "I have been trying to do right, and would like still to do so, but there is the old debt against me, and I have nothing to pay. O! what am I to do?" He saw clearly that of himself he could do nothing. There was a gap that he could not fill. At this point he had an interview with Faithful, who told him that a Person had come to this world on purpose to take up the old debts of all those who would sincerely call upon Him. But said Hopeful, "I cannot see that." "Well," said Faithful, "go and pray with all your heart and soul, 'Lord, show me the Savior; reveal Thy Son to me.'" So Hopeful prayed over and over again, but could get no answer, till at last he said, "One day when I was in the dumps lower than usual, thinking of my condition, I fell on my knees, and said, 'Lord, I am a guilty sinner; reveal Thy Son to me;' and all at once I saw The Christ who died in my stead." "Did you see Him with your bodily eyes?" he was asked. "Oh, no; I saw Him with the eyes of my understanding, and I saw that He had made that debt all right with God; and, although I still owed it, I could go free through His benevolence and His love." It was all fear with him till the Savior came, and then what was the result? Said he, "My heart was filled so much for love of the Savior that I thought if I had a thousand gallons of blood in my body, I could shed it all for His dear sake." Such was the effect of a revelation of the Savior by the Holy Ghost. When a man sees Christ in that fashion; when a man is ready to give his very life for those for whom his Master died, that man has the spirit of his Master, and that man is a saved soul.

Here comes home the question to you to-night: Have you received the Holy Ghost since you believed? No man can truly say that Jesus is The Christ till He breathes the breath of the living Word. You may know of Him, all that teachers teach you, and read of Him, all that is to be read in the Bible, but unless you know Him as a living Spirit in your own souls, and receive that Spirit into your inmost being, you are none of His. Nay, unless you receive the spirit by which you could die for man, even as your Master did, and become a living sacrifice of love for your fellow-creatures, Christ is not within you; you are yet dead in your sins. Have you the spirit of Christ? If you have not, how can you be Christians?

LECTURE XIX.

IGNORANCE, FEAR, AND TEMPORARY.

[SYNOPSIS OF CHAPTER.—This chapter has but little incident. The Pilgrims are yet in the Enchanted Ground, and almost home. They spend their time in talking with and about Ignorance, who, for the nonce, is a fellow-traveler, and one named Temporary, whom they mutually knew in the earlier part of their pilgrimage.]

THE chapter which I have partially read, and which forms the basis of the Lecture to-night, gives us three distinct subjects to speak of. We have, first, religious ignorance; secondly, the influence of fear in religious life; thirdly, the moral history of a backslider.

Ignorance, who is one of the spurious Christians of this Allegory, confesses that he was born in and comes from the country of Conceit; and, therefore, Bunyan introduces the character in his figurative way as connected with that quality. Bunyan was right, as he generally is, for ignorance and conceit usually go together. A conceited man is always an ignorant one; that is, he is relatively ignorant. He does not know as much as he thinks he does, or assumes to know. An ignorant man is generally conceited, while the man who feels that he knows nothing as he ought to know, is a man who knows something as he ought to know it. This character, in matters pertaining to religion, is a type of a considerable class who sometimes appear to be in the way of righteousness; who think to themselves, and who declare to others, that they are on the way to the Celestial City.

This person's conceit and ignorance combined made him careless about the proper entrance into the Way of Righteousness. When Hopeful asked him why he had not entered by the Wicket Gate, he replied that it was held by men with whom he lived in his part of the world, that the gate was too far out of the way for them to think of entering it;—the meaning of which I understand to be this, that Jesus Christ is so far away from conceited ignorance as not to be thought of as even the beginning of the Way of Righteousness; that the conceited think they can get into the Way of Righteousness and reach heaven, and be admitted there, without any reference whatever to Christ. This is as much as to say that a man can be a Christian, and yet need to know nothing of Christ. But, now, can he?

Is there not a great deal of such loose and false theory floating about? Are there not a great many people who say, like Ignorance, "I am a very good liver; I pay my debts; I am kind to all about me, and I am living in the way of righteousness; therefore I have no need of Christ; or, therefore, I am a Christian?" Well, now, I will ask you a question or two: Can I be a Mason without going through the initiatory Masonic services? True, I may be just as good a man as a Mason, and I believe I am as good as some of them; but can I be a Mason without going through your services? Will you give me your grips, and let me know your secrets? Or, can a man be a Mahometan without any faith in Mahomet as the prophet of God? Can a man be a Mormon without any faith in Joseph Smith, Brigham Young, or the Book of Mormon? Absurd! you say; and yet it is no less absurd to claim that a man can be a Christian without Christ. Christ says, "I am the door; by Me if any man enter in, he shall go in and out, and find pasture. I am the door, and whosoever climbeth up some other way, the same is a thief and a robber." What is absurd in theory is impossible in practice.

Again, the conceit in this character is seen in his anxiety to walk alone. You remember the narrative tells us that he kept a long way behind the Pilgrims, and when Christian and Hopeful spoke about his joining them, he preferred to be by himself. He was very happy with his own thoughts, and wanted to walk solitary in the way that led to the Celestial City. We find the counterpart of this every day upon the street—men and women who think themselves Christians, are desirous of walking alone.

A Christian Church is simply a collection of men and women, banded together to do good, to worship God, and to love one another. What is a Christian out of the Church? He is apt to be a man who thinks himself so strong and wise that he, at least, has no need to unite himself with his fellows. There are many like him; men who think they are under no necessity to unite themselves with the Christian Church—they are above such dependence.

Let us look and see if that is right Christian conduct. If you are a Christian man or woman, is it not your duty to fellowship with other men and women like-minded with yourself, that you may do them some good? O, but, you may say, I cannot get any good myself. If you say that it shows that you have not the Christian spirit, and I say it advisedly, you are not a Christian. The man who says, I won't joint a church because I cannot get any good from doing so, is not a Christian.

Perhaps another says, I wish to join the church in order that I may do some good. Now he is a Christian, for that is the Spirit of the Master, who being rich, for our sakes became poor and went through the bitterest of all poverty, that we might exchange our rags for robes of righteousness. A man who thinks he can stand apart from all human sympathy and make a church of himself, and a pastor of himself, and all the machinery of good works of himself, is an egregious embodiment of conceit.

Here was a compound of ignorance and conceit in this character. They finally get him into conversation, and his conversation illustrates first, that he was ignorant of himself. They ask him his reason for believing that he was a Christian, and what do you think he said? Why, that "He found he was full of good emotions, which came into his heart as he walked, in this way," and when they asked, what good emotions, he replied, "I think of God and heaven." Well, now, that is a good thought, to think of God and heaven; perhaps you say we think of God and heaven, but as Christian evidence it is equivocal; the very devils in hell—the spirits of the damned, think of God and heaven. That poor girl who died in her shame the other day, and whose shame helped to pay the city's taxes, thought of God and heaven. The worst men and the worst women in this or any other community, think of God and heaven. Thought merely does not make a Christian. This man thought it did. But while good men may think of God and heaven, so may bad men.

He went a step further; he also said he had a desire for God and heaven. A remark that many may make who are never likely to see their desires accomplished. The soul of the sluggard desireth and hath nothing. You may desire—I presume we all desire to be happy. We have read of heaven, and long to be there; and hope by some means or other we may get there; we greatly desire that, but it does not make us Christians. The worst creatures in the world desire God and heaven. Let a farmer desire a crop; that does not produce it. Some of us, perhaps, desire to do the Paris exposition next year, but only desiring does not take us there. It may be one step; we may desire and then determine to go; but some of us may not after all wish to undertake the long and tedious journey; so that we may desire and still be unwilling to go. And so a man may desire heaven and yet not be in the way thither, or take the trouble to go.

Another thing: this man was ignorant of his own heart, inasmuch as he trusted it. Here is a man who, in his self-conceit, was trusting to his own heart; but the Bible says—and it is not true because the Bible says so, the Bible says so because it is true—"The heart is deceitful above all things, and desperately wicked who can know it,"—fathom its deceitfulness? Such passages were quoted to this man, but of course he resented them. He said his heart, at least, was not deceitful; his heart was as good as the heart of a converted man, with a right to a hope of heaven. Now you may be just so far along as to say you have very great comfort in your soul in thinking of and desiring eternal joys and God and heaven. Your heart may tell you these flattering tales, but the heart's language is not to be trusted. Ask my fellow if I be a thief? Ask the heart to condemn itself, and I do not think it will.

My brethren, there is one person in this world whom we do not know very well. We may know our next door neighbors, our children, relatives, and friends; we may know those with whom we do business; but there is one person of all the world whom we do not know—and that is ourself. We do not know what we are capable of until we are plunged into a train of circumstances where we are liable to sin. We do not know what is locked up in our souls. A terrible volcano in our hearts may at any time belch forth flame and smoke and death. The heart is like a magazine of powder; there the deadly mixture may lie from year to year in quiet, but lay a train and touch a match, and watch the fire leap along, and hear the explosion, where silence has reigned for years. What man has done in the way of depravity, man may do. Men who have been blessed all their lives, have suddenly sunk to the lowest depths. Man must not trust his heart, for out of it proceed bad thoughts and salacious desires. All the wickedness of this world has come from the human heart; and, I repeat, what man has done, man may do; and he that trusteth his own heart, is a fool. What man is capable of, may well make us tremble.

We do not know ourselves, and for this reason: we are not honest with ourselves; we each of us have an ideal self before our minds. We know what we ought to be, and we know what we think we are; but what we really are, we are not willing to admit. To call ourselves by our own right names, is a thing we are unwilling to do. Why, here is a man who cheats in business; keeps back the truth and deceives. What is his name? Let him whom he has cheated answer. His name is Liar. I do not care by what other name men may call him, his name is Liar; for a man's name is given to him by his character. So it used to be in the old Bible times. It many be thought it is not so now, but when you find a man who sins in any way, that sin is certain to give him his true name—the name he will have to face to all eternity. This man trusted his heart, ignorant of what his heart was. He thought his heart was all right, and he said he had good thoughts, and then added that he lived a life according to the commandments.

A man must be exceedingly ignorant when he says that. Perhaps we have not broken all of the commandments, but we are pretty sure to have broken some. There is one I can think of which I am very apt to neglect, and another I am very apt to break. We are all creatures of temptation. I am tempted, perhaps, in a direction you are not, but who dares say, "I have kept all of the commandments?" You cannot say it literally. Take the simple question of obedience in all things. What saith the Book, and not only that, but all nature, in calm, in storm, mountain, sea and river? The whole universe re-echoes— "Cursed is the man that continueth not in all things that are written in the Book to do them." When a man, then, says he keeps the law of God, and that he follows a life entirely in accordance with His commandments, that man is absolutely ignorant of himself, for there is no man that does it. If there is, I should like to see him. I never have seen him, and neither have you. The fact is so notorious, that I ask no excuse for saying that you do not keep them. It is a fact; you do not, nor have you done it, and I question whether there may not be a doubt in your heart of hearts as to you possibly desiring it. Sins are sweet; exceedingly sweet. This is a world of sin, and it is unfashionable to be unwordly.

In the second place, the man was ignorant of the plan of salvation. To begin with, he fell into the fundamental error of separating religious from all other kinds of life. For instance, when he is asked this question: "How do you believe in Christ for justification?" he says, "I have an idea it is Christ who makes my duties acceptable to His Father, by virtue of His merit, and so I shall be justified." You see the idea in this ignorant person's mind. It was his duty, he thought, to perform certain religious service, which Christ would make acceptable to

God; for instance, worship, prayer, praise, in any and all their forms. It was his duty, he thought, to offer such service. You see, he separated religion from life. That is a very common mistake. It is very easy to be Christians on Sunday, but another thing to be Christians on Saturday night and Monday morning, and all the week through. Religion covers a man's life; a man's religion is his life, and a man's life his religion. Let us look at this.

Men will be judged by deeds done in the body, whether they be good or bad. That is the statement of Scripture. What deeds? His religious deeds? Let us look at the Judgment, and apply the statement. Suppose we hear Christ say to those on His right hand, "Come, ye blessed of My Father; you went to church on Sunday and heard sermons, and you went to prayer-meeting once a week, and some of you went to Sabbath-school, and some of you did not; you attended sewing-societies, and had tea-meetings, and festivals, and bazaars; you have done all these things, so now come." And suppose Him saying to the others, "Depart from Me, ye cursed, for you did not go to church, nor to prayer-meeting, and you did not attend to religious duties. Depart. But as to these others, they were religious, so come, ye blessed."

You know very well Christ will say nothing of the kind. What has He said? You shall be judged by the deeds done in the body, whatever they are. Come, ye blessed of My Father, for on Monday morning you saw a child hungry and fed it; on Tuesday, you found a poor widow with her children, sitting alone in her desolate house, and you brought relief; on Wednesday, you went to the prison and visited the prisoners; on Thursday, you saw a man sick, and alleviated his sufferings; on Saturday, you repeated yourself as best you could; and on Sunday, you went to the house of God, and praised Him, and got fresh heart and grace to sustain you in another week. Therefore, come, ye blessed of My Father, and inherit the kingdom prepared for you." And to the others He will say, "Oh, you went to church, you went to prayer-meeting, and you thought yourselves the very cream of creation; you were too good to touch the rags of the poor, and moved in too high society to visit prisoners; you forgot that you were human, and you forgot that you need to be saved yourselves; you forgot Me—My claims, too; so depart, ye cursed, into everlasting fire." And, I tell you, they will go right down to it. Some of you smile, but what are you, you who smile, doing for the poor? What are you doing for God's children who are living and dying in their sins? Are you doing anything? You think God will accept your religious service performed on Sundays with no inconvenience, but God will not do so. Do not be deceived; God is not mocked, for whatsoever a man soweth, that shall he also reap. If he sow to his flesh, he will of that reap corruption; but if he sow to his spirit, the spirit of self-denial, for God's and man's sake, he will of that spirit reap everlasting life.

But this person was also ignorant of the working of Christ within him. Christ, indeed, has done a work outside of us, in His life and in His death, and this man's idea was that Christ justified his actions. There is that word justification, the key-note of the Reformation, and oh, how terribly it is perverted! It does not mean to-day what Luther meant and what Bunyan meant; it has become nothing more or less than a hollow fiction. That man is justified whose heart is just, and men are justified because faith transforms them through the One, and to the One, in whom they believe. Our evil actions are not justified; our spirits are justified. A man has to believe in Christ, and is justified through believing. I say this person was ignorant of the working of Christ within him. What work does Christ do? Paul puts it beautifully: "I live, yet not I, but Christ within me. It pleased God to reveal His Son in me. God forbid I should glory save in the cross of our Lord Jesus Christ, by whom the world is crucified unto me, and I unto the world. I live, but my life is hid with Christ in God; Christ is in me the hope of glory." That is the working of Christ within us; Christ formed in our hearts by faith, with unfeigned love to all the brethren. But this man knew nothing of it. My friends, do you see your counterpart in him? Are you ignorant of yourselves, ignorant of God, ignorant of Christ, and of the work of

Christ within you? Do not be conceited. The best men are humble; the wisest are lowly. Trust not your own heart, for he who does is a fool. Trust only that true Word, which can never fail. Heaven and earth may pass, but the Word of God abideth forever. Rest your souls upon that. Trust every promise that God has made, and you will live forever and forever.

Now we come to another branch of the subject, and that is the power of fear. We see fear manifested early in Christian life, and a picture of it we find here in the lesson. We have all known men who, but for a hell to escape from, would not think of going to heaven; men and women are so afraid of that, they have no blush when they say that they would not think of heaven but for the fear of hell. And while that is all very well in one just beginning a Christian life, it argues little progress and low experience in the Pilgrimage. Yet fear has its use, else God would not have implanted it. You cannot find a man who does not fear; it is a principle in all our souls, and there are times and cases when it is the only motive to which the Gospel can appeal for a man's salvation.

Let us consider this a little. There is a wrong fear and a right fear. How is the latter caused? A man feels that he is a sinner, and, when he feels that, he dreads the consequences—for what are they? The wages of sin is death, and the soul that sinneth shall die, and whatsoever a man soweth shall he reap. That is the reply of nature as well as revelation, and no amount of philosophy can alter it. We cannot alter the eternal facts of this universe. It has been proven by the life and proven by the death of every sinner, that those awful words are true. It brings death and all the train of woes. I suppose we need not say a word more on that point. Now when a man is convinced that he has sinned, I say he dreads the consequences—he must do so, and it is a very mean soul, indeed, that does not fear the consequence of sin, for it cannot be magnified.

Then right fear, rising from conviction of sin, drives the soul to lay hold on salvation. Suppose we were at sea to-night, and a storm should rise, and the ship be threatened with destruction, and we were in a condition to be sensible of the danger; but suppose there was one too deeply sunk in drunken stupor to be conscious of the peril. The captain cries, "Leap into the life-boat." We all who are moved by fear obey, but he who is too insensible lingers behind, and sinks with the doomed vessel. In olden times, when men slew others unintentionally, a hue and cry followed, to take vengeance on the destroyer; so, to give the unfortunate a chance for life, cities of refuge were built, where, when the fugitive knew the slayer was upon his track, he could take refuge and be saved. What man who has sinned and feels that he has sinned, does not ask the all-important question, What shall I do to be saved? And if God has not provided an answer to that question, then God has mocked us. But God has made provision, and Christ is set before us, the sinner's hope and Saviour; and we are told that He saveth to the uttermost all who go to God through Him. So, then, this right fear not only leads the soul to lay hold on Christ for refuge, but fear abides with that soul, to keep the continual presence of the Savior in it.

Do you mean to say that Christians have fear? Yes, I do; and the best Christians have most fear; not, indeed, a slavish, selfish feeling, but a fear of offending God. We fear lest we should fall; we fear that after we have preached to others, we may ourselves be castaway—not a fear of punishment, but we are moved by fear to our salvation; a fear to grieve the great and good Being who has manifested His love by saving us from death. Yes, Christians are moved by fear, for God has given his Son, his only and best beloved, that great sacrifice. And when we see men living unworthily, we see that gift rejected, we see that Savior again stretched upon the cross; and when Christians look on sin, they must view it with trembling and with fear. Hence we are told the fear of the Lord is the beginning of wisdom. The fear of the Lord is also the continuance of it. This is right fear, and the effect of it on the soul is wholesome and salutary.

I know of no better expression of this sense of fear than in the immortal verse of Binney:—

> "Eternal light! eternal light!
> How pure the soul must be,
> When placed within Thy searching sight
> It shrinks not, but with calm delight
> Can live, and look on Thee!

> "The spirits that surround Thy throne
> May bear the burning bliss;
> But that is surely theirs alone,
> Since they have never, never known
> A fallen world like this.

> "Oh! how shall I, whose native sphere
> Is dark, whose mind is dim,
> Before the ineffable appear,
> And on my naked spirit bear
> That uncreated beam?

> "There is a way for man to rise
> To that sublime abode:—
> An offering and a sacrifice,
> A Holy Spirit's energies,
> An Advocate with God:—

> "These, these prepare us for the sight
> Of holiness above:
> The Sons of Ignorance and Night
> May dwell in the Eternal Light
> Through the Eternal Love!"

Of the wrong kind of fear we see examples when we come to the history of backsliders. In our own day we see created by our church systems a large number of spurious Christians. At periods of revival encouraged by the Church, we have men and women who are converted at every one. Ever since they were boys and girls, on to old age, at every revival, they are converted. There are many who put off the subject of conversion to times of revival; and I say our systems do encourage and create this ephemeral class of believers. We have seen men making a profession of religion, and a very loud one, and a very encouraging profession, too; and by-and-by turn back. These examples were not wanting in Paul's time: "Ye did run well; what did hinder you?" Bunyan introduces one, whom he calls Temporary, who dwelt in the town of Graceless, next door to one Turnback. What is the philosophy of the Allegory here? How is it that these men get what we call religion, and in a very short time turn back, and are apparently worse men than before—how is it? Bunyan has told us. We will merely give his thoughts without repeating the language. He says, in these men, conscience is awakened to think a good deal about the punishment of sin, that punishment is preached in very vivid colors, and men tremble in view of the consequences of their conduct, so that their consciences become, as it is called, awakened; for they are awakened as if out of deep slumber. Does that awakening make a Christian? Certainly not. We see that these did not become Christians; or, did not remain so. Why not? Simply because to make a Christian a man's mind and soul must both be changed. Awakening does not—the fear of hell does not make Christians, but change of heart; and hence Christ told Nicodemus, who knew so much that was good; o know is not enough; you must be born again; your heart, your life, must be changed. This is what we preach. For instance: A murderer stands in the dock. He has heard his trial; the evidence is against him; the jury find him guilty; and when the judge puts on the black cap, he sees his doom and trembles. He is simply awakened to a sense of his condition; his awakening does not prove a change of heart or disposition, for though he trembles, society would protest against his being let loose again, on the ground of his sense of his condition. So, when man faces the consequences of sin, he may tremble and yet not be cured of sin. The Master says he must be changed: "Except ye be converted and become as little children ye shall in no wise enter the kingdom of heaven." To whom did he say that? He said it to his disciples. And he said to the wise Nicodemus, "You must lead a new life; you must have a new birth." What does that mean? The wind bloweth where it listeth, and ye hear the sound thereof, yet cannot tell whence it cometh or whither it goeth; even so with this new birth. All birth is mysterious, whether physical or spiritual; but the fact of life no one can gainsay. Though Christ has thus spoken, and though we see the absolute necessity of the case, men shrink back and say, "why should I pass through this change of heart? Is it not hard in God to impose such conditions?" My friends, it is for your sake—not for his. He is no hard and cruel Master. There is no other way; you must be born again.

Thus far we have considered the backsliding of new converts, but we have also in this lesson examples of another kind: backsliders, who, for a long time, have lived the Christian life, and then fallen away. Do men fall from grace? Bunyan thought so. But you say, I thought Bunyan was a Calvinist, and believed in the perseverance of the saints. Well, I met a man a while ago, and he was drunk; he happened to be in my church one Sunday morning, and as he met me the following week, said, in thick-tongued speech, "Mr. N.,—hic—I agree with you entirely; I am so glad you believe in—hic—election; I was —hic—elected seventeen years ago." "Well," said I, "you have not kept your trust, have you?" "But," said he, "I believe in the perseverance of the saints;—hic—you know that's part of the Calvinistic system." "All right," said I, "but you seem somehow to have gotten out of the system." Now, here was a man who believed in the perseverance of the saints, and yet was walking after the flesh. There are some who do not believe in men going back, and some who do. Some make provision for it in their church schedules, and others make none at all. But it is not a matter of theology or ecclesiasticism, but a matter of fact.

My friends, what do you say? Some of you know you have gone back. You have a name to live while you are dead. You know very well you have lost something. Ah, my friends, these are awful, terrible matters, and it seems to me God alone can understand them.

Let us look further into the moral history of backsliding. How does it begin? We have here its genesis. First, they draw off their thoughts from God and Judgment. Yes, all backsliding begins from that. First distinct thoughts, then a habit, and at length a confirmed character. They first draw off their thoughts from the remembrance of God; God is no longer in all their thoughts, until they get so far as to say, Well, after all, there will be no Judgment such as that described in the Scriptures. Ah, my friends, I know it—it will be ten thousand times more dreadful than language can describe; and we are preparing ourselves for the Judgment to-night.

Then they cast off the fetters of private duty. I suppose I need hardly trace these steps—they are only too well known. Secret prayer is neglected; nobody hears in the closet; nobody knows anything about that. Christ says nothing about praying in public, but He says when thou prayest enter into thy closet and pray to thy Father, who seeth in secret. Do you think I pray out of the inmost heart in the public congregation? Do you pray your best here when you bow your heads so reverently? Possibly you may, but the sad fact is, that in public not much true prayer is made. No; men pray at home, and when they are alone, if they pray at all. The backslider begins by neglecting private prayer; then forgets to curb his lust; forgets to be watchful. Yet to be watchful is the Christian's duty, and not to see how near he can come to temptation without yielding, but to keep out of the way of it. Sorrow for sin soon ceases with backsliders, and they become dead Christians. We know how true that is, for half of our churches are filled with dead Christians; not buried, but we shall all be buried by and by. Decay begins at the root, and at last appears above ground. After habitual neglect of private duty, we see then, perhaps, excuses for open vice, and it may be on the ground—a very specious one—of a want of perfection in professed Christians. How perfection in the Christian church can be expected, I can not for my life understand. That creatures endowed with reason should pretend to expect it, is the greatest puzzle to me imaginable—if it were not for the sophistry of self-deception. Well, after this, they will begin associating publicly with the carnal and wanton; with men whose talk is salacious; possibly men who stand at the corners of the streets and think themselves manly in saying beastly things of women who pass by. Young men, you know what I mean, some of you; I need not say another word. They begin with little sins in secret; then excuse them openly; and at last sink right down in the uncovered sloughs of vice. Such is Bunyan's genesis of the backslider. How far do you think it is true? How far have you gone in the awful course? "Ye did run well; what did hinder you?" Has not the hindrance been in your own selves? It began in your own soul; began where religion is vital; began where your Christian life was secret, dark, and hid from men; where all moral decay commences. It is not by neglect of public means of grace that the downfall of the Christian commences. He begins to die from within. Such is the sad story of the professor of religion who has turned his back upon his Savior.

Look over the theme again. Men are lost because they are ignorant. Men are lost because they are hardened, and do not fear. Men are lost because they allow sin to enter into their most secret souls.

And now, my friends, can I say another word to bring you to a better life—to the life of a living Christian? Every plant has a root which must strike into the soil and send down its little tendrils deep into the fertile moisture, to bring up the elements of its nature. The plant must go down in the earth after its flowers, and fruit, and seed; the roots must be right, if the plant would be thriving. It is what your secret lives are, that make or mar you. What kind of men and women are you when you think yourselves alone, and when you are in the presence only of your Maker—when you unlock your heart and look it over as you might perhaps a drawer, to take account of what is in it?

My friends, if I may give advice, do not think of your public religious life; let that be a secondary matter. No professing Christian has need to wait and calculate whether he shall do a good act or not. No, let the good deed come out quick and hot, like bread from an oven. It is this secret life that is important. What are you in secret, where men have no chance to watch you; when you are hid from all other eyes but God's? What are you in your heart of hearts, where God requires wisdom and truth? What are you there? Are you men—the men you profess to be—the men you think you are? Or, do you find that you deceive yourselves? Brothers and sisters, do not deceive yourselves. Be honest, be true, and before your God above all things. Know yourselves, and having learned to know yourselves, seek further to know the Lord Jesus Christ.

"Oh Thou pure light of souls that love,
True joy of every human breast,
Sower of life's immortal seed,
Our Saviour and Redeemer blest.

"Be Thou our guide, be Thou our goal,
Be Thou our pathway to the skies,
Our joy, when sorrow fills the soul,
In death our everlasting prize."

LECTURE XX.

THE CELESTIAL CITY.

[SYNOPSIS OF CHAPTER.—The dangers of the Enchanted Ground are safely passed, and the Pilgrims are now in the Land of Beulah, where the birds sing and flowers bloom all the day, and where they every moment get more perfect views of the Celestial City. Between themselves and the city is a bridgeless river. Across it was the way to their destination. In the stream Christian had much difficulty, while Hopeful went through with ease. On the other side they were met by two shining inhabitants of the city. These escorted them to the gates thereof. Here an innumerable host met them, and gave them royal welcome. As they entered the gate they were transfigured, and had raiment put on that shone like gold. Harps and crowns were given them. Ignorance soon got over the river. He boldly asked admission at the gate; but when his certificate was demanded, he had none. Two shining ones, at the command of the King, had him away. The Dreamer saw that there was a way to hell, even from the gates of heaven, as well as from the City of Destruction. So he awoke, and behold, it was a dream!]

IN APPROACHING the last lecture of this series, one thing has deeply impressed my mind; a very simple thought, yet very important, and when rightly looked at, a solemn one: *all things must end.* Some five months ago, on a wet Sabbath evening, to less than an ordinary congregation, we began the exposition of Bunyan's Pilgrim's Progress. It is a grateful reflection that during this time we have all been preserved in health and strength, and not one, I think, who heard me on the first occasion, or in the earlier portion of the lectures, has suffered any severe or painful illness—not one has died. For such blessings we ought to be thankful, and I feel extremely so to-night. I hope you will indulge me in these personal remarks. I presume the reason why my thoughts dwell so earnestly at this time upon a truth so common, is, that these Pilgrims who to some may seem, as they did to me, mere visionary creations, have come to appear to me like real persons, and I feel to-night as if I were about to part with old friends. It is truly said that there are thoughts too deep for tears; let this express my feelings, as I bring before you now the closing scene of this most remarkable Pilgrimage.

From the beginning we have had this end in view; each of us, no doubt, expecting such a triumphant ending as the Immortal Dreamer has portrayed. Every end should be worth looking forward to and working for. Let me bid you, my friends, ask yourselves, each one, Am I working towards a designed end—is the end for which I am living worth living for? The questions you ask, you alone can answer. If you answer yes, it is well; if you cannot answer yes, if you cannot positively say it is your deepest conviction that the end for which you live is a worthy one, you had better at once begin a new life; seek a nobler end, for life is nothing of itself; the end alone can give it dignity and worthiness. The student applies himself at school or college, wears himself almost to a skeleton, to make of himself a profound scholar; a man toils from morning until midnight, with scarcely any rest, that the end of his days may be free from toil, bowered in comfort and repose. We call these both worthy ends. But the end in this life sought for should be a worthy beginning of another, for it ought not to be forgotten, that every end is also a beginning. The corn grown last year you eat, then in various forms deposit in the earth again; and so the end of last year's harvest becomes the beginning of the present year's crop. In like manner the end of this life is the beginning of eternity, and just what our lives here have been, they must also be in the world to come.

In this closing scene, Bunyan describes death as a river. A very old-fashioned, very familiar idea, and one which men have wrought into their literature in all time. The Jew, the Chris-

—36

tian, and the heathen, the ignorant and the learned, have all of them portrayed death as a river through which all must pass. But before they came to the river they reached a border land, which is called by Bunyan, Beulah. This word means married; its Scriptural use alludes to the fond union between a longing Church and a loving Savior. It is taken from the fervid apostrophe of the old prophet to his people, "Thou shalt no more be termed forsaken, neither shall thy land any more be called desolate, but thou shalt be called Hephzibah, and thy land Beulah; for the Lord delighteth in thee, and thy land shall be married," the verse closing, "as the bridegroom rejoiceth over the bride, so shall thy God rejoice over thee." The idea of the application of the term here, is, that just before the Pilgrims come to the stream of death in the border land, they enter into a close union with God and heaven, so that while still on earth gleams of the glory from the Immortal Grounds just beyond, shine into their hearts warm with a growing sense of the Savior's love; therefore the land is called Beulah. There the Pilgrims have many a rich experience; and the further they go the richer their experiences become.

We are to take Christian and Hopeful as types of ordinary followers of Christ, living out the allotted term of life in the ordinary way. The story has furnished types of the extraordinary; one, for instance, died a martyr's death. But these two have lived to a ripe old age in righteousness, and we picture them grey and venerable, just on the threshold of the house with many mansions, waiting for the Master's call. Flowers burst into their noblest bloom just before their fall. Fruit becomes more rich and tempting as the gathering draws nigh. So, too, we see aged Christians—dear old souls, whose faces are just like children's, and whose thoughts are just as innocent—looking back upon lives well spent, waiting cheerfully for death; expecting, like good children, a Father's loving arms soon to bear them home.

Every Christian who lives to good old age, may expect that his later hours will be more full of comfort than those of the beginning or middle of his course. When I first came to this country, people asked, Have you any Indian Summer in England? Oh, no, I replied, we have no such season there. Well, then, they said, you have no weather there. And I have since thought perhaps they were correct, for certainly I have never seen any season to compare with the rich, soft glory of the Indian Summer. I wondered what it could be that everbody had so much to say about, till one still autumn morning I rose to find a mellow halo over the earth, and as, in quiet ecstacy, I drank in the golden blessedness, it seemed that a part of heaven itself had clothed the earth. Like that the aged Christian's life may be. After the toils of life, a halo from the skies drops over him an Indian Summer of the soul.

These Pilgrims had the remembrance of past bitterness to sweeten triumph. You remember that the elder one, when he set forth, had to tear himself from home, wife and children; then he fell into a slough; next, astray, he found himself under the threatenings of Sinai; further on, he encountered the Hill of Difficulty; afterwards, fought with Appolyon, passed through the Valley of the Shadow of Death, struggled through Vanity Fair, pined in the Giant's dungeon, and, lastly, writhed in the hideous toils of the Deceiver. Many a time his heart had failed him, when Hope's promise seemed withdrawn and the Celestial City too far away. We have seen days begin with clouds and end in sunshine; we have seen other days begin in brightness, then choke up with clouds, and at last close in golden glory. So it is in life. It is only when the sun sets in the midst of clouds that its setting is most beautiful; for, as the apostle said, "These light afflictions, which are but for a moment, work out for us a far more exceeding and eternal weight of glory."

But in that lovely border-land, besides the rich fruits of which they partook on every hand, the Pilgrims encountered a still more rare and curious experience. Instead of resting satisfied in the midst of such delights, they became afflicted with a divine longing and heartsick desire for Christ, crying out, in the language of the Song of Songs, "If you see my Beloved, tell Him I am sick of love." We all know what homesickness means; or, when loved ones are absent, with what yearning we await their return, or our return to them. So I have known Christians and, perhaps, you have too, who seemed really reluctant to linger, waiting for the Master to call them home. They longed to depart and be with Christ.

> "And whence this weariness,
>   This gathering cloud of gloom?
> Whence this dull weight of loneliness,
>   These greedy cravings for the tomb?
> These greedier cravings for the hopes that lie
> Beyond the tomb, beyond the things that die,
> Beyond the smiles and joys that come and go,
> Fevering the spirit with their fitful flow,
> Beyond the circle where their shadows fall;
> Within the region where my God is all.
>
> "It is not that the path
>   Is rough and perilous, beset with foes
> From the first step down to its weary close,
>   Strewn with the flint, the briar and the thorn
>   That wound my limbs, and cleave my raiment torn;
> But I am homesick!
>
> "It is not that this earth
>   Has grown less bright and fair; that these grey hills,
>   These ever-lapsing, ever-lulling rills,
>   And these breeze-haunted woods, that ocean clear,
>   Have now become less beautiful, less dear;
> But I am homesick!"

Now, friends, if this be a true Christian experience, and it is, let me ask you one question: Will the course of life you are pursuing make you sick with longing to die—will it? I cannot answer the question; you must. Suppose you should live to grow old, will the life you now live, if lived as long as your physical strength will endure, give you this sickness—will it? When life has no more charms; when earthly appetites and senses are decaying, and when there seems at last nothing more to live for, will that condition be as unlikely as it seems to-day? That I cannot answer. I put to you the question. Answer ye?

Now, turning our attention to the Pilgrims in the River of Death, one peculiar fact attracts our attention. There is an idea entertained by nearly every one that Christians all die happily, and worldly men all die miserably. The general prevalence of this opinion I need not attempt to prove, for it is sufficiently well known. Whenever a man dies, the first question that arises in connection with the news of his death is, Did he die happily? According to the manner of the person's death is the opinion of that person's religious condition. When a noted man of the world passes away, people are anxious to obtain news as to the manner of his death; the mental and spiritual condition of his last moments. If it appears that he died in mental distress or gloom, the fact is published as very significant of the state of his soul. On the other hand, Christians have a morbid interest in the condition of dying Christians, watch for their last words, treasure them, and publish them to the world as very important evidence of the genuineness of their faith. If it should happen that a Christian dies, and gives no sign of cheerful hope or confidence as to his future, we are apt to think that there must be something secret and hidden in the life of that individual, which caused the failure of the expected evidence. I wish to-night to explode that idea. I would like to drive it from your hearts and minds forever. I want to bring to your attention the fact that some Christians die in intense misery, and, on the other hand, some unbelievers, infidels and Atheists die as cheerfully and contentedly as men can wish. You may say that is hardly orthodox, but never mind; orthodox or not, it is too true—and that is the worst of it. I say there are some Christians who die miserably, and there are some sinners who die happily. There was a man who committed a foul murder, some two or three years ago. That murder was but the natural result of the sort of life he had led; and when he came to meet his sentence, he walked to the scaffold and mounted to his fate without the quiver of a nerve or the twitch of a muscle—died calmly, positively calm. Some of the worst men that have ever lived have died with the utmost coolness, and with a joke freezing on their icy lips. On the other hand, many a Christian has shrunk from death; shuddered on its approach, shivered in its embraces, and been afraid to meet it. I wish you to learn that the manner of a man's death does not reflect the piety or impiety of his life, and gives no clue whatever to his destiny in eternity.

We frequently hear the expression, "Let me die the death of the righteous, and let my last end be like His." Certainly, take the old text and weave it into your prayers, if you will, but take it with all its true conditions. Do not pervert it. Don't pray this way, Let me die so as to save my miserable, little, selfish soul, by dying the death of the righteous. Let me so shape my last end as to save my poor, sordid heart from the powers of hell, by imitating the manner of the death of the righteous. That is what is generally the secret meaning of the expression in its perversion. Remember this, that no unrighteous man, however he may have appeared, has ever really died the death of the righteous. Remember this, that no ungodly man has ever really died the death of the godly; and, therefore, whether the prevalent feeling of the righteous man's death be miserable or happy, it is best to die the death of the righteous. The circumstances and seeming of the death-bed have nothing whatever to do with its real character. Man is not to be judged by the way he dies, but by the way he lives; not by his struggles in the waves of the dark river, but by the manly steadfastness, perseverance, energy and patience he has maintained in the way of righteousness. No one of you is going to be saved because of a chance smile on your lips in dying; but if you are saved at all, it will be only with the spirit of the Lord Jesus Christ in your heart.

Let us now turn to the chapter and take Bunyan's testimony on this point, for whatever you may think of me, Bunyan at least you will believe, for he is orthodox; you will take him, I know, on this question; and what does he say? You see how he describes the last hours of Christian, our first, eldest, original Pilgrim in this story; the man who fought so many noble fights of faith; the man whom every one of us would like to emulate, and to whose worthiness we would all like to attain. Watch his conduct in the flood of death. We are told that as they approached the stream they learned that it was deep, and that it had no bridge. As they passed in they were stunned at the sight. There are special moments in life, my friends, when we are all given a realization of the solemnity of death; when our children disappear, or our parents, brothers, or sisters are taken away; or when the hearse stands at a neighbor's door; it may be while a whole city is draped in mourning, and a whole nation halts to weep at a loss universally lamented. At such times we get in our minds a glimpse of the same awful river, the sight of which stunned these Pilgrims.

Before that stream we all stand alike; we know not exactly when, we only know the time is sure to come to each, when we, too, must descend into the dark tide. And again, we know each must meet those waves alone. The hope, confidence and comfort of others can go with us only in memory; none can die with us; alone we must pass through the deep and bridgeless river. The time set for that lonely passage God only knows; but we know that it must come. Fair maiden, the bloom on your bright cheek must fade; your lovely form must moulder away. Strong young man, a mightier wrestler, a more accomplished athlete, will yet throw thee, nor hast thou any skill to compete with him. Wise man, thou hast no science to evade him. Rich man, thou has no gold to bribe him. Good man, he will not spare thee. Bad man, thou too must fall before him. Frivolous man, he will touch thee with his fateful wand, and freeze on thy face thy idiotic grin in death. We must all die, and die alone. And it is well for us now and then to catch a glimpse of the river.

As to our Pilgrims; their experiences varied in life, and it would not be strange if in death they also varied. All Christian experiences do. When they came to the river, he whose toils and sorrows we have followed longest, began to despond, because he could see no way of escape. But they addressed themselves to the water, and as they entered, Christian began to sink—it was not easy for him to die—and he cried out, "I sink in deep waters; the billows go over my head; all the waves go over me." Again he says, "The sorrows of death compass me round about; I shall not live to see the land that floweth with milk and honey." And with that a great darkness and horror fell upon him, so that he could not see before him. In a great measure he lost his senses, and was troubled about the sins he had committed, both since and before he became a Pilgrim, and appeared haunted by all sorts of wild fancies, apparitions of hobgoblins and spirits of evil, about which he raved in his misery. Nothing his companion could say seemed to encourage him. He felt that each soul's experience was its own, and therefore his reply to the cheerful suggestion of Hopeful, describing what to him appeared to be awaiting them, was, "No, no; all that is for you, and you only. You have a right to be hopeful; but, ah! if I were to be saved, too, my Savior would come to me now; but, on account of my sins, He has led me into this snare, and left me." Then replied Hopeful, in the significant language of an old Bible text respecting the wicked, reminding Christian that he had quite forgotten it, "There are no bands in their death but their strength is firm; they are not troubled as other men, neither are they plagued like other men." So Hopeful tried to assure Christian that his troubles and distresses in the river were no sign whatever that God had forgotten such real evidence as had been afforded by the sincerity of his life, or that his Savior would forsake a true and faithful follower. This is the important truth that I wish to impress on you: It is not your experience in death, but the manner of your life, that must save you; not the way you die, but the way you live; not what you feel, but what you do—that gives you entrance to the better world. The mode of death is mainly a matter of temperament, as we see illustrated next in the experience of Hopeful; for while Christian was sinking, Hopeful said, "I feel the bottom, and it is good." He had such an abundance of confidence that he overflowed in help to his companion. In his buoyant frame of mind the promises of God were recalled, and while Christian quoted texts of despair only, Hopeful responded, "Be of good cheer; Jesus Christ maketh you whole." Such hope at last proved infectious, so that Christian, in reply, broke out in a loud voice, saying, "I see Him now, and He tells me, 'When thou passest through the water, I will be with thee; and through the rivers, they shall not overflow thee.'" And then they both took courage; and after that the enemy—that is, Fear —was as still as a stone until they were gone over.

This, however, is not the end of the description, for we are told that, upon the bank of the river on the other side, there came to the river two shining ones, whose acquaintance had already been made in the Border-land, by whom they were led toward the gate. Meanwhile, the Dreamer also saw Ignorance draw near to the river, who, with the aid of a ferryman named Vain Hope, crossed without any trouble whatever—thus illustrating the text quoted by Hopeful, to the effect that those whose lives afford no ground for hope, may yet in death fail to be troubled like other men.

How is such a phenomenon to be accounted for?

As I have said, the mode of death is much a matter of temperament. But there is a further explanation to be found in the various degrees of refinement of the moral senses; for as all special senses are capable of special culture, so it is possible to educate the conscience to an extreme delicacy. You know you can refine the painter's sense of beauty, till the daub that tickled the fancy of his boyhood gives his mature taste positive displeasure. You know, too, the ear of a musician may be so refined that thumps and knocks, which to the uneducated ear may seem melodious, will strike his skilled nerve with actual pain. In the same way, the conscience of a Christian enters upon a progressive course of refined distinctions, till what was at first rude enough, at last attains a conception so exalted of the contrast between the heart and its ideal, as to inspire a horror of death. So Christians may shrink from death because of an extreme refinement of conscience, while duller souls pass through unfearing.

Now, beyond the River of Death, I am sorry there exists no detailed record, for there is this peculiarity in the Bible, that it enters into no particulars, but lays down only a few general principles, leaving each to work out the problem for himself. Still faith does not leave us without a glimpse, such as that embodied in the close of Bunyan's dream. He says that the Pilgrims, aided by the two shining ones, helping them by the arm, mounted the hill toward the city, going up sweetly talking; and that as they drew toward the gate, a company of the heavenly host came out to meet them, to whom they were introduced by their conductors, whereupon the host gave a great shout, crying, "Blessed are they who are called to the marriage supper of the Lamb." So Lazarus, from the rich man's gate, where men loathed him and dogs licked his sores, was lifted to Abraham's bosom. An abundant entrance was given to the Pilgrims. Perhaps some of you may have seen the triumphal procession of a king or conqueror: heralds go before; the city is filled with banners; flowers strew the way; eager throngs press round, and, as the hero draws nigh, the air throbs with peals of welcome. Such, we may suppose, is a very faint type of the honors given to these Pilgrims. We are told that they were met by choirs in shining dress, who hailed them with sweet instruments and voices; and as the throng drew near the gate, the Pilgrims looked up and read inscribed above it, in letters of gold, "Blessed are they that do His commandments, that they may have right to the Tree of Life, and may enter in through the gates into the city."

Do you see it, my friends? Blessed are they who do His commandments. But some one says, I thought we were going to heaven through Jesus Christ? So you are, if you go at all; through keeping Jesus Christ's commandments. That is the only way. There it is, over the gate: "Blessed are they who do His commandments." Oh! but you say, That is a hard way to heaven. Very well; it is the only way; and I know nothing worth having, that is not hard to get. We all know how hard it is to get gold; how hard to get a home; how hard to get knowledge; how hard to get anything worth having. Is heaven worth having? They only will get there who do Christ's commandments. Is there no way out of this? I will tell you what the Master himself says, "If ye keep my commandments, ye shall abide in my love." "Take my yoke upon you." But you say, That is too heavy. Christ says, "My yoke is easy and my burden is light." You only need to put your neck into the yoke, and it is done. Work in it. His commandments are not grievous; they are full of comfort. But there is the inscription right over the gate of heaven: "None enter here but those who keep the commandments."

Then the Pilgrims were transfigured; they went into the river clad in mortal flesh; this robing they left behind them, and the new raiment they put on shone like gold. Those who met them gave them harps and crowns—the harps for praise, and the crowns in honor. Then, says the Dreamer, I heard all the bells in the city ring again for joy, and it was said to them, "Enter ye into the joy of our Lord," and I heard also the men themselves, saying, "Blessing and honor and glory and power be unto Him that sitteth upon the Throne, and unto the Lamb forever and ever." And as the gates opened the city shone like the sun, and the throng wore crowns on their heads and bore palms and harps, and some of them had wings, and they chanted as they did fly, Holy, holy, holy is the Lord."

We Christians on earth had better be careful how we treat our fellows. When the poor drunkard rises from his slough of sin, they sing to him that song of triumph; and though we say, "Why, he was never worth much," God only knows, and, alas, God only cares, for men do not care for their brethren; while we reproach them, God forgives them, and heaven is glad when they repent, and angels chant their welcome home. Ah, if Christ's spirit were ours we might receive sinners into our churches as God receives them into heaven with joy.

When the Pilgrims were transfigured, the Dreamer tells us, and they had passed in, the gates were shut; which, he says, when I had seen, I wished myself among them. And so do we. We wish to be among the holy and happy in the eternal glory. Do you not? But wishing alone will not take take you there. There needs something else. If the prodigal, when far from home, had been content with wishing to arise and go to his Father, that wish would not have taken him. It was only when he said, "I will arise and go to my Father," that he came to his Father.

In my old parish I gave a course of lectures on the Pilgrim's Progress—not these exactly, but I dare say something like them—and in my congregation was a lad who was quite simple, too simple to work, too simple to get an education, but he began with Christian, starting from the City of Destruction, and followed him intently all the way through. Several times during the course he spoke to me and asked if I thought it was possible to get that man "through." And I remember he would sit listening with all attention, as I unfolded the steps of the Progress. I was very glad to be able to preach so that he could understand, for he seemed to do so. When we had finished the last lecture, he stood upon the steps outside the church, and as I came out took me by the hand and said, "I say, we got him through—didn't we get him through?" He walked all the way home with me, and to everybody he met said, "We got him through." As he was telling it the next day, I said, "William, when are you going to be a Pilgrim?" That silenced him. Now, I dare say, few of you would like to be told that you are simple, but all rather pride yourselves on being able to listen to a course of lectures on the Pilgrim's Progress with intelligent interest, and so human and vital is the story that perhaps to-night you are sighing with a sense of relief, and ready to whisper to one another, Well, we have got him through. But, friends, what about getting yourselves through? Have you yet to become pilgrims? We have been warning you of the dangers of sin, and have been telling you something of the strife of godly living; we have been trying to bring you to the Cross and under the teachings of the Holy Spirit, and at last, to-night, we have led you to the brink of death's deep, bridgeless river. We have followed the Pilgrims home, and now what about yourselves? Are you Pilgrims? Some of you may say, Well, I am not religious, and don't expect to be. My friends, you will bear me witness that I have never preached to you about being religious, but I have been preaching to you about being righteous through faith in Christ. Is there nothing in your lives that you condemn? Do you not feel that there is some need to make your peace with God? Are you living the sort of life you ought to live, or are you sensible of defection and failure? You cannot get through safely unless you live the right life, and I do not care how you die, if you do but live well. God does not care how you die if you live well; you will die right if you live right. Now will you begin to live right?

Then, says Bunyan, I awoke and behold it was a dream. But dreams after all are never as good as reality. We wake from a frightful dream, and are thankful that it is not real; we wake from a pleasant dream, and wish that it were true. But sometimes in life we meet things much more delightful than the brightest dream could depict or the liveliest fancy portray. And so, brethren, there are in the Christian life, from beginning to end, things better, nobler, richer, and dearer than in this dream. As the Scripture says, There are things that the eye hath not seen and the ear hath not heard, and which have not entered into the heart of man to conceive—things known only to the Spirit, and spoken in the sacred recesses of the soul by the Spirit that searcheth all things; yea, the deep things of God.

Will you be Pilgrims? Reading Bunyan's story will not make you one. Looking through a railway guide does not make you a traveler; poring over a dictionary does not make you eloquent; mere reading and wishing cannot make Pilgrims of you. The only way to become a Pilgrim is this, start from the City of Destruction; go to the Wicket Gate; go to Him who says, "I am the door." Go to the Lord Jesus Christ, and in your prayers tell Him that you are sinful, and ask Him for forgiveness; ask Him to sustain you in the way of righteousness; and in this way only may God help you to be a Pilgrim.

"'Twas not a vision of my sleep nor dream that fancy paints;
It was a view of heaven itself, the dwelling place of saints;
It was the glory of the Lord, the Spirit hath revealed,
The final happiness of those that God the Father sealed,—
This was the sight from which I woke, and looked and looked again,
And though their pilgrimage was o'er, I yet was on the plain;

> And in the rugged wilderness I looked and sighed in prayer,
> 'O God, complete my pilgrimage, conduct me safely there!'"

Fellow Pilgrim, earnestly press that petition. "Safely there!" in the land of holiness, of joyfulness, of perfection, of beauty, free from care, temptation, sin, sorrow, and death. "Safely there!" in the Paradise of God, where are the many mansions, and where sorrow and sighing are done away. "Safely there!" where Jesus is, and the spirits of just men, made perfect with glowing seraphim and cherubim, praise Him forever. "Safely there!" in *our* eternal home; *ours* by Jesus' grace; *ours* by the sacrifice of Christ; *ours* by the earnest of the Spirit in our hearts. "Safely there!" after we have one by one crossed the river; O God, most Merciful, God most True, may we be found!

ADDENDUM.

[Refer to p. 38.]

A SCHOOLMATE of mine lately committed murder. He was a foremost man in a church. He was nearly fifty years of age. Through thirty years he had suffered from an unhappy marriage. God knows what his trials had been. But the man was sane. He was in health. Not a whisper has been raised in his defense, although he is to be tried for his life in a few weeks. Coming home from an evening gathering, his wife and he passed into their house together, apparently at peace with each other. Half an hour later, when she was asleep, the monster with an axe took his wife's life.

Do not avert your gaze, my friends, from this lurid point of light. The narrative is of a piece with much else that has actually happened in the nights and days of our softly rolling globe; and yet you say it is not philosophy. I affirm that events like these are facts, and that philosophy must face facts of every description, or once for all cease to call itself scientific. This piercing gleam out of experience is blue fire, indeed; but not a little radiance of that sort has crept before now through the volcanic crevices of the world. When by this ominous but actual lamp you gaze intently upon the glitter of this axe, and upon the flashing of the afterward dripping blood, you will find that many problems as to the peace of the soul are here exposed to view, under a flame intense enough to permit their scientific examination.

Both these persons were my schoolmates. I knew each of them well, and think I have some reason to say that I understand what, probably, the whole interior sky was in this man. One of the things that proved his guilt, aside from his confession, which he made at the end of a week, was a remark which he curiously enough repeated to his neighbors months before his crime: "Can I not repent, even if I do a great wrong, and so repent as to go to heaven? Is it not taught that a man may repent and be saved, although he does something very bad?" This man was not well educated. He had in his mind the query, whether one might not commit some atrocity, and yet repent, and by the good grace of the Almighty God, who is of too pure eyes to behold iniquity, be saved though the Atonement?

* * * * * * * * * *

This man, befogged, but not insane, took up the theory—this was proved before the jury—that he might commit murder, and yet afterward repent, and go to heaven. And he committed murder; and I think his chief temptation, aside from vexatious married life, was that lie whispered to him out of the very bowels of Gehenna, that the Atonement is enough to save a man who makes a bargain of it, and tries to cheat God. That man did on a large scale what it is possible you and I have been trying to do on a small scale. We do not commit murder; but we would, if we had our own way, very gladly cheat God of half our lives at least, because we remember that we can repent at last, and all will come out well. Some men think that, if they repent after they go out of this life, all will be well: that is rather a large application of this principle.

"ORTHODOXY," by Joseph Cook. Lecture V., pp. 141, 142, 143.

FINIS.

www.ingramcontent.com/pod-product-compliance
Lightning Source LLC
Chambersburg PA
CBHW032053220426
43664CB00008B/979